THE PIRATE WORLD

OSPREY
PUBLISHING

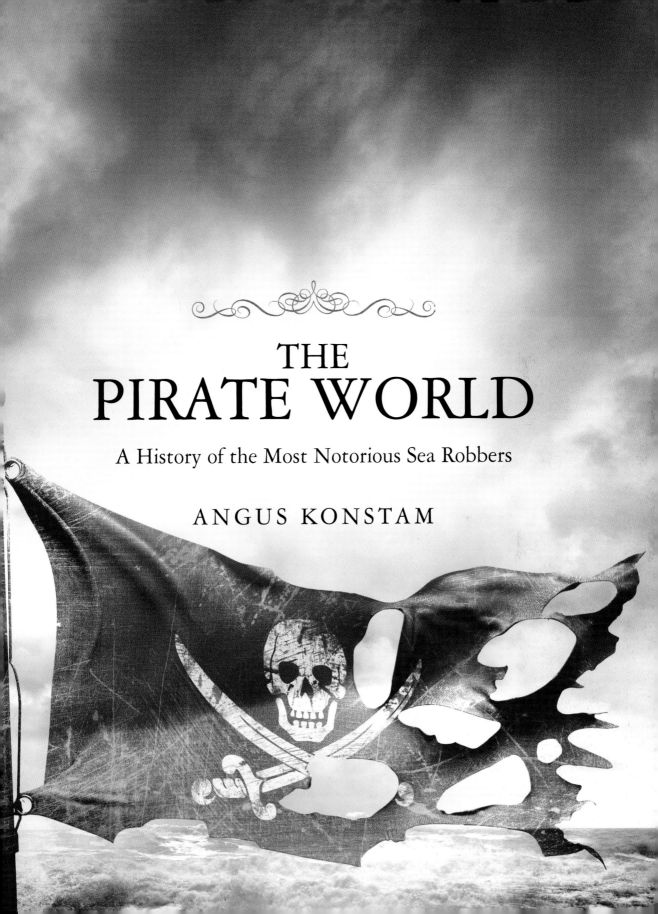

THE
PIRATE WORLD

A History of the Most Notorious Sea Robbers

ANGUS KONSTAM

OSPREY PUBLISHING
Bloomsbury Publishing Plc
PO Box 883, Oxford, OX1 9PL, UK
1385 Broadway, 5th Floor, New York, NY 10018, USA
E-mail: info@ospreypublishing.com
www.ospreypublishing.com

OSPREY is a trademark of Osprey Publishing Ltd

First published in Great Britain in 2019

A catalogue record for this book is available from the British Library.

ISBN: HB 978 1 4728 3097 5; eBook 978 1 4728 3096 8; ePDF 978 1 4728 3098 2; XML 978 1 4728 3099 9

19 20 21 22 23   10 9 8 7 6 5 4 3 2 1

Maps by Nick Buxey
Index by Zoe Ross
Originated by PDQ Digital Media Solutions, Bungay, UK
Printed in Hong Kong through World Print Ltd.

Front cover and page header images from iStock.
Back cover: A painting of Blackbeard's last fight by Jean Leon Gerome Ferris. (SuperStock/Getty Images)
Back flap: Angus Konstam, pictured at the Edinburgh International Book Festival. (Photo by Colin McPherson/Corbis via Getty Images)

Unless otherwise specified, all images in this book are from The Stratford Archive.

Osprey Publishing supports the Woodland Trust, the UK's leading woodland conservation charity.

To find out more about our authors and books visit **www.ospreypublishing.com**. Here you will find extracts, author interviews, details of forthcoming events and the option to sign up for our newsletter.

CONTENTS

INTRODUCTION

Crime, and the public's fascination with it, are as old as civilization itself. So, it wasn't surprising that in 1724, when a London publisher produced a book called *A General History of the Robberies and Murders of the Most Notorious Pyrates*, this lurid pirate exposé became a best-seller. It 'lifted the lid' on a world of violent criminals operating on the high seas. It told of men (and a few women) who rebelled against society, and who lived by their own piratical code. Of course it also helped that most pirates met a colourfully violent end. Three centuries later the fascination with them still remains.

For most people the word 'pirate' conjures up an image of a slightly comical seaborne ruffian with a parrot, a peg leg and a bandana. This comes from a century or more of cartoonish depictions of pirates in *Peter Pan*, *Treasure Island* and *The Pirates of the Caribbean*. Nowadays these sanitized pirates are used to sell everything from rum to home insurance. Similarly, like the pirate himself, his skull and crossbones motif has become an instantly recognizable symbol whose meaning is far removed from its dark and sinister origins.

In fact, all this began long before *Treasure Island*, with Captain Charles Johnson, the author who wrote that bestseller back in 1724. His descriptions of Blackbeard and 'Black Bart' Roberts, of 'Calico Jack' Rackam and Charles Vane, captured the public imagination, and have ensured that his book is still in print almost three centuries later.

His pirates, though, were real people. Nowadays, fictional pirates are usually portrayed either as romantic characters, or as figures of fun. Even historians have added to the problem by using a term that conjures up romance rather than the grim reality of robbery on the high seas. The phrase 'the Golden Age of Piracy' was first coined by the creators of pirate fiction rather than by people who experienced piracy for themselves. There was nothing golden or romantic about the real thing. Still, the term serves as a useful historical shorthand for a time when some of the best-known pirates in history were sailing the world's oceans in search of prey.

Even the term 'pirate' has been changed over the years. Scriptwriters continually manage to confuse the name with others, such as 'privateer', 'buccaneer', 'filibuster', 'corsair', 'freebooter' and 'swashbuckler'. All of them have their own separate meanings. A 'privateer' was a government-sanctioned pirate who did not attack his own people. The French called these people 'corsairs', although even this term became associated with Mediterranean 'pirates' instead of 'privateers'. A 'buccaneer' was a 17th-century raider who preyed on the Spanish in the Caribbean, while a 'filibuster' (or 'freebooter') was simply a French word for a 'buccaneer'. As for 'swashbuckler', the term meant a 16th-century brigand, or a 17th-century swordsman, but in the 20th century it was adopted by the writers of pirate fiction, and then by Hollywood. In the piratical heyday most of these terms were never used the way they are today. Finally, there were 'pirates'. The dictionary specifies that a 'pirate' is someone who robs from others at sea, and who acts beyond the law. Usually, they attacked whatever ships they came across, regardless of nationality. So that term at least should be pretty clear.

Sometimes, though, these 'pirates' themselves crossed the line from one category to another. For example, Captain Kidd was a 'privateer' who later turned to 'piracy'. Francis Drake was a 'privateer', although the Spanish simply called him a 'pirate'. To muddy the waters further, Henry Morgan was a 'buccaneer' operating as an English 'privateer', although technically much of the time he acted as a 'pirate'! While this all sounds pretty confusing nowadays, in fact for most seafarers from the past it all made perfect sense. One of my tasks in this book is to unravel it all, and explain just what piracy actually meant.

This book gives you a window into this piratical past. In these pages we'll cover the whole history of piracy, from the time of the Egyptian pharaohs to the present day. However, we'll be concentrating mostly on the real heyday of piracy. This falls neatly into two halves. The first is the colourful era of the 17th-century buccaneers who preyed on the Spanish Main – men like Henry Morgan or the bloodthirsty François L'Olonnais. The second is what we'll reluctantly call the 'Golden Age of Piracy'. This was the brief but heady period in the early 18th century when the likes of Blackbeard, Black Bart and Charles Vane roamed the seas. So, while giving you an overall picture of piracy through the ages, we'll also look more deeply at these two key periods, and explain why piracy was so prevalent back then.

The main aim of this book is to strip away the myths and inventions from these historical figures to reveal the brutal but utterly fascinating world of piracy as it really was. This book tells the story of the real pirates of history – the men for whom shipwreck, starvation, disease and violent death were a constant threat, and whose careers were usually measured in months rather than years. The notion that their lives were in any way romantic would have been hugely amusing to them.

Angus Konstam
Edinburgh, 2018

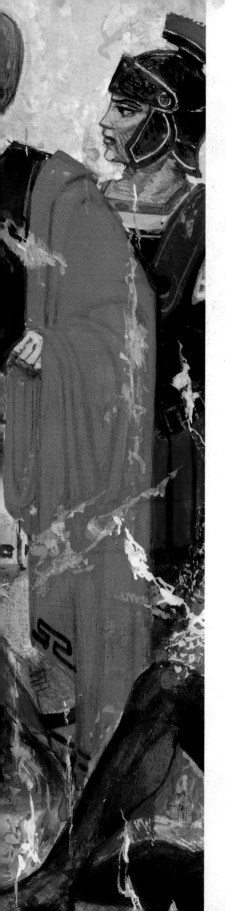

Chapter One

PIRATES OF THE ANCIENT WORLD

THE SEA PEOPLES

Piracy has probably been around since man first took to the sea. However, it first appeared in the historical records before the building of the Egyptian pyramids. As in any period, piracy in the ancient world flourished when there was a lack of central control, and in areas beyond the reach of major powers. The first known pirate group was the Lukkans, a group of sea raiders based on the south-eastern coast of Asia Minor (now modern Turkey). In the 14th century BC, Egyptian scribes recorded that they raided Cyprus, then allied themselves with Egypt's rivals, the Hittites. A century later the Lukkans drop from the records, their disappearance linked to the emergence of a new maritime threat. It is now believed that these pirates became assimilated into a confederation of maritime nomads known as the 'sea peoples'.

This colourful modern mural celebrates the capture of the young Julius Caesar by Cilician pirates in 75 BC. They held him hostage for just over a month, until his ransom was negotiated. Once freed, Caesar gathered a Roman punitive force together, captured the pirates in their island lair, and had them crucified. (DEA PICTURE LIBRARY/Getty Images)

THE MEDITERRANEAN AND THE SEA PEOPLES

Historians have blamed these sea raiders for the collapse of the Bronze Age cultures of the eastern Mediterranean, the end of the Mycenaean Greek civilization, and the destruction of the Hittite Empire. It seems that only the Egyptians weathered this storm. The term 'sea peoples' was first coined by Egyptian chroniclers, who claimed the invaders were migrating tribes who originated in the Aegean and Adriatic. These nomads raided and fought, but they also traded, developing sea routes that spanned the eastern Mediterranean. The same sources mention that the sea peoples were divided into several tribes – the Shardana, Denyen, Peleset, Shekelesh, Weshesh and Tjeker. Later

KEY

- - - - Trade routes   ◄───── Pirate raids   ✗ Battle

1. Around 1250 BC: Attacks into late Bronze Age Greece from northern 'barbarians' begin, and lead to the collapse of Mycenaean Greece.
2. When the 'barbarian' Dorian Greeks finally conquer the Greek mainland, Mycenaean Greek refugees flee to Crete, Cyprus and southern Italy.
3. The Lycians (or Lukkans) are the first of the sea peoples, and develop a reputation as pirates.
4. 1340 BC: The Lycians raid Cyprus.
5. 1285 BC: The Egyptians inflict a major victory on the Hittites at the battle of Kadesh.
6. Early 12th century BC: The Hittite Empire collapses after being invaded by barbarians who attacked it from the west.
7. Late 13th century BC: Desert peoples invade Egypt from the west, but are repulsed.
8. Around 1200 BC: Ugarit and other neighbouring cities are attacked and destroyed by the sea peoples.
9. 1200 BC: The Cypriot city of Enkomi is destroyed by the sea peoples, and the rest of the island ravaged.
10. Early 12th century BC: The sea peoples begin raiding the Egyptian coast.
11. *c.*1175 BC: The sea peoples are defeated in a decisive sea battle fought in the Nile Delta. The survivors flee from Egyptian waters, never to return.
12. The remaining sea peoples conquer the coast of what is now Israel and settle there. By the 6th century BC this evolves into Phoenicia, a growing maritime mercantile power.

historians added two more – the Tursha and Lycians (or Lukkans). The Shardana, Shekelesh and Peleset tribes may have originated in the northern Adriatic, but the Shardana have also been linked to Sardinia. Others probably came from Anatolia. Whatever their origins, these sea raiders formed the first known pirate confederation in history.

The best evidence for them comes from inscriptions in the great temple at Karnak and from the tomb of the pharaoh Rameses III 'the Great' at Medinet Habu. In Medinet Habu the inscriptions record a great sea battle fought off the Nile Delta around 1175 BC. In it, the Egyptian fleet led by Rameses III comprehensively defeated this pirate confederation. The bas-relief carving of the battle provides us with the first depiction of pirates in action, and the earliest illustration of a sea battle. Incidentally these inscriptions mention that the sea raiders allied themselves with Egypt's other enemies, but Rameses broke up this nascent alliance before it could threaten his empire. Although effectively the sea raiders operated like hostile migratory tribes with ships, their actions still represent piracy on a grand scale, and this is exactly how they were viewed by the Egyptians.

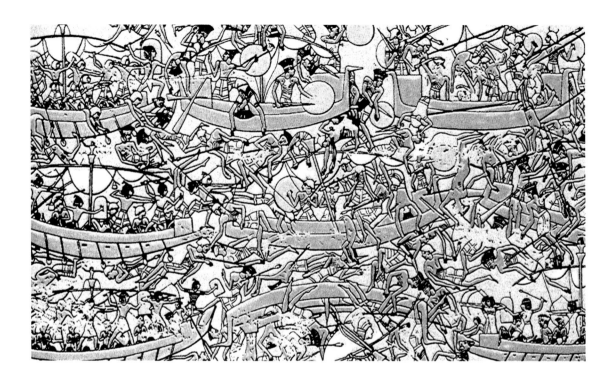

Around 1175 BC the Egyptian pharaoh Rameses III repulsed a major invasion by the sea peoples in a naval battle fought off the Nile Delta. This bas-relief from the temple of Medinet Habu was almost certainly produced to celebrate this victory, and so is probably the world's first depiction of pirates in action.

One of the Medinet Habu bas-reliefs tells us how these pirates fought. The 'sea peoples' are shown in smaller and flimsier ships than those of the Egyptians, and they appear to lack armour, bows and arrows. The carving supports the idea that the 'sea peoples' depended on light raiding craft, and their style of fighting relied on speed and stealth rather than on brute force. Still, Mycenaean accounts describe the 'sea peoples' as being great warriors and seamen, armed with long swords and helmets. They seem to have defeated everyone they came up against – until they met the Egyptians.

The battle with the Egyptians may well have marked the beginning of the end for the 'sea peoples'. The evidence suggests that from around 1220 until the battle in *c.*1175 BC they enjoyed an almost total control of the eastern Mediterranean. After the battle they quickly disappeared from history, which suggests that Rameses effectively put an end to the pirate threat. After their defeat the surviving 'sea peoples' settled in Palestine. The Tjeker tribe continued to trade throughout the region until the 9th century BC, and indulged in piracy on the side. The remains of Tjeker settlements found near Dor in Israel may therefore be the world's oldest surviving pirate havens. Trading eventually replaced piracy as their main source of income, and within a century the Tjekers had amalgamated with the Phoenicians, another major sea power of the ancient world.

THE PIRATES OF ANCIENT GREECE

Piracy was still commonplace throughout the eastern Mediterranean after the collapse of the 'sea peoples', and it would continue until the Romans finally managed to establish their control over the whole Mare Internum (the Inner Sea). While the Ancient Greeks are best remembered for their contribution to Western civilization, they also produced some of the most prenicious pirates of the ancient world. In fact, some Greek city-states actively encouraged piracy as a means of generating wealth. Others, such as the Athenians, formed anti-piracy fleets to keep the sea lanes clear for their own trading ships.

One of the first known pirate havens was Crete, which sat astride the sea lanes between Greece and the rest of the eastern Mediterranean. In the 10th century BC the last remnants of the Minoan civilization on the island were destroyed by the Dorian Greeks. The invaders then used the island as a base for pirate raids throughout the Aegean. Cretan cities such as Cydonia and Eleutherna became thriving marketplaces for slaves and plunder. In Homer's *Odyssey* the Cretans are described as being especially notorious pirates. They continued to be until the rise of Athens as a naval power in the 5th century BC. Then the rapacity of the Cretan pirates was greatly curbed by the Athenians, although they remained an irritant to mariners until the end of the 2nd century BC.

Further north, Plutarch told of the Samians, who were driven from their island by invaders, and so moved to Mycale, where they established themselves as pirates. The Athenians finally managed to crush the Samian pirates, and, following a raid on Athens by pirates from Lemnos, the Athenian navy campaigned to clear all pirates from the Aegean. Apart from Mycale and Lemnos, other pirate strongholds on Cithnos, Mykonos and the Sporades were

This detail of a 4th-century BC Greek vase decoration shows the execution of captured pirates by 'keelhauling': tying the victims up, throwing them overboard, and then dragging them beneath the hull of a ship.

In another decoration from a 4th-century BC Greek vase, two opposing groups of Greek hoplites (well-armoured infantry) do battle at sea, as oarsmen manoeuvre their galleys into battle. All naval battles or pirate attacks of this period were conducted in this manner.

destroyed by Athenian anti-piracy expeditions during the 5th century BC. Herodotus provides us with vivid accounts of pirate attacks, and of these Athenian anti-piracy operations.

During the 3rd century BC the Aetolian League became the dominant power in central Greece. Part of its success was due to its use of piracy as a means of waging economic warfare against its enemies. Soon Aetolian pirates dominated the waters of the Aegean basin. It was not until the League's defeat by the Romans in 192 BC that this particular piratical scourge came to an end. By then, though, many of the pirates had simply moved to Cilicia on the south coast of Asia Minor. These Cilician pirates would soon become the largest and most notorious pirate community in the ancient world.

Piracy also flourished on the other side of Greece, along the eastern coast of the Adriatic. The Illyrians and Dalmatians raided the Greek and Italian coasts, and even ventured into the central Mediterranean. Their depredations reached a peak in the 3rd century BC. The Illyrian pirate menace was curbed somewhat when the Romans conquered the region, but even after the Roman annexation of Illyria in 168 BC the pirates continued their attacks from relatively secure bases on the Dalmatian coast, and from the islands of Corfu and Cephalonia.

During the 2nd century BC Roman punitive expeditions finally cleared most of the Dalmatian mainland of pirates, but they still maintained a presence in the islands until the mid-1st century BC, when 'Pompey the Great' dealt with the problem once and for all. During this period which saw the growth of Rome as a major power, piracy was also rife in the Tyrrhenian Sea, on the far side of Italy. In fact the very name 'Tyrrhenian' effectively meant the same as 'pirate'. As early as the 5th century BC Thucydides recorded several pirate attacks in these waters, carried out by 'barbarians' based on the islands of Elba, Corsica and Sardinia. These attacks continued for another two centuries. Other well-known pirate bases existed in the Lipari Islands off the north-east corner of Sicily, the Balearic Islands and the Ligurian coast of what is now the French

Riviera. This pirate activity was clearly no sudden phenomenon. Earlier Greek mythology tells how the god Dionysus was captured by Tyrrhenian pirates, who mistook him for the son of a wealthy merchant. Dionysus thought it all a hilarious escapade, but he still turned the pirates into dolphins as punishment for their temerity. Later, in the 3rd century BC, the Romans also accused the Sicilians of piracy, although in truth the Greek rulers of the island sanctioned legitimate privateering rather than piracy. However, the establishment of a Roman hegemony in the western Mediterranean finally ended any form of organized piracy in the region.

THOSE TROUBLESOME CILICIANS

If anywhere deserved the reputation of being the cradle of piracy in the ancient world, it was Cilicia. A narrow strip of land in Asia Minor (now south-eastern Turkey), Cilicia perched between the towering Taurus mountains and the Mediterranean Sea. This inhospitable region remained largely unsettled, apart from a few small coastal towns. The coastline itself was broken up by rocky headlands, hidden bays and well-protected anchorages. It was also ideally placed for attacks on shipping sailing between Syria and Greece or Italy, as pirates could strike unexpectedly, then quickly return to their secret hideaway before anyone could track them down. In effect this rocky coast was the perfect hideout for pirates. This was therefore the region that attracted the Aetolian pirates driven out of the Aegean in the early 2nd century BC.

These Aetolian pirates began to arrive in Cilicia at exactly the same time that the Seleucid kings of Syria stopped their regular naval patrols. The decisive Roman victory over the Seleucids at Magnesia (190 BC) resulted in the western part of Asia Minor becoming a Roman protectorate. The Seleucid navy was withdrawn but the Romans lacked the inclination to maintain their own naval presence in the area. Consequently, the pirates were allowed to develop their power base without military interference. Their communities expanded, and soon they became strong enough to counter just about any naval force that could be sent against them.

As a young man, Gaius Julius Caesar (100–44 BC) was captured by pirates in the Aegean Sea, and held to ransom by them. On his release he returned to the pirate lair at the head of a punitive expedition, and crucified his former captors.

This bas-relief carving from a Roman sarcophagus from Sidon in Lebanon shows a Roman merchant ship of the kind that plied the Mediterranean for much of the Roman era. Frequent civil wars and rebellions within the empire led to the re-emergence of pirates during this period, and ships like this were their prey.

At first the Cilician pirates limited their attacks to the eastern Mediterranean, gradually spreading their influence further along the sea lanes until they reached the shores of Crete, Palestine and Egypt. They also raided coastal towns, gathering captives whom they then sold in Cretan markets. Richer prisoners were held to ransom, while plunder was sold in the nearby cities of Miletus, Ephesus and Smyrna, all of which were within the borders of the Roman protectorate in Asia Minor. This continued for decades, until the expansion of Roman trade and influence into the eastern Mediterranean meant that the Romans themselves became the principal victims of piratical attacks. Their most celebrated victim was the young Julius Caesar, who was captured by them in 75 BC.

According to the Greek historian Plutarch, when the pirates demanded a ransom of twenty talents, Caesar volunteered to pay fifty. He was held prisoner for thirty-eight days, all the time threatening to crucify them once he was released. Once the ransom finally arrived from Miletus he was set free. Caesar sailed to Miletus, gathered a punitive expedition together, and returned to the pirate lair. He captured almost all of the pirates, took their plunder as spoils of war and imprisoned his captives. He then crucified them all, just as he had threatened to do while languishing as their prisoner.

During the early 1st century BC the Cilician pirates began to operate in the Aegean and Adriatic, areas the Romans regarded as their own. They even began raiding the coast of Italy in search of slaves. The Roman Senate responded by passing its first anti-piracy law. Now, pirates could no longer trade within the Roman sphere. The pirates, of course, simply took their plunder elsewhere. In 86 BC, a pirate squadron defeated a Roman naval force off Brundisium in south-east Italy, disrupting communications between Rome and Greece. The Romans sent warships to counter the pirate threat, and a succession of Roman provincial governors led punitive but ultimately indecisive expeditions against the pirates. Then, in 74 BC, Marcus Antonius Creticus (the father of Mark Antony) was defeated while attacking the Cretan pirates, and he died shortly afterwards. As a result, Roman attitudes hardened, especially when Cilician pirates supported the slave revolt led by Spartacus (73–71 BC). Roman punitive expeditions could temporarily subdue the Cilician pirates, but not eradicate the threat they posed. In order to properly protect Roman trade, a much more dramatic response was needed.

The bireme became the standard pirate-hunting ship in the Mediterranean. Not only was it fast and agile, but it carried a contingent of highly trained Roman marines. This bas-relief is from the Temple of Fortuna Primigenia in Praeneste.

POMPEY AND THE PIRATES

POMPEY AGAINST THE PIRATES

Today, Pompey the Great is best remembered as the bitter enemy of Julius Caesar during the Roman Civil War. Before that, though, Pompey was regarded as the 'First Man in Rome' and the saviour of the Roman Republic. Much of this acclaim stemmed from his successful war against the pirates, which effectively ended piracy in the Mediterranean. Following the revolt of Spartacus and the support given to him by the Cilician pirates, the Senate decided to completely eradicate piracy in the Mediterranean. This task would stretch the resources of Rome to its limits. Consequently, in 67 BC Pompey was offered an

KEY

---- Trade routes   ◄—— Pirate raids   ◄—— Pompey's voyage to Cilicia

1. The Roman Republic consolidates its control over Italy in the wake of the Second Punic War (218–201 BC).

2. The troublesome pirate dens along the Illyrian coast are cleared after Rome gains control of the region in the early 2nd century BC and it becomes a Roman province.

3. 146 BC: Rome gains control of Greece and Macedonia, and they become Roman provinces. As a result, the Achaean (or southern Greek) pirates are driven from the mainland and forced to re-establish themselves in the Aegean islands.

4. As Roman control extends into the Aegean, the pirates are driven east and establish themselves along the Cilician coast. In 133 BC this region becomes a Roman province, but the pirate scourge continues.

5. Mithridates of Pontus (134–63 BC) encourages piracy in the Eastern Mediterranean as a means of countering the expansion of Roman influence.

6. 75 BC: Julius Caesar is captured by pirates based on the island of Pharmakonisi. He is released when a ransom is paid, but he returns with a naval force and captures and crucifies the pirates.

7. 72 BC: Cilician pirates aid Spartacus, who is leading a slave revolt in Italy. Although Spartacus is defeated the following year, this pirate alliance galvanises the Romans to deal with the Cilician threat.

8. 67 BC: the Roman Senate awards Pompey the Great an *imperium* and unlimited funds, with orders to clear the Mediterranean of pirates.

9. 67 BC: Pompey divides the Mediterranean into 13 areas, and then moves eastwards, destroying pirate bases and driving the survivors ahead of him. By the end of the year all remaining pirates are concentrated in Cilicia, which he left open to them.

10. Finally, Pompey blockades Cilicia, and his troops methodically clear the region until they capture the final pirate stronghold at Coracesium (now Alanya). The Mediterranean is now completely free of pirates and will remain so for several centuries.

imperium (military dictatorship) and ordered to drive the pirates from the Mare Nostrum, or Mediterranean Sea.

Pompey's *imperium* granted him sweeping powers, an immense budget and a military force of some 500 ships including 200 war galleys, and 120,000 Roman legionaries. The sheer scale of this enterprise – the equivalent today would be the diversion of over half the US budget and armed forces – showed just how seriously the Roman Senate took the pirate threat. Pompey had fought the pirates before – and he knew exactly how to go about the operation. The majority of his pirate-hunting warships were fast enough to pursue the pirates on the high seas and trap them. These lighter craft

Gnaeus Pompeius Magnus (106–48 BC), or Pompey the Great, is best known for his opposition to Julius Caesar, but arguably his greatest achievement was to rid the Mediterranean of pirates.

were supported by a fleet of heavier warships, filled with veteran Roman legionaries. Pompey divided the Mediterranean into 13 districts, and he placed each of them under the command of a legate (deputy commander). In a co-ordinated strike, each legate led his forces against the pirate bases and blockaded them, then sent other ships to scout for unknown pirate lairs. Then Roman troops destroyed the pirate bases. Many pirates surrendered; while ringleaders were executed, others were interrogated, ransomed and released. The attacks were launched simultaneously throughout the Mediterranean, with the deliberate exception of Cilicia, which was not attacked.

Next, Pompey led his fleets in a sweep through the Mediterranean, working eastwards from Gibraltar, driving any surviving pirates ahead of him. Many pirates ran into the blockades established by the legates and were defeated. The rest were driven towards Cilicia. In 40 days Pompey had successfully cleared the Mediterranean of pirates, apart from Cilicia, which he now blockaded. All attempts to break out were repulsed. Then Pompey tightened the cordon, pushing inwards along the coast to reduce the size of the pirate enclave. Legionaries were sent ashore to explore every inlet and gully to make sure that nobody slipped through the net as the pirates were gradually driven towards the main pirate stronghold of Coracesium, sited on a remote Cilician peninsula. Then Pompey sent in his legionaries. The Cilicians were no match for Roman veterans, and within weeks they were forced to surrender.

Once again Pompey was surprisingly lenient, executing only the ringleaders and exiling the rest to the hinterland. Pompey returned to Rome in triumph. In three months he had destroyed 120 pirate bases, killed 10,000 pirates, captured 500 ships and secured a fortune in pirate booty, which was shared equally among Pompey, his men and the Senate. As a result, for the first time in history, the Mediterranean was cleared of pirates. In the Mare Nostrum, Roman shipping would remain safe from attack for another four centuries. The Pax Romana (Roman Peace) would break down only following the collapse of the Western Roman Empire, at which point the anti-piracy mantle was passed to the Eastern Romans. In the guise of the Byzantine Empire, the war against piracy would continue to be fought well into the Middle Ages – until Byzantium itself finally succumbed to the Turks. However, by then piracy was once again big business in the Mediterranean, although the centre of piratical activity had moved from Asia Minor to the shores of North Africa.

OPPOSITE A late Roman cargo ship of the 4th century AD in a mosaic showing the embarkation of exotic animals. As Roman military power declined, merchant ships of this kind became easy prey for a new breed of pirates, operating in the Adriatic and Aegean Seas.

Chapter Two

MEDIEVAL PIRATES

THE SEA RAIDERS

Most people don't always think of the Vikings as pirates. They rarely robbed at sea, although certainly there were those who made their living from piracy. Rather, they were sea raiders, raiding coastal targets. Although the Vikings were not the first of Europe's Dark Age sea raiders, they were arguably the most successful. For over two centuries they terrorized northern Europe, then returned to conquer, and to rule. Although not strictly pirates, they did rely on their ships for speed, mobility and surprise – all hallmarks of the sea raider.

Most Vikings began as small-scale raiders, using one or two ships, but by the end of the era they operated in large fleets, capable of landing substantial armies. The Anglo-Saxon cleric Alcuin dated the coming of the Vikings to the morning of 8 June AD 793. That day a Viking band descended upon the monastic island of

The *Anglo-Saxon Chronicle* entry for AD 793 recorded that on 8 June 'Heathen men came and miserably destroyed God's church on Lindisfarne, with plunder and slaughter.' The attack on Lindisfarne marked the start of a devastating series of Viking raids on the British Isles. (Photo by Werner Forman/Universal Images Group/Getty Images)

Lindisfarne, off the north-east coast of England, and put the monks to the sword. It then pillaged the monastery and set it on fire. Even in an age when murder was commonplace, this seemed an unprecedented atrocity. A chronicler described the raid as 'an attack on both the body and soul of Christian England'. Alcuin went further, claiming that 'never before had such a terror appeared in Britain as we now have suffered from a pagan race'.

The attack on Lindisfarne was only the beginning. Just a year later, in 794, an Irish monk recorded 'the devastation of all the islands of Britain by the gentiles' as Viking attacks were launched along Britain's eastern seaboard. Over the following years the monastery of Iona off Scotland's western coast was plundered, as were several others.

By 798 the Vikings were raiding the northern coast of Ireland, using their winter camp in Orkney as a base. Raids were launched increasingly further afield, until by the start of the 9th century it seemed as if no coastal community was safe. The monks who bore the brunt of these likened the fury of the Norsemen to the apocalypse. The Book of Jeremiah produced a suitably appropriate quote: 'Out of the north an evil shall break forth upon all the inhabitants of the land'. To these monks, the arrival of the Vikings presaged the end of the world. Although this day of judgement never came, the Viking raids would continue.

By the 820s a new breed of Norse overlord was appearing, willing to offer British coastal communities their protection in return for money. The era of the Viking raiders was starting to give way to a new phase of conquest, in which Britain became the battleground of warlords rather than a destination for plunderers. However, the raids would continue in Ireland for another decade. In 820 a cleric wrote in the *Annals of Ulster* that 'The sea spewed forth floods of foreigners into Erin, so that no haven, no landing place, no stronghold, no fort and no castle might be found, but it was submerged by waves of Vikings and pirates'. Even settlements that had been considered far enough from the coast to be safe from attack now fell prey to the Norsemen.

During the late 830s the Viking leader Turgeis followed up these attacks by seizing control of Ulster. Then the Vikings captured Dublin, and established a new power base.

For the most part the Vikings who raided the shores of Celtic Scotland and Ireland were Norsemen – from Norway. The raiders who devastated much of Anglo-Saxon England during the late 8th and early 9th centuries were Danish. The *Anglo-Saxon Chronicle* entry for 835 declared that 'In this year the heathen devastated Sheppey' – an island on the Thames Estuary. From that point on the

A large Viking force landing on the coast of Anglo-Saxon England. While this illustration accompanied a 12th-century English manuscript chronicling St Edmund the Martyr, the scene it depicts still captures the general menacing appearance of Viking raiding parties of the 9th century.

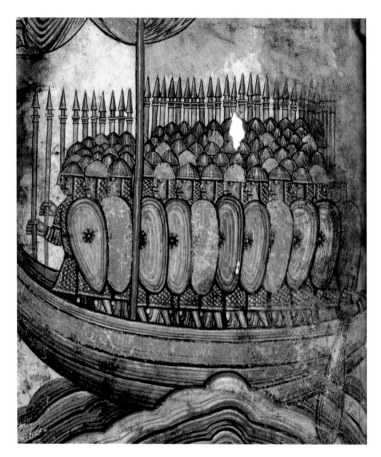

A Viking longship filled with heavily armed warriors, as depicted in an illustration from a 12th-century Frankish manuscript, the *Life of St Aubin*. The warriors of a real Viking raiding party would have been less uniformly dressed and equipped, and would probably have had a less disciplined appearance.

Chronicle reported that each year the raids became larger and more numerous. During the 850s the Vikings established themselves in Kent on the islands of Thanet and Sheppey, which provided secure bases for expansion. This heralded a change of emphasis from raiding to conquest.

The Anglo-Saxons and the Celts were not the only peoples to suffer from Viking attacks. 'In the year of our Lord 845, the vast army of the Northmen breached the frontier of the Christians.' This was how a friar in the monastery of St Germain-des-Prés near Paris recorded the arrival of a large Viking force at the very gates of Paris. Actually the first Viking raiders had arrived in the Frankish kingdom 25 years earlier when they raided the Frisian (Dutch) coastline and probed the defences of the river Seine. In 841 the Vikings plundered Rouen, then extorted *danegeld* (protection money) from the locals. This was followed by the great attack on Paris in 845, when the sack of the city was only prevented by the payment of a horde of silver. Within six years the Vikings had established a permanent settlement on the lower Seine, which duly became Normandy, the land of the Norsemen.

In Europe the Viking raids lasted little more than half a century, a period that ended because there was little left to plunder, and because the Vikings had developed a taste for conquest. Whether these raiders can be dubbed pirates is open to question, although contemporaries viewed the term as virtually interchangeable with Viking. In effect the activities of individual Viking bands had become subsumed into a larger movement, influenced in turn by the development of a national Scandinavian identity. Although the Viking age would continue into the mid-11th century, by the middle of the 9th century the days of the sea raider were over.

PREYING ON THE HANSE

While the ascendancy of the Viking sea raider might have ended, the era of the Scandinavian sea trader would continue, forming part of a greater mercantile empire that would transform the economy of Europe. By the 12th century a new series of major ports had developed along the Baltic and North Sea coasts – Hamburg, Lübeck, Bremen, Stettin, Danzig and Rostock being the most prominent.

In 1241, Lübeck and Hamburg joined forces to form the Hanseatic League, a merchant guild that supervised maritime trade in the region, and provided some protection against pirates. Other ports soon joined the League, until by 1300 the Hanse had become a major power in the Baltic and North Seas. The League dominated north European trade, which in turn reduced the power of individual states in the region. The Danes in particular were staunch opponents of the League, and they waged a low-key war against this mercantile monopoly that lasted well into the 14th century. This conflict also attracted those who sought to claim their own share of this Hanseatic wealth.

One such group was the confederation known as the Cinque Ports on England's south-east coast. The organization was formed in the early 14th century to protect local English shipping from pirates and to encourage trade. However, while the Hanseatic League remained a legitimate trading organization, its English equivalent also operated as an extortion racket, a semi-legal piratical organization that safeguarded its own shipping and those of its 'clients', but attacked shipping that had not paid for 'protection'.

In the Baltic, a group of German mercenaries and pirates formed their own brotherhood. Known as the *Vitalienbrüder*, or 'Victual Brothers', a name coined after running supplies into a beleaguered Stockholm in 1392, they then spent a decade fighting an undeclared war against both the Danes and the Hanseatic port of Lübeck. In 1393 the brothers sacked the Hanse ports of Bergen in Norway and Malmö in Sweden. The following year they seized Visby on the Baltic island of Gotland, and the island became their major base. This, however, coincided with a political union that united Sweden, Denmark and Norway under the Danish crown, and meant the brothers now had a powerful enemy.

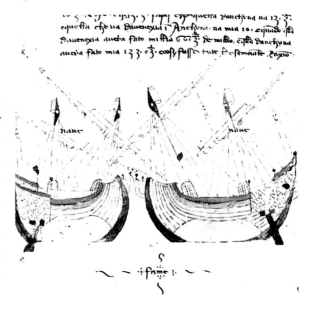

Although these merchant ships are depicted in a 14th-century Venetian manuscript, they actually show much older vessels, of the kind used by Italian traders operating in the Aegean, Adriatic and eastern Mediterranean from the 12th century on.

KLAUS STÖRTEBEKER AND THE VICTUAL BROTHERS

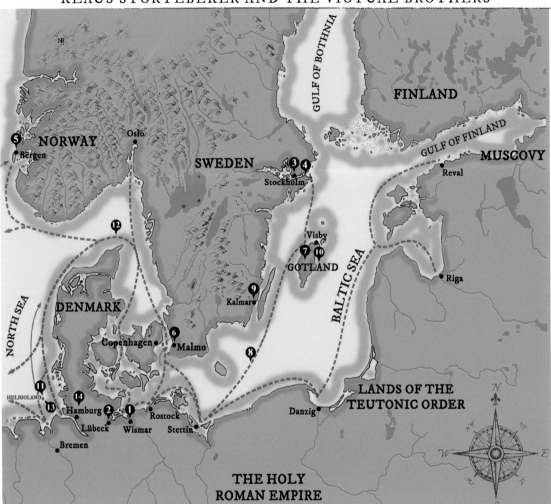

Still, the brothers continued their attacks on Danish and Hanseatic ships, until in 1398 Denmark leased Gotland to the Teutonic Knights. This powerful military brotherhood duly invaded Gotland and drove the pirates from the island. Then the survivors of the brotherhood established new bases on the Ems estuary on the modern German–Dutch border, and on the North Sea island of Heligoland. This new brotherhood called itself the Likedeelers, which meant sharing things in equal measure.

Their most famous pirate leader was Klaus 'Störtebeker'. It is probable that his given name was Nikolaus Storzenbecher, and that he was born in Wismar

KEY

---- Trade routes   ◄—— Pirate raids

1. Around 1360: Klaus Störtebeker is born in Wismar.

2. 1367: The Hanseatic League declares war on Denmark, the dominant power in the Baltic. The Danes suffer several defeats, and in 1370 they sue for peace. The Hanse are now the region's major power.

3. 1389: The Danish Queen Margaret invades Sweden and besieges Stockholm.

4. 1392: The Victual Brothers – a pirate organisation – side with the Swedes against the Danes and relieve Stockholm. The pirates are also aided by the Hanseatic League.

5. 1393: The Victual Brothers raid the Hanseatic port of Bergen, and the League declares war on the pirates.

6. Early 1394: The Victual Brothers sack Malmö, and go on to raid dozens of smaller ports in Sweden and further afield.

7. Late 1394: The Victual Brothers seize the island of Gotland, and Visby becomes their main pirate base.

8. By the winter of 1394/95, maritime trade in the Baltic is at a standstill thanks to pirate attacks on the sea lanes. Both the Hanseatic League and the Danes suffer from this.

9. 1397: The Kalmar Union is founded, as Denmark, Sweden and Norway are united under the rule of Queen Margaret.

10. 1398: The Kalmar Union hires the Teutonic Knights to deal with the pirate threat. The Knights invade Gotland, Visby is captured, and the surviving Victual Brothers flee the island.

11. 1399: What remains of the pirate brotherhood re-establishes itself on the island of Heligoland.

12. 1400: Störtebeker becomes the head of the pirate brotherhood, which now calls itself the Likedeelers. They prey on Hanseatic and Danish ships alike.

13. 1401: A Hanseatic fleet attacks the Likedeelers, and in a sea battle fought off Heligoland the pirates are crushed and Störtebeker and the other survivors are taken prisoner.

14. 1401: Störtebeker and his men are executed in the Hanseatic port of Hamburg.

---

around 1360. Störtebeker was one of the brotherhood who escaped from Gotland, and he rose to command the Likedeelers. His pirate flagship was allegedly called the *Seetiger* (*Sea Tiger*), and was the largest ship in the pirate fleet. Heligoland was ideally placed for attacks on shipping sailing in and out of Hamburg, which by then was a thriving Hanseatic port. This made the Likedeelers a serious threat.

Störtebeker finally met his match in 1401, when the Hanse sent a fleet led by Simon of Utrecht to capture the island. The two forces met off Heligoland, and after a long-running battle the *Seetiger* was captured, as were Störtebeker and 71 of his men. They were taken to Hamburg to face trial, and that October Störtebeker was condemned to death. Even then he struck a deal. Pardons would be granted to all of the crewmen whom he could walk past after his head was cut off. As the legend goes, he staggered past 11 of his shipmates before he was tripped by the executioner. The heads of the pirates were stuck on spikes along the banks of the river Elbe. Today Klaus Störtebeker is something of a German hero, a cross between Robin Hood and Sir Francis Drake.

THE PIRATE KNIGHTS OF THE MEDITERRANEAN

In the early 5th century AD, when the Western Roman Empire collapsed in the face of barbarian invasion, the Eastern Empire somehow managed to weather the storm. In fact, as the Byzantine Empire it survived as a political entity for another millennium. The Byzantine Empire was effectively founded in AD 330 when the emperor Constantine established a new capital in Byzantium, which he renamed Constantinople. The city soon became a major commercial centre which thrived on its maritime trade. Byzantine warships patrolled these sea lanes, protecting the empire from seaborne attack and keeping pirates at bay.

This all started to unravel during the late 11th century. First came a catastrophic military defeat at the hands of the Turks at the battle of Manzikert (1071), which led to the loss of much of Asia Minor. Then the Crusaders appeared, who regarded the Greek Orthodox Byzantines as almost as much of a religious enemy as the Muslims. In the aftermath of Manzikert the Byzantine navy had been neglected, and so in 1189 the Byzantine emperor Isaac II signed a naval treaty with the Venetians. This policy backfired spectacularly, as in 1204 these Italians stormed and sacked Constantinople. What remained of the Byzantine navy was destroyed, and while the tattered remnants of the empire survived, its ability to control the seas did not. So from 1204 onwards the waters of the eastern Mediterranean were once again a haven for pirates.

This new infestation took root amid the patchwork of petty states where a new breed of Latin overlord saw piracy as a useful source of revenue. Seizing this opportunity, Italian adventurers took to piracy in large numbers. They established themselves in remote bases, well away from Venetian patrols or from Byzantine authority. Crete was a favourite haunt of theirs, as was Monemvasia in southern Greece. This harbour, known as the 'Rock', was a medieval fortress built on a rocky outcrop, joined to the mainland by a small causeway. This near-impregnable base became a major pirate haven during the 13th century, as did the nearby Mani peninsula to the west.

Other busy pirate havens were found in the Dalmatian Islands of the central Adriatic – now part of Croatia's picturesque Dalmatian coast. The region was then known as Maria, and it had been infested by pirates before the establishment of Byzantine control. Now, like the Peloponnese, Maria provided pirates with a secure base astride the rich Venetian sea lanes.

Their most successful pirate leader was Margaritone of Brindisi (1149–97), an Italian knight who began his maritime career as a pirate. He then became a privateer working for the Norman rulers of Sicily, who rewarded him with high office. In 1185 he seized control of the Dalmatian Islands from the Byzantines, and turned them into a major privateering base. His end finally came while assisting the Sicilians by helping to defend Naples. In 1194 he was captured when the city fell to the Holy Roman Empire, and he died in a German prison. Still, the Dalmatian Islands remained a pirate base for another decade, until the archipelago was attacked and captured by the Venetian fleet in 1204. During the century that followed local pirates established new havens on Corfu, Zante and Cephalonia, and these islands remained active pirate bases until the late 14th century.

The real pirate heyday in Greek waters came in the later 13th century. The emperor Michael III recaptured Constantinople from the Italians, but he lacked the resources to rebuild the navy. Instead he hired pirates as privateers, and under the Byzantine banner they preyed on Italian ships throughout the eastern Mediterranean. The irony was that most of these pirates were Italians, from Venice or Genoa. One of these Byzantine privateers, Giovanni de lo Cavo, seized Rhodes from the Genoese in 1278, and became overlord of the island, ruling in the name of the Byzantine emperor. Rhodes remained a thriving pirate haven until 1306, when the Knights Hospitaller conquered the island.

This 14th-century seal depicts a cog, the round-hulled and commodious little ship that was used as both merchant vessel and warship during this period. This example shows a rudimentary quarterdeck and forecastle.

By that time the rest of the region had been subjugated by the Turks, the Byzantines or the Italians. The growing naval power of the Ottoman Empire and the regional dominance of the Venetians and the Knights Hospitaller meant that lawlessness was curbed and maritime trade encouraged. After the capture of Rhodes, only remaining pirate refuge on the Greek coast of the Aegean was Athens. From 1311 on, pirates flourished under the protection of Duke Manfred of Athens, a Catalan mercenary who hired his services to Latin and Byzantine rulers alike. His so-called 'Catalan pirates' remained a scourge in the region until the Turkish conquest of Athens in 1458.

By the late 14th century the centre of piratical activity in the Mediterranean had moved west to the Mediterranean coast of North Africa. At a time when the merchants of northern Europe were re-establishing long-abandoned maritime trading routes, the Mediterranean was being divided into a religious battleground, where piracy and naval power would be combined to deadly effect.

PIRACY AROUND THE BRITISH ISLES

One of the characteristics of the feudal system was that the central power of the crown was limited. This made it difficult to maintain a state navy powerful enough to root out pirate dens. Therefore, in British waters, piracy thrived wherever it could, particularly in the English Channel and the Irish Sea. In the Channel Islands pirates even became semi-feudal lords themselves, benefiting from the dynastic struggle between England and France. By the early 13th century piracy had become such a serious problem in the English Channel that only the best-protected ships were guaranteed a safe passage. One of the most notable of these pirates was Eustace the Monk, also known as the Black Monk,

In this depiction of a late 14th-century cog from an English seal, the forecastle and sterncastle structures are more integrated into the hull of the ship, providing a better platform for fighting.

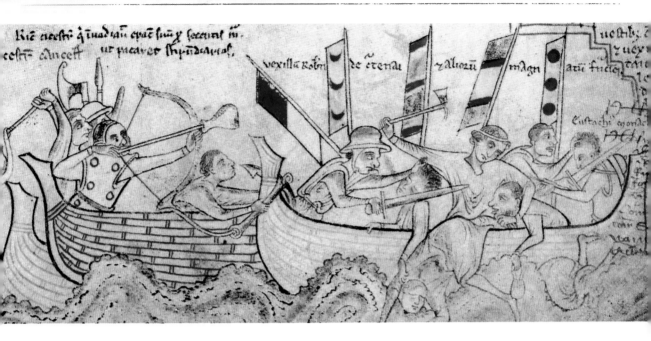

who was simultaneously hired as a privateer by both King John of England and King Philip II of France. From his base in Jersey he dominated the waters of the English Channel, demanding protection money from shipping and attacking those who refused to co-operate.

From 1205 until 1212 he served King John, leading raids on the French coast from Calais to Brest. Then in 1217 Eustace used his fleet to transport a rebel English army across the Channel. This pirate fleet was lying at anchor off Sandwich on the south-east coast of England when it was surprised and destroyed by a larger English force. Eustace was captured, and together with his fellow pirates he was put to the sword.

By the mid-13th century both the English and French governments found a way to contain the pirate problem by issuing formal privateering licences. This was the first time that privateering 'letters-of-marque' were used to control would-be pirates, and to channel their energies into attacking a state's enemies. As long as the pirates did the bidding of their chosen monarch, then they enjoyed the protection of the crown. If they attacked the shipping of the ruler's country, however, they would find themselves branded as pirates and hunted down.

On the Celtic fringes of Britain, in the west of Scotland and in Ireland, small-time piracy continued to thrive well into the 16th century. The Lords of the Isles were descendants of the Vikings who once controlled the west coast of Scotland, and they operated in much the same way as Eustace, attacking passing

A late 13th-century manuscript illustration depicting the activities of Eustace the Monk, a pirate who preyed on shipping in the English Channel during the late 12th and early 13th centuries. He was finally defeated and killed in a battle off Sandwich in 1217.

ships that refused to pay them their 'feudal' dues. It was not until the 17th century that the Scottish crown managed to end this extortion racket.

In Ireland the lack of central authority meant that pirates enjoyed the same immunity. Probably the most notorious Irish pirate – and certainly the most unusual – was Gráinne Ní Mháille (or Granuaile), known to the English as Grace O'Malley (c.1530–1603). In Irish legend she enjoys the marvellous title of the 'Sea Queen of Connemara'. Her father, the clan chief of the Ní Mháille (O'Malley), controlled much of the coastline of what is now County Mayo, charging taxes on fishermen using his coastal waters. In 1546 she married Donal O'Flaherty, heir to the O'Flaherty title, and bore three children to him before he was killed in 1564. His wife took over his small-time pirate operation, establishing herself on her father's fortified stronghold on Clare Island off the west coast of County Mayo. Tiring of this in 1577, the authorities sent a force to besiege her stronghold, and she was captured and imprisoned. Granuaile was eventually released, but her children were kept in prison as surety for her good behaviour. She sailed to London, and was granted an audience with Queen Elizabeth I. The result was that her children were freed, and the now elderly 'pirate queen' continued her small-scale raiding until her death. While much of this story is shrouded in Irish legend, her visit to the court generated sufficient interest for her life to be chronicled by English-speaking contemporaries. Despite the relatively small scale of her activities, her sex guaranteed that she would be remembered long after the raids carried out by other minor Irish pirates and clan leaders were long forgotten. However, set against the activities of the English sea raiders of the same era, she was little more than a local tear-away.

This 16th-century German woodcut depicts the execution of pirates – in this case a band led by a pirate captain called Henszlien, who operated in the North Sea until his capture by Hanseatic warships and his execution in Hamburg.

OPIDVM S. Augustini lignis tantum constructum,
amœnissimos habuit hortos, vtq; suis frueretur, homo
anobis vero cum inde soluertur iuxta, iam incineres redactum. Præsidium hic erat, eo lustimans
aliud, item eodem numero ad duodecim Equites erant
Versus leucas in loco S Helena dicto, hinc progressis
scilicet quemadmodum canes in prœspexum; eho consulto desueta
erant nisi ad prohendos Emitur et Galeo a destructam
regionum quæ prorsus media iacet, occuparent

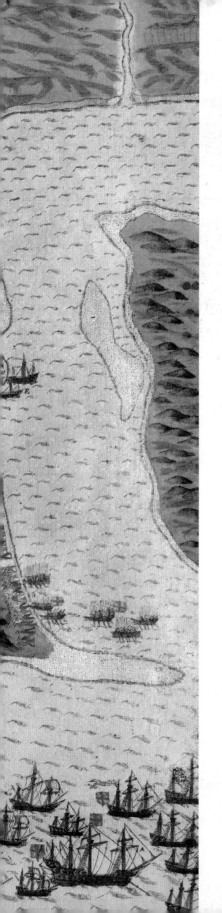

Chapter Three

THE SEA DOGS
OF THE
RENAISSANCE

SEA DOGS: PRIVATEERS
OR PIRATES?

There is truth in the notion that one country's privateer is another country's pirate. The famously swashbuckling age of Elizabethan 'sea dogs' was a time when national and individual interests could be pursued in tandem, and a fortune could be won while ostensibly serving the state. For much of this period Catholic Spain and Protestant England were 'cold war' rivals. In 1585, after three decades of low-level conflict, this turned into a full-blown war. This long-awaited struggle was largely brought on by the actions of sea captains such as Francis Drake, whose raids on the Spanish Main effectively constituted acts of war. Still, now freed from diplomatic restraints, Queen Elizabeth I was able to let slip her sea

After his capture of Cartagena in 1572, Francis Drake sailed around Cuba and up the east coast of Florida. In late May he came upon the Spanish settlement of St Augustine, almost hidden in a coastal inlet. He captured the settlement and its fort but found little of value there. (Photo by VCG Wilson/Corbis via Getty Images)

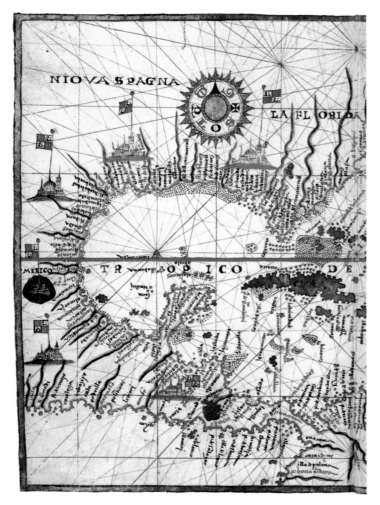

An early 16th-century Spanish map of the New World, bisected by the tropic of Cancer. The Spanish viewed the whole region as their exclusive preserve, and hunted down other European 'interlopers' who tried to encroach on their territory in the Caribbean basin.

dogs, and for two decades they terrorized the Spanish in the New World and thwarted Spanish attempts to invade England.

However, the English were not the only national group to attack Spain's overseas empire. Others saw the potential offered by streams of specie – silver ingots, gold bars and coins – being shipped to Spain. The French began attacking Spanish treasure ships in the 1520s, some four decades before the English began their attacks on the Spanish Main. Then Dutch fleets began preying on Spanish convoys in American waters.

Throughout this period the Spanish regarded other Europeans who ventured into the Caribbean as dangerous 'interlopers'. The phrase 'no peace beyond the line' referred to the division of the New World into Spanish and Portuguese sectors. According to the Treaty of Tordesillas (1494), the longitudinal line of 36° 47' West, which ran through Brazil, set the boundaries of the Spanish New World. Everything to the west of this line belonged to Spain. Clearly other emerging maritime powers felt they were being excluded, and so the scene was set for centuries of conflict. For the Spanish the situation was very simple. With the exception of Brazil, they considered the Americas to be Spanish territory, and so would resist any attempt by outsiders to establish their own colonies 'beyond the line'. Therefore they regarded 'interlopers' as pirates, even if they arrived to trade rather than to fight. This heavy-handed reaction inevitably fuelled the steady drift into open conflict. For example, Queen Elizabeth issued 'letters of reprisal', which allowed privateers to attack the Spanish in redress of losses suffered at Spanish hands. In law, 'reprisal' was considered a perfectly legal act.

A privateer was an individual or crew who was given a licence or 'letter-of-marque' by their national government, which allowed them to attack the shipping of another belligerent state. Privateering was governed by an internationally recognized set of rules, which in theory meant that if caught by the enemy, then the privateer was considered an enemy combatant rather than a pirate. In return for this legal protection the state that had issued the letter-of-marque usually received a percentage of the profits. As long as they abided by the rules, privateers could not be legally hanged as pirates.

However, the Spanish refused to observe these niceties, particularly if the privateers operated 'beyond the line'. While the English regarded Sir Francis Drake as a national hero, the Spanish likened him to the Devil and labelled him as a pirate, to be hunted down without mercy.

THE SPANISH MAIN

Pirateers leaving from one of the ports in England's West Country for the New World would begin by running down to the Canary Islands, or Cape Verde. There they would pick up the north-east trade winds, which took them across the Atlantic. They would make landfall in the Lesser Antilles, where they would take on water and supplies. The islands were not settled by the Spanish, so for the moment they were safe. However, from that point on the ship would be operating in the Spanish Main.

Potosi in Peru was literally a mountain of silver, and soon became the source for most of that specie transported from the Spanish New World to Europe by means of the treasure fleets. This vast wealth naturally attracted pirates and privateers who sought to garner their own share of this treasure.

The so-called Pearl Islands off the Spanish Main, now the Isla de Margarita and its neighbours off the coast of Venezuela, as depicted in a 16th-century Spanish engraving. 'Interlopers' found these to be a valuable and poorly defended source of plunder.

In theory, this term referred to the northern coastline of the South American mainland – the region Spanish settlers called the Tierra Firme, or 'dry land'. However, the term 'main', or sea, was soon extended far beyond these coastal waters, and by the mid-16th century it had become synonymous with anywhere in the Caribbean basin. To avoid confusion, the Caribbean Sea itself soon became labelled the Mar del Norte (North Sea). This meant that once past the Lesser Antilles, any privateer would be regarded as an 'interloper'.

The Caribbean basin itself contained numerous islands, the largest being Cuba, which separated the Gulf of Mexico from the Mar del Norte. To the east lay Hispaniola, with Puerto Rico beyond it. Then the chain of islands that formed the Lesser Antilles curved southwards towards the Tierra Firme. To the north of Cuba lay the Lucayos, or Bahamas.

In the midst of this tract of warm seas and tropical islands lay the Spanish settlements, ranging from substantial cities such as Havana and Cartagena to smaller harbours and settlements. Ports such as Havana, Cartagena, Vera Cruz and Nombre de Dios were well protected but many smaller ports lay open to attack.

From 1524 on this ramshackle overseas empire was administered by the Council of the Indies, which controlled shipping to and from the New World, and the transport of specie. In 1535 the Council established the viceroyalty of New Spain, based in Mexico City, and in 1544 a second viceroyalty was created in Peru.

Eventually smaller regional *audencias* were created, administered by one of the two viceroys. *Audencias* were Spanish administrative districts in the New World, each ruled by a governor. While on paper all this sounded impressive, the system itself was open to misuse, corruption and neglect.

A ceremonial mask made from gold, one of a number of similar objects wrought by native goldsmiths from what is now Colombia, a region the Spanish claimed for themselves as part of the 'Spanish Main'. It was the arrival of objects such as these in Europe which first attracted non-Spanish 'interlopers' in the area, eager for their own share of the plunder.

THE TREASURE FLEETS

The impetus behind Spanish conquest in the New World was the search for gold. While the conquistadors and the administrators who followed were entitled to the largest share, the Spanish crown claimed its *quinto*, or fifth. By the 1520s Spanish ships were transporting this specie back to Spain. From 1526 on, after Spain lost several treasure ships to French pirates, these shipments were transported as part of a *flota*, or fleet. From then on this annual convoy transported the wealth of the New World back to Spain, presenting the Spanish crown with a windfall and 'interlopers' with a tantalizing opportunity for plunder.

For almost two centuries this convoy followed a set routine. There were two treasure fleets. The first of these, the New Spain fleet, sailed from Seville in April, and after a transatlantic crossing it made landfall in the southern part of the Lesser Antilles. In September the Tierra Firme fleet followed the same route, but once in the Spanish Main it took a different direction. After collecting the silver produced in Mexican mines the New Spain fleet wintered in Vera Cruz, then sailed on to Havana in the early summer. The Tierra Firme fleet wintered in Cartagena, where it collected Colombian emeralds and Venezuelan gold. In the spring it continued on to Nombre de Dios, where it picked up a huge cargo

THE DEFENCES OF THE SPANISH MAIN

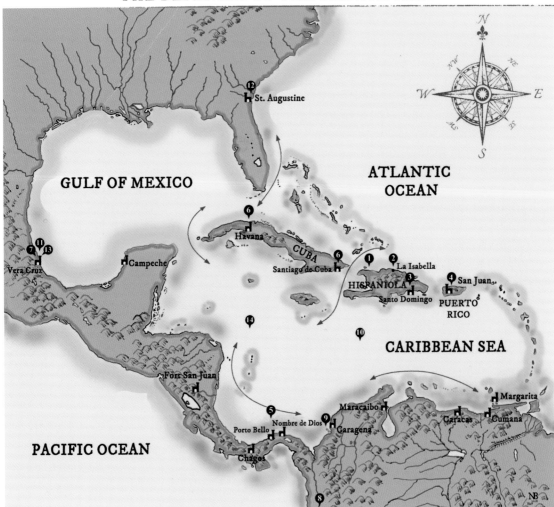

of silver, which had been transported there from Lima. Following Drake's attack on the town in 1572, the treasure terminus was moved just up the coast to Porto Bello. The *flota* then sailed on to join the New Spain fleet in Havana.

Usually the two *flotas* returned home separately. The New Spain fleet usually arrived in Seville first, in the early autumn, followed a month later by the Tierra Firma fleet. However, in time of war the two convoys would band together for protection. This involved a risk, as it could delay departure well into the hurricane season, which lasts from June to November. The *flotas* of 1544, 1622 and 1715 were all overtaken by major hurricanes. So the safe arrival of a treasure

KEY

←— Regular Spanish Naval Patrols   🏰 Fortification

1. 1492: Columbus discovers the Americas and establishes a settlement at La Navidad on Hispaniola.
2. 1494: The larger settlement of La Isabela is founded, but it is abandoned within four years.
3. 1498: Santo Domingo is founded on the southern coast of Hispaniola. It becomes the first fortified Spanish settlement in the Americas.
4. 1508: The Spanish conquistador Juan Ponce de León builds a settlement at San Juan in Puerto Rico.
5. 1510: On the isthmus of Panama, the settlement of Nombre de Dios is founded and fortified.
6. 1511: Cuba is settled, and settlements are soon established at Havana and Santiago de Cuba.
7. 1519: Hernán Cortés invades Mexico and establishes a port at Vera Cruz. Soon all of Aztec Mexico is under his control.
8. 1526: Francisco Pizarro marches south from Panama and invades the Incan Empire. Within a decade all of Peru is under Spanish control.
9. 1533: A well-defended settlement is founded at Cartagena.
10. 1535: The first French 'interlopers' enter the Caribbean and attack Spanish shipping and settlements.
11. 1558: Extensive defences are built at Vera Cruz.
12. 1565: A colony is established at St Augustine in Florida.
13. 1568: English 'interlopers' are defeated at San Juan de Ulúa, the fortress protecting Vera Cruz.
14. During the 1560s, the Spanish begin a major fortress-building programme in the New World to improve the defences of their American colonies.

The island of Hispaniola was the site of the first Spanish colony in the New World, and one where the Spanish first clashed with the indigenous population. By the mid-16th century, though, it was a stable and reasonably prosperous island, dominated by the port of Santo Domingo.

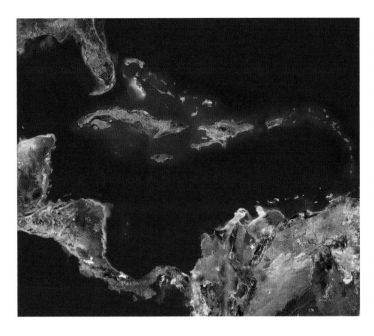

During the age of sail, shipping in the Caribbean was dependent on the prevailing winds, which generally blew westwards. North of Cuba though, the winds blew eastwards, through the Florida Straits and the Bahamas Channel. The Spanish treasure *flotas* followed a clockwise route through the Caribbean to take advantage of these winds. (Planet Observer/Getty Images)

fleet was a cause for rejoicing in Seville, and on the few occasions when the fleet never arrived, then the Spanish economy suffered.

Naturally enough, these treasure fleets were attractive targets for 'interlopers'. However, even Sir Francis Drake found the well-guarded treasure fleets too difficult a target. The only occasion in which a *flota* was captured in its entirety was in 1628, when a Dutch squadron drove one ashore off Cuba. However, Drake found a weak point in the system. Many of the treasure ports were still poorly defended, as was the road used to transport silver across the isthmus of Panama. So a well-planned attack could seize a fortune in plunder. Then there was always the chance that a treasure ship could be caught on its own, as shipments from Spanish possessions in the Philippines to Mexico were still made by single ships, called Manila galleons. For much of this period the Spanish would make every effort to preserve the flow of specie from the New World to the Old. For their part, men like Drake regarded the Spanish Main as their hunting ground, and the treasure fleets as their prey.

THE FRENCH CORSAIRS

The first serious attack on Spain's overseas empire came just two years after the conquistador Hernán Cortés captured Tenochtitlán, the capital city of the Aztecs. A portion of the Aztec gold seized by Cortés was shipped back to Spain. In May 1523, the three treasure ships made their landfall at Cape Sagres, the south-west corner of the Portuguese coast. Their voyage had been uneventful, and Seville was now just three days' sail away. It was then that lookouts spotted five strange sails to the north. The Spanish turned away, but within hours the five ships overhauled the Spaniards. Outmatched, the Spanish were forced to surrender. The mystery ships were French privateers, commanded by the 'corsair' Jean Fleury (or Florin) of Honfleur. To the French, 'corsair' was synonymous with 'privateer'; the word was derived from the French term *la course*, which in nautical terms meant a cruise. France and Spain had been intermittently at war with each other since 1494, and by 1523 the two nations were still fighting. The French crown issued a privateering licence to Fleury, who duly set off in search of Spanish plunder. Off Cape Sagres he hit the jackpot.

The plunder reputedly included chests filled with golden Aztec statues, exquisite jewels including an emerald the size of a fist, bejewelled headdresses and even a live jaguar. The total value was placed at 800,000 ducats. When Fleury returned to Dieppe, the news of his success caused a sensation. For the first time, the rest of Europe understood the full scale of Spain's plunders and conquests in the New World. After Fleury's encounter, a wave of French corsairs put to sea, and many ventured 'beyond the line'. Fleury never lived long enough to join them, though. In 1527 he was captured by the Spanish, who tortured him and then executed him as a pirate. This, though, didn't curb these attacks. For example, between 1534 and 1547 alone, 24 unescorted Spanish merchant ships were lost to French corsairs in the Spanish Main, with further ships taken

The Spanish conquistador Hernán Cortéz, leading his men in an assault of the Aztec capital Tenochtitlán. This paved the way to the Spanish conquest of all of Central America, and the establishment of the province of New Spain.

A convoy of Spanish merchant ships are attacked off the northern coast of Cuba by a small squadron of French corsairs. In the foreground, Spanish settlers do what they can to rescue their countrymen. During the 1540s and 1550s French corsairs regularly operated in Cuban waters.

in European waters. In 1537 unescorted ship losses were so great that the Spanish royal income from the New World in the form of taxation and trading duty was cut by half. The initial French attacks resulted in the creation of the *flota* system for treasure ships in 1526, which at least ensured the bulk of the annual treasure shipment would reach Spain without interference. However, the losses among unescorted ships continued. Spanish ships were not the only victims. In 1536 a group of French 'interlopers' attacked the port of Havana, while the following year smaller Spanish settlements in Honduras and Panama were sacked. In 1540 the corsairs captured San Juan in Puerto Rico, and in 1541 Havana was plundered again. In 1544 it was the turn of Cartagena, one of the largest settlements on the Spanish Main.

The most successful of these French privateers was François le Clerc, a corsair known as 'Pegleg' (Jambe de Bois). In 1553 he ravaged Puerto Rico and Hispaniola, then early the next year he captured Santiago de Cuba, and held the town to ransom. Although le Clerc returned home with his plunder, his lieutenant Jacques de Sores remained behind with three ships. In July 1555 he descended on Havana, and after a siege lasting two days the governor was forced to yield the city to the corsairs. After plundering what he could, de Sores burned the long-suffering city to the ground.

SPANISH COINAGE

In the 16th century the basic unit of Spanish coinage was the *maravedi* – the equivalent of an English penny. Across Europe the standard unit of international currency was an 8oz (227g) gold coin called the *ducat*, whose stability was assured by its adoption by German and Italian banking houses. The Spanish crown introduced its own golden equivalent – the *mark* – but in 1537 this gave way to the *escudo*, which was valued at 374 maravedis. In 1566 the Spanish also minted a half-escudo coin and also a two-escudo coin called the *doblon* – more famously known as the *doubloon*. Later, other larger coins were minted, worth four and eight escudos apiece. In 16th- and 17th-century England the *pound* (coin) was the equivalent of a pound (weight) of silver, and was therefore the equivalent of an escudo.

The silver coin used by the Spanish was the *real*, which contained an ounce of silver. Before the depreciation of silver prices caused by the huge influx of specie from Peru, 11 silver reales were the equivalent of one gold escudo. However, from the 1560s on the rate was set at 16 reales to the escudo. These coins were minted in half-, one-, two-, four- and eight-real denominations, although the most common was the eight-real coin – also known as the silver *dollar* or *peso*. This coin became popularly known as a *piece-of-eight*. This meant that a golden doubloon was the equivalent of four silver pieces-of-eight.

In 1544, French corsairs attacked, looted and burned the port of Cartagena. Despite the wealth of the settlement it was poorly defended, and the French made off with plunder valued at 150,000 ducats.

HUGUENOT CORSAIRS IN THE SPANISH MAIN

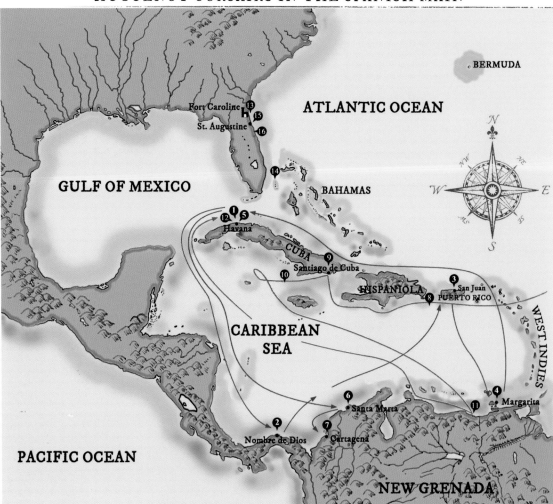

It was de Sores who introduced a sectarian element to these attacks. He was a Protestant and a follower of John Calvin (1509–64), the French-born reformer. Calvinists viewed the Spanish as their religious enemies, and therefore privateering expeditions took on a religious aspect.

Although peace was declared in 1559, a clause in the treaty stated: 'West of the prime meridian … violence by either party to the other side shall not be regarded as a contravention of the treaties.' In other words there would be no peace 'beyond the line'. In France, the end of the Spanish war was followed by the French Wars of Religion (1562–98). The withdrawal of state-sponsored

KEY

◄— First French attacks   ◄— Raids of le Clerc and de Sores   ▌▌ Fortification

The First Attacks

1. 1536: French 'interlopers' attack and plunder Havana.
2. 1537: Nombre de Dios is sacked.
3. 1540: San Juan in Puerto Rico is captured and plundered by French raiders.
4. 1541: French corsairs loot the rich pearl fields of Margarita.
5. 1541: Havana is looted for the second time in six years.
6. 1544: Santa Marta is ransacked and burned.
7. 1544: Cartagena is captured by the French.

François le Clerc and Jacques de Sores

8. 1553: François le Clerc raids Spanish settlements on Hispaniola and Puerto Rico.
9. Spring 1554: Le Clerc sacks Santiago de Cuba.
10. Summer: Le Clerc returns to France, but his deputy Jacques de Sores takes command of the remaining Huguenot corsairs.
11. Spring 1555: De Sores leads raids along the coast of the Spanish Main.
12. Summer: The French capture Havana after a brief siege, and the city is burned.

Jean Ribault

13. 1564: The French settlement of Fort Caroline is established on the coast of Florida.
14. 1565: Pedro Menéndez de Avilés is sent to deal with the French 'interlopers' in Florida.
15. September 1565: After landing at St Augustine, the Spanish march north, capture Fort Caroline and destroy the settlement. The French there are massacred.
16. October 1565: Jean Ribault's fleet is wrecked by a hurricane. The survivors are massacred by the Spanish.

privateers offered Spain a respite, but then after the French Protestants (Huguenots) suffered a string of reverses in this civil war and were driven from their homes, some of these exiles decided to establish settlements of their own in the New World.

In 1564, French Huguenots founded a colony on the banks of the St Johns River, near the modern city of Jacksonville, Florida. This settlement, named La Caroline (or Fort Caroline), was established near the spot where two years earlier the French explorer Jean Ribault had raised a stone marker, proclaiming that the area belonged to France. The Spanish had other ideas. Their fear was that a rival European power would manage to establish a base within striking range of their Caribbean settlements, which would then serve as a haven for

Havana, the principal Spanish port in Cuba, was attacked and burned by French corsairs twice in ten years. This shows the assault by the corsair Jacques de Sores, carried out in 1555.

The French stronghold of Fort Caroline in Florida, established in 1564, was situated on the banks of the St Johns River. The river protected its earth and timber palisades on one of its three sides, while the other two were enhanced by a moat. There was only one entrance, served by a drawbridge and covered by artillery.

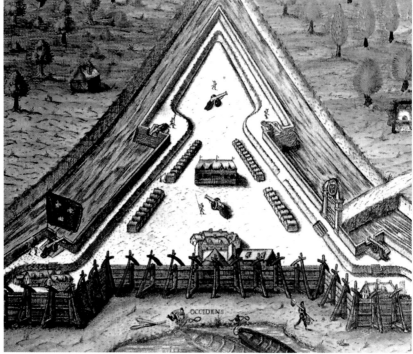

pirates and 'interlopers'. So a Spanish force under Pedro Menéndez de Avilés was sent to remind the Huguenots that Florida belonged to Spain.

First, the Spanish expedition established a forward base at St Augustine, some 30 miles (48km) south of La Caroline. Ribault and his followers put to sea in an attempt to intercept the Spanish ships. Instead, they were caught by a hurricane, and were shipwrecked on the Florida coast. Meanwhile Pedro Menéndez de Avilés marched north from his base, and in September 1565 he attacked the remaining garrison of La Caroline. Heavily outnumbered, the French defenders were quickly overwhelmed. After putting all male prisoners to the sword, the Spanish marched south again to round up the survivors of Ribault's squadron. Around 350 Frenchmen were captured, and this time all of them were massacred. The Spanish must have congratulated themselves on dealing with a serious threat to their overseas empire. However, an even more serious one was looming just over the horizon.

HAWKINS AND THE ARRIVAL OF THE ENGLISH

When word of Spain's New World riches reached the rest of Europe, few powers were able to take advantage of the opportunities this presented. Henry VIII of England was a Spanish ally until 1527, when he temporarily switched his

In September 1565 a Spanish force led by Pedro Menéndez de Avilés stormed and captured the French stronghold of Fort Caroline, sited on Florida's St Johns River. Most of the fort's small garrison were massacred.

JOHN HAWKINS IN THE SPANISH MAIN

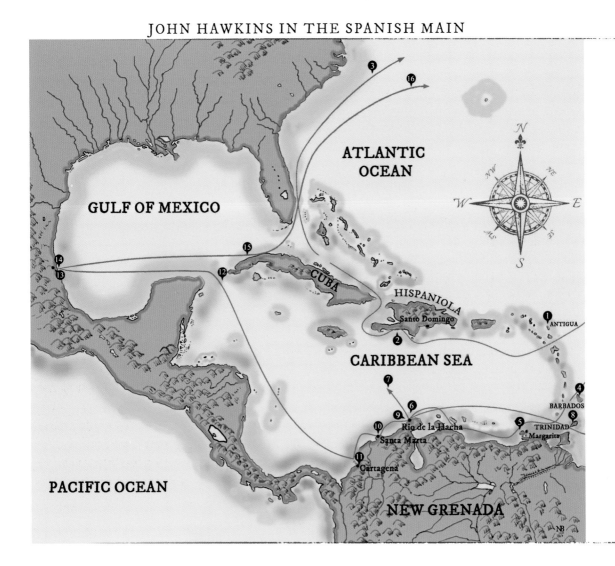

allegiance to the French. A few letters-of-marque were issued, and later that year the Spanish recorded the first English 'interloper' beyond the line. This unnamed English captain landed a force on Hispaniola, plundered what he could, and then withdrew. While this process was repeated several times over the next four decades, the political status quo dictated against English interference in the Spanish Main. France remained England's main rival, and so an alliance with Spain made sound political sense. Trading expeditions to the Spanish Main were forbidden, and while the French made the most of these opportunities for plunder, the English had to content themselves with privateering voyages closer to home. However,

KEY

◄──── First voyage   ◄──── Second voyage   ◄──── Third voyage

First Voyage

1. 1563: Hawkins makes a landfall at Antigua, then sails west into the Caribbean.
2. He lands on the coast of Hispaniola to the west of Santo Domingo and sells his cargo of slaves.
3. He returns to Plymouth by way of the Windward Passage and the Bahamas Channel.

Second Voyage

4. 1565: Hawkins makes a landfall at Barbados, then sails south towards the Tierra Firme coast.
5. He is unsuccessful in selling his slaves at Margarita.
6. He finally sells his human cargo at Rio de la Hacha, after threatening to fire at the town.
7. Once again he returns home through the Windward Passage.

Third Voyage

8. 1568: Hawkins makes landfall at Trinidad and sails up the Tierra Firme coast.
9. June: The inhabitants of Rio de la Hacha refuse to trade with him.
10. July: He sells part of his human cargo at Santa Marta, after threatening to bombard the settlement.
11. August: Hawkins attempts to enter Cartagena, but is fired upon and forced to withdraw.
12. September: His squadron is hit by a hurricane in the Yucatán Channel.
13. Hawkins is forced to put in to Vera Cruz to make repairs. To safeguard his ships, he captures the fortress island of San Juan de Ulúa. Two days later the Spanish treasure fleet arrives, and a truce is arranged.
14. 23 September: The Spanish launch a surprise attack, and San Juan de Ulúa is recaptured. The Spaniards turn the fort's guns on the English ships, and Hawkins is forced to flee in the *Minion*, accompanied by Drake in the *Judith*. The rest of his squadron is captured.
15. October: Over a hundred of Hawkins' men demand to be put ashore, rather than face starvation. They are duly captured by the Spanish.
16. The *Minion* and the *Judith* return home through the Bahamas Channel, their crews racked by hunger and disease.

following the accession of Elizabeth I in 1558, relations between England and Spain cooled considerably. As an active Protestant, Elizabeth saw Spain as a religious rival. Although open war was avoided, the 'cold war' between the two countries provided ample opportunities for English sea captains.

John Hawkins (1532–95) was the first of these. His first voyage in 1562 was more of a slave trading expedition than an attempt to break the Spanish monopoly in the New

Sir John Hawkins (1532–95) was one of the great figures of the Elizabethan age. While he began his career as a merchant and slave trader, he soon developed into a skilled sea dog, before becoming a naval commander. He also oversaw the transformation of the English royal fleet, whose ships proved far superior to their Spanish counterparts.

Pictured here in the 1540s, the 700-ton *Jesus of Lubeck* was once part of Henry VIII's fleet, but Hawkins modernized her, turning the old Tudor warship into a forerunner of his later 'race-built' English galleons. She was captured by the Spanish during the battle off San Juan de Ulúa in 1568.

World. After collecting a cargo of slaves on the West African coast, Hawkins crossed the Atlantic, making landfall near Antigua in the spring of 1563. His three small ships carried 300 Africans, whom Hawkins hoped to sell in Hispaniola. Avoiding Santo Domingo, Hawkins landed his human cargo some miles up the coast and opened negotiations with local landowners. The captain of a cavalry squadron even offered to protect the English in return for a cut of the profits. Hawkins returned to England a wealthy man, the richest in Plymouth.

It was inevitable that Hawkins would try again. This time he was offered royal backing and lent a royal warship, the 700-ton *Jesus of Lubeck*. Although she was imposing, she was also old and obsolete, so Hawkins modernized her at his own expense, Once again Hawkins picked up a cargo of slaves in West Africa, but this time the Spanish were less willing to co-operate. Turned away from the island of Margarita off the Venezuelan coast, he tried elsewhere, eventually selling his slaves at Rio de la Hacha. Still, in late 1565 Hawkins returned home with an even greater profit than before, although this time his actions earned a formal complaint from the Spanish ambassador. Hawkins had proved that, if he wanted to, he could break the Spanish trade monopoly.

Hawkins then embarked on a third attempt. This time the *Jesus of Lubeck* was accompanied by a second royal warship, the 120-ton *Minion*, as well as Hawkins' own ships *Swallow*, *Solomon* and *Judith*, the last of these commanded by Hawkins' young kinsman Francis Drake. The expedition left Plymouth in October 1567 and made for the West African coast. A slaving raid near Cape Verde ended with the deaths of eight sailors, killed by poisoned arrows as Hawkins was forced to retreat back to his ships. Then, in what is now Sierra Leone, Hawkins discovered that two local chiefs were at war. He sided with one against the other, and helped his new-found ally capture Conga, his enemy's capital. The Englishman's reward was a cargo of 500 Congalese slaves. Hawkins then sailed for the Spanish Main, his holds filled with human cargo.

In June 1568 he visited Rio de la Hacha again, but this time the defenders drove him off. Still, he managed to sell half of his slaves at Santa Marta further up the coast. This sale involved a pretence. The locals put up a token resistance, and Hawkins threatened to bombard the town, thereby 'forcing' them to trade with him. Hawkins hoped to sell the rest of his slaves at Cartagena, but again he was driven off by gunfire.

Hawkins sailed north, but in September 1568 his fleet ran into a hurricane off Cuba, and he was forced to put in to Vera Cruz in Mexico for repairs. This was the treasure port for Mexican silver, and was known to be protected by a fort on a small island in front of the harbour. So Hawkins decided to use subterfuge. His squadron flew the Spanish flag as they entered port, and then his men quickly seized the port's defences before the garrison realized they had been tricked. Hawkins thought he could repair his fleet in peace, but two days

A large English 'race-built' galleon of the 1580s. Unlike Spanish galleons with their towering superstructure, these vessels, the design of which was supervised by Hawkins, had a sleeker appearance, and made better use of the guns they carried. This gave them a decided edge over their Spanish opponents in a naval battle.

A late 17th-century depiction of the Spanish fortifications of San Juan de Ulúa, protecting Vera Cruz, the principal Caribbean port of New Spain (now Mexico). It was here in September 1568 that Hawkins and Drake fought their way out of a Spanish trap.

later the annual Spanish treasure *flota* arrived, a powerful force commanded by Admiral Francisco Luján. The English were now outnumbered.

A temporary truce was arranged, but Martín Enríquez, the governor of New Spain, had no intention of being dictated to by Hawkins. Under cover of darkness Spanish troops were hidden in a cargo ship moored between the two fleets. As dawn rose on 23 September, the Spanish leaped ashore and overran the English garrison on San Juan de Ulúa, the island in Vera Cruz's harbour where the ships were moored. Having captured the shore batteries, the Spaniards turned the guns on the English ships. The fight lasted all day, but it was clear that Hawkins was in a hopeless position. Finally he gave orders to cut and run.

The *Jesus of Lubeck* was trapped, as was most of the rest of Hawkins' fleet, but eventually Hawkins in the *Minion* and Drake in the *Judith* ran the Spanish gauntlet and escaped to the open sea. The two English ships had no provisions, so a hundred crewmen demanded to be put ashore. Disease and starvation took its toll on many of the rest. By the time the ships limped back into Plymouth only a handful of men were left alive, including Hawkins and Drake. The expedition had been a disaster, but it awoke in both Hawkins and Drake a burning hatred of the Spanish, whom they viewed as breaking their word. While Hawkins then concentrated on rebuilding Elizabeth's Navy Royal, Drake vowed to return to the Spanish Main and to take the fight to the enemy. What would begin as a private war would end up as a clash between nations.

DRAKE'S FIRST RAIDS

Francis Drake (*c*.1540–96) was already an experienced sea captain in 1570, having been at sea since his teens. After participating in his second cousin John Hawkins' expeditions, he had more knowledge of the Spanish Main than most other Englishmen. In 1570 the queen granted him a 'letter of reprisal' – a peacetime version of a privateering letter-of-marque. It allowed him to attack the Spanish and to seek redress for the losses he had suffered at San Juan de Ulúa. In 1570 Drake led the first of three small annual expeditions 'beyond the line'. His first force comprised just two small ships. Little is known about what exactly he did on the Spanish Main that year, although he probably treated the raid more as a reconnaissance than as a privateering cruise. In any event, there is no record of plunder being brought back.

The English sea dog Sir Francis Drake (*c*.1540–96) made a career out of harassing the Spanish in the New World, although his most lucrative success came in 1579, with his capture of a treasure ship in the Pacific. Queen Elizabeth of England once described him as 'my pirate'.

We know a little more about what happened the following year, when Drake returned in the 25-ton *Swan*. He cruised off Nombre de Dios, before teaming up with a French Huguenot privateer. Together they captured several prizes, and by the time Drake returned to Plymouth the *Swan*'s hold contained a rich haul in plunder. Drake's reputation was secured. His backers were delighted, and they promptly financed a new expedition. So in 1572 Drake left Plymouth in two ships, the 70-ton *Pasco* (or *Pasha*) and the smaller *Swan*. By July Drake was back off Nombre de Dios, having established a secret base on the coast which he called Port

OF SHIPS AND GUNS

The popular myth of the period is that the Spanish sailed in large, cumbersome ships, while the English preferred smaller, faster ships. Like all such myths, the story contains an element of truth and a few misleading generalizations.

The galleon was a Spanish invention – a faster and more manoeuvrable version of its predecessor the cumbersome *carrack* (or *nao*). Until the 1520s most large warships were carracks – three-masted square-rigged ships with high forecastles and sterncastles. These ships made excellent warships as they were large and stable enough to carry artillery. When it first appeared in the 1530s the galleon was a streamlined version of the carrack, with a lower superstructure and better sailing qualities. Originally designed as a treasure carrier for the *flotas*, the galleon was soon used as a warship. Under Hawkins' guidance English shipbuilders developed the design to produce their own 'race-built' galleons. These same features were also found in smaller privateers such as the 100-ton *Golden Hind*, built to carry 18 heavy guns.

This armament was important, as the English regarded gunnery as the key to victory. While the Spanish tactics called for guns to be fired once, just before boarding, the English liked to keep their distance. Most Spanish carriages were two-wheeled, while the English preferred more sophisticated four-wheeled carriages, which could be reloaded faster. The Spanish advantage was the quality of their sea soldiers. The two protagonists of the era followed different tactical doctrines, one emphasizing firepower and the other close combat.

Conditions on board were primitive. The *Golden Hind* was less than 70ft (21.4m) long, with a 20ft (6.1m) beam. Below decks space was taken up by stores, guns and ammunition, and by the crew of 80 sailors. While Drake had his own tiny cabin, his senior officers only had alcoves on the deck below. The crew slung their hammocks between the guns. Still, Drake circumnavigated the globe in this little floating world.

Pheasant. It was there that a third English ship joined Drake's, commanded by Captain James Raunce (or Ranse). Deciding to attack the port, Drake left Raunce in charge of the ships, and on the evening of 28 July he landed 70 men on the beach a few miles from the town. What should have been a straightforward night attack, however, soon went badly wrong.

A watchful sentry raised the alarm just as the Englishmen were approaching the town, and so the local militia were ready for them. In the fighting that followed

Drake was wounded in the leg. The Spanish were eventually driven off, but they regrouped, and were reinforced by the garrison of the town's forts. A rainstorm kept the two sides apart, but the English realized that they were now heavily outnumbered. When Drake fainted from loss of blood, his men retreated back to their ships. Drake's first real attack on the Spanish Main had ended in failure.

Raunce decided to quit the expedition, leaving Drake with just two ships and 60 men. Drake now had too few crew to sail his ships properly, let alone to continue raiding. He scuttled the *Swan* and moved his crew onto the *Pasco*, then began cruising the Main in search of prizes before he returned home. So far his expedition had little to show for its efforts. In January 1573 he decided to return to Nombre de Dios, and intercept the annual convoy of Peruvian silver which was due to be transported across the isthmus. The timing was crucial. Drake had to intercept the mule train before it reached Nombre de Dios and also avoid the Tierra Firme fleet, which was due there in January.

On returning to the Panama coast, Drake recruited Cimaroons (runaway slaves living in the jungle) as guides. Hiding his ships, Drake led a small force inland, then set up an ambush astride the 'Royal Road'. Now all Drake had to do was stay in hiding and trip the ambush at the right moment. Unfortunately, Drake reckoned without Robert Pike. The sailor had been drinking heavily, and when he heard the pack train approaching he leaped up and cheered. His companions dragged him back into cover, but he was spotted and the alarm was raised. The mule train was turned around and Drake had no option but to order his men back into the jungle.

Soon after returning to their ships, the Englishmen encountered a French Huguenot pirate, Guillaume le Testu (or Têtu). Together they decided to have another go at the treasure train, which was now back in Panama. Once more Drake recruited the Cimaroons, and soon his 40 men – half French and the rest English – were lying in ambush again. This time everything went smoothly. The mule train was captured after a short, sharp fight. Drake found it contained 15 tons of silver – too much to carry – as well as smaller gold bars. Drake decided to bury the silver for the moment, and made off with what they could transport.

The only casualty in the fighting had been le Testu, who was too badly wounded to move. So he was left behind, and was captured and executed by the Spanish. The Spanish pursued the 'interlopers' and caught a Frenchman, who was tortured until he revealed where the silver was buried. So all Drake had left was the gold, which he shared with his French allies. In August 1573, Drake returned to Plymouth, having made just enough to please his investors and to clear his debts.

DRAKE'S CARIBBEAN RAID

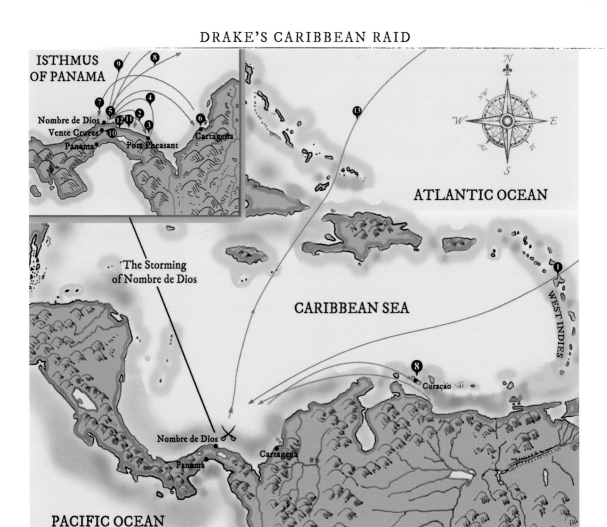

The sea dog would return to the Spanish Main, but in the meantime he found himself something of a celebrity, and a favourite of the queen. He duly proposed a new enterprise, a voyage into the Pacific. By entering what the Spanish considered a private sea, Drake could prey on the wealthy Manila galleons. Queen Elizabeth shared his enthusiasm, but for diplomatic reasons she was unable to give her official sanction. Instead she became a secret shareholder in the clandestine pirate expedition.

KEY

◄──── 1572 expedition   ◄──── 1573 expedition   ✕ Battle

1572

1. May: Drake makes landfall in the Windward Islands and sets a course towards Nombre de Dios.
2. July: Drake arrives off Nombre de Dios, and sails east, looking for a secure base.
3. August: He establishes a hidden base at Port Pheasant, where he is joined by another English ship.
4. 26 July: Drake lands his men a little way from Nombre de Dios and marches towards the town.
5. 28 July: His dawn attack is successful, but Drake is wounded, the local militia rally, and in the battle that follows the English raiders are forced to retire to their ships.
6. Autumn: Drake sails west towards Cartagena.
7. Winter: Having captured a handful of prizes, Drake abandons the *Pasco*, and returns west in his remaining ship, the *Swan*.

1573

8. January: Drake heads west as far as Curaço in search of prizes.
9. March: He returns to the isthmus of Panama, having decided to intercept the cross-country shipment of silver from Panama to Nombre de Dios.
10. Drake attempts to attack the mule train carrying the silver, but his ambush is detected, and the English raiders return to their ships. There he joins forces with a group of French corsairs.
11. April: Drake lands well to the east of Nombre de Dios and makes another attempt on the mule train. This time he captures it.
12. The Spanish pursue Drake, and he is forced to abandon most of his plunder. The Spanish eventually recover it.
13. June: Drake sails home through the Windward Passage.

Today, Cartagena in Colombia is a bustling Latin American metropolis, but when the city was just a fortified settlement, it was the target of attacks by Spain's enemies. During Drake's capture of the city in 1573, the fighting raged in this square as the Spanish defenders tried unsuccessfully to drive off their English assailants. (VW Pics by Universal Images Group at Getty Images)

DRAKE'S SECRET VOYAGE

In December 1577 Drake sailed from Plymouth with five ships: the *Pelican* and *Elizabeth*, the smaller *Swan* (II) and *Marigold*, and the store ship *Christopher*. They headed to the Cape Verde Islands, where Drake plundered Portuguese shipping, then set a course across the Atlantic, making landfall off Brazil in early April. Drake continued south, but that leg of the voyage was marred by two incidents: the abandonment of the *Swan* and *Christopher* due to their poor condition, and the execution of one of his captains, whom Drake accused of plotting against him. He also renamed the *Pelican*, which became the *Golden Hind*.

On reaching the continent's southern tip, Drake's ships threaded through the Straits of Magellan. However, as soon as they entered the Pacific they were struck by a tempest. The *Marigold* foundered with all hands, while the *Elizabeth* and the *Golden Hind* were separated. Captain Wynter of the *Elizabeth* waited for Drake off the Peruvian coast, but when his leader didn't appear he took his ship back home the way he had come.

For his part Drake had been driven south, and was almost wrecked by the Antarctic ice. When the storm abated he sailed north, following the coast as far as Valparaiso, where he captured a Spanish ship and plundered the town. Finding no sign of Wynter he continued north, attacking Arica and Callao, but found little worth taking. However, Drake did lay hands on Spanish charts of the Pacific coast, which he used to plan his next move. He also learned that the treasure ship *Nuestra Señora de la Concepción* had left Callao

In late 1577 Francis Drake left Plymouth with a squadron of five small ships, the largest of which was the *Pelican*. He later renamed her the *Golden Hind*. This was the ship he used to capture the Spanish treasure galleon *Nuestra Señora de la Concepción,* and then to circumnavigate the globe. (Photo by DeAgostini/Getty Images)

a few days earlier, and was on her way to Panama. Drake immediately set off in pursuit.

After several days Drake spotted his prey ahead of him. He used the old trick of increasing sail but dragging objects behind the ship to make his vessel appear slower than she actually was. On the evening of 1 March the *Golden Hind* came within hailing distance of the *Concepción*. Her captain San Juan de Anton still thought the other ship was a Spanish merchantman, so when Drake opened his gunports he was taken completely by surprise. A broadside fired at point-blank range brought down the galleon's mizzenmast, and then Drake's men boarded her through the smoke. Within minutes the *Concepción* was in Drake's hands.

The haul of plunder was breathtaking. The *Concepción* carried 26 tons of silver ingots, 80 pounds of gold and 14 chests filled with pieces-of-eight. The total haul was later valued at 400,000 pesos, or £200,000 in Elizabethan England – a little more than half the annual income of the English crown. It was an astounding haul, and for Drake and his men their fortunes were made. All they had to do now was to make it home with their plunder.

Drake avoided Acapulco and continued north up the Pacific coast, hoping to find the North-West Passage, a sea route around the top of the Americas. Beaten by the ice and cold, Drake headed south again, and put in to the coast of what is now California. He realized that the only safe way home was across the Pacific. First, though, he needed to careen his ship and replenish her provisions. The location of the anchorage where he did this is the subject of continued debate, but a likely candidate is Drake's Bay, near modern-day San Francisco. He named the area Nova Albion (New England), and stayed there for five weeks. Finally, on 23 July, the *Golden Hind* headed west towards the setting sun.

In terms of piracy, the rest of Drake's voyage was unexceptional. However, as a piece of maritime history it was a monumental achievement – the first circumnavigation of the globe by an English captain. In late September 1580 Drake returned to Plymouth as a hero and a rich man. The queen was delighted, and after dining on board Elizabeth knighted Drake on the quarterdeck of his own ship. Sir Francis Drake was at the height of his fame and fortune. After all, when the queen secretly called you 'my pirate', you could do little wrong.

In March 1579, while sailing up the Pacific coast of South America, Francis Drake in the *Golden Hind* chased and overhauled a Spanish treasure galleon, bound from Callao to Panama. She was the *Nuestra Señora de la Concepción* (nicknamed the 'Cacafuego'), and Drake captured her after a short one-sided battle. She was carrying a fortune in silver and jewels.

THE GREAT RAID

By 1585 the 'cold war' between England and Spain was hotting up. Barring a miracle, war between the two powers was now inevitable. The previous year the Spanish had impounded all English ships in Spanish ports, so Elizabeth offered the ship owners the right of 'retribution'. Meanwhile, Elizabeth's spymaster Sir Francis Walsingham planned a full-scale 'retaliatory' raid on the Spanish Main. Drake was given command of this state-sponsored expedition, and during the summer of 1585 he busied himself gathering ships and men. Once again this was organized as a business venture, with the queen being just one of many investors. Her stake was the lease of two royal warships, the *Elizabeth Bonaventure*, which became Drake's flagship, and the smaller *Aid*. Drake's deputy was Martin Frobisher, who flew his flag in the *Primrose*, an armed merchantman.

This was no half-hearted raiding party. Including the two royal warships, Drake's fleet comprised 21 well-armed ships, 1,000 crew and 800 soldiers, the latter commanded by Captain Christopher Carleille. This was a force capable of striking virtually anywhere it wanted. However, the queen was now having second thoughts. So Drake hurriedly put to sea on 14 September, before he could be recalled. His first stop was Vigo in north-western Spain, which he seized while riding out a bad storm. He then headed to the Canary Islands, where he failed to intercept the returning Spanish treasure *flota*. Undeterred, Drake continued on to the Cape Verde Islands. On 16 November Drake's men assaulted Santiago (now Praia), but found little there worth plundering. This action took its toll on the fleet during the transatlantic voyage, as the men were struck by a disease brought on board during the raid. By the time Drake made his landfall at St Kitts he had lost some 300 men. Despite this, Drake planned to attack Santo Domingo on Hispaniola to test the potential of his powerful fleet.

The English arrived there in late December, and Carleille was landed further up the coast. Drake returned to the port, and at 8am on 1 January 1586 he began his bombardment. Simultaneously, Carleille's men emerged from hiding and stormed the town's main gate, driving the garrison into the jungle. Drake was now the master of the city. While his men searched for plunder, Drake opened negotiations with the Spanish, proposing to spare Santo Domingo in return for a ransom. When the negotiations stalled Drake's men levelled the city's principal buildings, and by the end of the month Drake had his ransom. He re-embarked his men and sailed away leaving the Spanish to reclaim their battered city.

For his next attack Drake selected Cartagena, a major destination for the Tierra Firme *flota* and a city regarded as the richest prize in the Americas. It was

well defended, and this time the Englishman realized there would be no easy victory. The Spanish governor already knew the English were coming, and so had prepared his defences before Drake arrived on 19 February. Drake began by probing the city's fortifications, but soon realized that a conventional assault was doomed to failure. Instead he landed his soldiers on the tip of a coastal spur that ran westwards from the city, dividing the outer roads from the sea. The Spaniards had built strong defences on the seaward and landward sides of the town, but the earthworks covering the narrow spit were only half-finished. As at Santo Domingo, Drake was merely a spectator, and it was Carleille who led the assault. He landed his men under cover of darkness, but a Spanish cavalry patrol raised the alarm, and the element of surprise was now lost. Carleille kept going. As dawn broke, the English appeared in front of the barricade and Carleille led an immediate assault. Despite heavy casualties he stormed the defences, then chased the Spanish troops into the city beyond them.

Francis Drake's assault on Santo Domingo in Hispaniola in 1586 demonstrated just how vulnerable Spanish New World cities were to attack. Drake bombarded the city from the sea, then launched a land assault that easily breached the settlement's defences. He then held the city to ransom. (Photo by VCG Wilson / Corbis via Getty Images)

CIVITAS CARTHAGENA in Indie occidentalie continente
sita, portu commodissimo, ad mercaturam inter Hispaniam et
Peru exercendam

CARTAGENA

In 1586, Francis Drake attacked Cartagena, the largest city on the Spanish Main. This shows his assault forces storming the city's defences in a dawn attack, having approached them along the beach. Meanwhile the English fleet has forced its way into the lagoon that formed the port's outer harbour.

Carleille's soldiers fought their way through the streets to Cartagena's marketplace, defeating all attempts by Governor Fernandez to organize a new line of defence. His Spanish troops gathered to make a last stand in front of the city's cathedral, but the firepower of the English troops soon broke their will. With his men now in headlong flight, the governor bowed to the inevitable and joined them. Against the odds, Drake had won the day – at the cost of just 30 casualties.

Once again, as his men plundered the town, Drake demanded a ransom. He held the city for almost two months but eventually the Spanish paid up, and Drake sailed away almost half a million pieces-of-eight richer. His force had been whittled down by disease, but he still planned to launch one more dramatic assault before heading home. Drake considered an assault on Havana, but a reconnaissance showed that the city was too well defended. So he headed north towards the Carolinas, where he planned to put in at Sir Walter Raleigh's new settlement at Roanoke. However, the route took him past the Spanish settlement of St Augustine, on the eastern coast of Florida. Until now, the existence of this small colony had been unknown to the English. This changed on 27 May, when Drake's lookouts spotted the coastal watchtower that marked the mouth of the Matanzas River. A prisoner Carleille captured there revealed that the Spanish settlement lay a few miles further inland. Once again Carleille's troops were landed on the beach and marched across the dunes until they came to the town, which lay on the far bank of the Matanzas River. A night-time attack by Indians loyal to the Spaniards was repulsed, and at dawn the English soldiers crossed the river in boats and stormed the town. They found it deserted, the Spaniards having fled inland during the night. All that the victors captured of any value was a strongbox in the fort containing the garrison's wages. Drake ordered the settlement razed, then continued his voyage northwards. Few would have guessed it at the time, but this was Drake's last fully successful raid on the Spanish Main.

The expedition put in to Roanoke, where the struggling English settlers accepted Drake's offer of a passage home. The fleet arrived back in Plymouth in mid-July to find that the long-awaited war had finally broken out. As a plundering expedition, Drake's raid of 1585 was unsuccessful; his force was simply too large to ensure everyone made a substantial profit. However, as a means of discomfiting the Spanish the raid had worked perfectly, proving that the Spanish Main was now open to attack by anyone with ships, men and determination.

PLUNDERING FOR THE GREATER GOOD

War brought a temporary halt to these expeditions, as the sea dogs were called up for service with the Navy Royal. In theory this should have reduced the opportunities for piratical acts, but in effect it made little difference. The balance between patriotism and profit was a fine one in Elizabethan England, and men like Drake did their duty to their queen while still finding a way to make a profit.

The most notorious example of this was the capture of the *Nuestra Señora del Rosario*. During the first battle of the Spanish Armada campaign fought off Plymouth on 31 July 1588, the *Rosario* was damaged in a collision. Attempts to tow her to safety were thwarted by rough seas, and as night fell the galleon fell behind the rest of the fleet. Drake had orders to shadow the

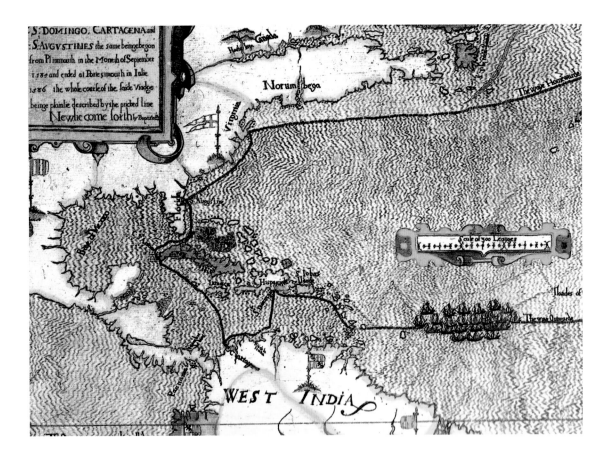

During his campaign of 1585–86 Drake led a powerful English fleet across the Atlantic with the sole purpose of attacking and plundering Spanish cities in the New World. This shows the route taken by his expedition during this campaign, which saw successful raids carried out on Santo Domingo, Cartagena and St Augustine.

Spanish fleet. Instead, he set off in pursuit of the stricken *Rosario*. As the sun rose, the Spanish captain Don Pedro de Valdés found Drake lying off his stern and preparing to fire a broadside into his ship. After some prevarication Valdés surrendered, and the *Rosario* was towed into Dartmouth. On board was a chest containing 100,000 pieces-of-eight. Drake came in for some sharp criticism afterwards, particularly when the queen discovered that half of the plunder had mysteriously disappeared. After that the cloud of distrust surrounding Drake never quite went away.

The Armada campaign itself is not really part of this story, nor are the attacks launched by Elizabeth's fleet on the Spanish coast both before and after 1588. However, by using privateers such as Drake, Frobisher, Raleigh, Grenville and Hawkins as her naval commanders, the English monarch blurred the line between private enterprise and public service. This was further exacerbated by her tendency to run these expeditions as financial enterprises, even though they were ostensibly conducted as official naval operations. It is therefore hardly surprising that the majority of English seamen saw such ventures as little more than an opportunity to plunder on a grand scale.

For example, in 1592 two English ships commanded by Robert Crosse were cruising off the Azores when they encountered the treasure galleon *Madre de Dios*, commanded by Fernando de Mendoza. The Spanish ship was taken after an epic fight. According to Mendoza, his galleon was carrying specie worth one million pieces-of-eight. However, only 300,000 pesos was handed over to the queen's assessors, and soon accusations began flying. Inevitably Crosse was accused of stealing the rest of the plunder. Eventually Elizabeth appointed Drake to sort out the mess. After all, he was probably an expert in the business of hidden treasure. However, apart from a paltry 18,000 pieces-of-eight, the missing plunder was never recovered.

As well as these 'official' expeditions, numerous smaller privateering raids were carried out. It has been estimated that between 1589 and 1591, a total of 236 English privateering ships were at sea. Not all of these privateers were successful. For instance, in 1592 Captain John Myddelton, commanding the 50-ton *Moonshine*, was driven off when he tried to attack the *ranchería* (pearl fishing station) at Margarita, off the Venezuelan coast. He then joined up with another privateering squadron, but their cruise proved equally fruitless. However, in early 1597 a Captain Parker successfully looted the *ranchería*, and went on to plunder the Mexican port of Campeche before returning to England. His backers were delighted, and funded another equally successful raid in 1600. These successes were unusual. The Earl of Cumberland financed over a dozen such raids, only one of which turned a profit. Still, the overall climate was one of fiscal greed and opportunism, despite the failure of many of these expeditions. However, none of these small raids was powerful enough to take on the treasure *flotas*, or to capture the Spanish treasure ports. So, it was left to the old sea dogs Drake and Hawkins to show the others how it was done.

THE LAST OF THE SEA DOGS

In 1595, Elizabeth's advisor William Cecil devised a plan to renew the offensive against the Spanish. An expedition jointly commanded by Sir Francis Drake and Sir John Hawkins would descend on the Spanish Main, where it would cause as much damage as it could. A secondary objective was the establishment of a permanent English settlement within the Caribbean. To achieve this, they had a fleet of 27 ships, including six royal warships, crewed by 2,500 men. Unfortunately animosity between the two commanders did much to limit the expedition's effectiveness. The kinsmen had fallen out when Hawkins publicly censured Drake for his capture of the *Rosario*, back in 1588. After that the two ageing sea dogs found it hard to agree on anything.

The expedition sailed from Plymouth in August 1595, and a major attack on the Canary Islands was thwarted by heavy seas. The English even had to leave a boatload of men behind. Under torture the prisoners revealed the fleet's destination, and so a fast ship was sent to warn the governor of San Juan that the English were coming. The fleet reached Puerto Rico on 12 November, having made landfall in Dominica. By that time Hawkins was dying from fever, as were many of his men. He finally succumbed some days later, leaving Drake in sole command of the expedition.

Drake found San Juan too well defended to attack, and so after probing its defences he withdrew in search of easier pickings. He considered that Cartagena was now too strong to assault again, so instead he raided Rio de la Hacha and Santa Marta on the Spanish Main. Next the fleet headed west and Drake arrived off Nombre de Dios on 6 January 1596. The port was no longer the all-important Caribbean terminus of the silver mines in Peru; this had moved to Porto Bello, just down the coast. The town was undefended, so Drake established a base there, and prepared his men for an assault on Panama, 30 miles (48km) away on the Pacific side of the isthmus.

He sent Sir Thomas Baskerville and his soldiers inland, but when they reached the mountain barrier at the centre of the isthmus they found that

During the 16th century, Havana, the largest Spanish settlement on Cuba, was raided three times by French corsairs. So in 1589, work began on a substantial stone-built fort, the Castillo del Morro, which dominated the entrance to the harbour – the rendezvous for homebound treasure fleets. (Michael Marquand/Getty Images)

Spanish troops were dug in across the only pass. Baskerville launched three fruitless assaults before retiring to Nombre de Dios. After burning the port Drake headed back out to sea. His plan was to raid the coast of Honduras, but many of his men were now sick with yellow fever. Within days Drake himself caught the fever himself, and on the evening of 27 January the sea dog died. Drake's body was placed in a lead-lined coffin and buried at sea within sight of Porto Bello. It was now time to leave. Not only was Drake dead, but a powerful Spanish fleet had gathered to destroy the English expedition. It caught up with them off the Cuban Isle of Pines, but the English managed to repulse the Spanish attack and escape. The ships arrived back in Plymouth in April 1596, where rumours of the deaths of Hawkins and Drake were finally confirmed.

The deaths of these two men marked the end of an era. Within a few years Elizabeth herself would also be dead, and her passing marked both the end of the Tudor dynasty and what many regarded as a golden age. Her successor, James I of England and VI of Scotland, united the monarchy of those two kingdoms, made peace with Spain, and ushered in a time when merchants rather than pirates or privateers dominated the waters of Europe and the Americas. The days of the sea dogs had passed into history. However, within a few short years a new breed of seaman would turn the Spanish Main into its hunting ground. At least the Elizabethan sea dogs followed the established gentlemanly rules of war. The buccaneers who followed them would have no such inhibitions.

Chapter Four

MEDITERRANEAN CORSAIRS

GREEK PIRATES AND MUSLIM CORSAIRS

Following the collapse of the Roman Empire the western Mediterranean became something of a backwater. Rather than develop trade, the 'barbarian' states established there preferred to eke out a living from fishing, raiding and piracy. To the east Byzantium remained a bastion of order in the Mediterranean for several centuries. However, by the late 12th century its power was limited to Greece and western Asia Minor. Following the sacking of Constantinople in 1204, the Byzantine navy could barely patrol its own home waters. Consequently, piracy developed in the Aegean. Further west the Ionian islands of the Adriatic also became pirate dens. By the 13th century piracy thrived in Greek waters, although many pirates were actually Italian. Other Greek and Balkan pirates also operated in Grecian waters, many of them being local fishermen who made a living moonlighting as pirates on the side.

Spanish warships bombarding La Goletta near Tunis, in a detail of a scene depicting the capture of Tunis by the emperor Charles V in 1535. Very accurately, the galleys are shown going into action with their masts stepped to reduce the risk of damage.

This detail from Joan Blaeu's *Atlas Maior* (Amsterdam, 1662–65) shows the geography of the Barbary coast (marked 'Barbaria'), with Algier, Tunis, Tripoli and Djerba all marked. Inland from the port cities, though, there was little apart from desert.

Then from the late 13th century the naval vacuum was partly filled by the rise of three navies. Rhodes became a stronghold of the Knights of St John, who maintained a small but effective galley fleet. The Venetians hunted pirates in the Adriatic and southern Aegean, and supported the Rhodeans in anti-piracy operations. By the 1360s the Ottoman Turks controlled the western coast of Asia Minor, so their galleys could now patrol the Aegean. However, the Turks relied heavily on privateers to augment their regular navy.

On the African shore of the Mediterranean a similar transformation was taking place. Following the Arab conquests of the 7th and 8th centuries the entire coast of North Africa fell under Muslim control, as did Sicily and most of Spain. Although these vast territories were united by religion, there was little or no political unity. A string of petty states dotted the African coast from Morocco to Libya. The reconquest of Sicily by the Normans in the late 11th century and the beginning of the Reconquista in Spain meant that by the late 14th century these North African states now formed a frontier between religious rivals. By then intermittent religious wars fought between Christian and Muslim were raging in Spain to the west and Greece to the east. It was inevitable that North Africa would eventually be drawn into this pan-Mediterranean struggle.

Although pirates had operated along the North African coast since the collapse of the Western Roman Empire, it was not until the expansion of European commence in the late 15th century that piracy became a serious threat. The ports of Algiers, Tunis and Tripoli were ideally located to serve as privateering bases from which to harass passing shipping. As these 'Barbary ports' lay on the edge of the Sahara Desert, any riches had to come from the sea. Consequently, during the late 15th and early 16th centuries local rulers encouraged corsairs to use their ports. In return, these rulers (known as beys, meaning 'governors') expected a percentage of the profits. Privateering was a hugely profitable business, and their ports soon became bustling markets for the sale of slaves and plunder.

THE BARBARY CORSAIRS

In theory, the rulers of the Barbary States owed feudal allegiance to the Ottoman sultan. However, following the Turkish conquest of Constantinople (now Istanbul) in 1453, the sultan established his court in the former Byzantine capital. This was far enough away from the North African coast for the beys of the Barbary coast to be left alone, unless the sultan needed their help in fighting a war. While the privateering fleets of the Barbary coast took part in several major naval campaigns during the 16th century, for the most part they operated independently of both the Turks and each other, and limited their activities to the western and central Mediterranean.

While the Barbary galleys would accurately be described as 'privateers' – operating under a licence issued by the bey – the terms 'corsair' and 'pirate' were both used freely. Technically the French term 'corsair' means 'privateer', although by the 16th century it was also used to describe pirates who operated in the Mediterranean. The term 'pirate' was rarely used at the time. The

A depiction of the battle of Zonchio (1499), showing Venetian sailing carracks being attacked by Barbary corsairs led by Kemal Reis (labelled 'Chmali' here). He was one of the founding leaders of the Barbary pirates.

RIGHT Christian captives being landed in Algiers, after being captured by Barbary corsairs. While the depiction of the city's harbour front is fanciful, the subject is not – the slave trade underpinned the economy of the Barbary states throughout their existence.

BELOW Domestic Christian slaves serving their Berber masters in 17th-century Algiers. These slaves were fortunate. Although they wore chains, many others worked in the city's stone quarries, in the fields, or else served as galley slaves.

difference was only appreciated later, when the maritime powers of Europe refused to recognize the authority of the Barbary rulers. The American assault on the Barbary ports in the early 19th century was carried out as an anti-piracy operation, and therefore it was expedient to call the Barbary sailors 'pirates' rather than 'privateers'. For clarity, we will stick to the term 'corsair' during the period up to the mid-17th century. After that we will use the term 'pirate' to reflect their lack of international recognition.

By the early 16th century many of the beys were elected from the ranks of the corsairs, which meant that privateering became an integral part of the political framework of the Barbary coast. They were certainly well organized. A ruling captains' council called the Taife Raisi supervised the running of the ports and the corsair fleet, but remained answerable to the bey. The Taife Raisi ruled over any disputes, supervised the sale of plunder and slaves, and made sure that the bey was given his share of the spoils. While he nominally served the Ottoman

Empire and his bey, each privateering captain (or *rais*) owned his own ship, and had almost complete freedom of action. He was assisted by the *agha*, who commanded the boarding party, and a scribe appointed by the Taife Raisi who ensured that any booty would be registered. Typically, the local bey would claim 10 per cent, plus a port fee. As the Barbary ports provided excellent markets for the sale of contraband and captured slaves, the arrangement suited everyone, apart from the captives.

However, as privateers the Barbary corsairs had to abide by the terms of their letters-of-marque. This meant that they had to limit their attacks to non-Muslim shipping, and collect only non-Muslim slaves. Also, as the sultan was their overlord, the corsairs had to abide by the terms of treaties arranged between the sultan and Christian rulers. For instance, Venice was often at peace with the Turks, and therefore attacks on Venetian ships were forbidden.

Feudal obligations between the Barbary States and the Ottoman sultan worked both ways. The city-states of the Barbary coast were technically considered part of the Ottoman Empire, and so Turkish troops helped the local bey defend his territory. Conversely, the corsairs often combined piratical attacks with service in the Ottoman navy, and corsair commanders fought in all of the major galley battles of the 16th century. However, the corsairs had an enemy much closer to home. The Spanish followed their Reconquista by launching assaults against the ports of the Barbary coast, initiating a long-running struggle for control of the North African shore.

This rivalry began with the expulsion of the Moors from Spain in 1492. The exiles settled in the North African ports, and sought revenge by launching attacks on Spanish shipping. They were assisted by the Barbary rulers, and by Muslim adventurers from the eastern Mediterranean. The Spanish retaliated by assaulting the major Barbary ports – Oran, Algiers and Tunis – forcing the local beys to appeal for help to the sultan. In 1529 the Turkish counter-attack began, which eventually drove the Spanish from most of their coastal enclaves. Ultimately this conflict with Spain ended in a stalemate as the 16th century drew to a close, largely because through a series of peace treaties the Spanish

European Christian propagandists frequently exaggerated the 'barbarity' of the Barbary rulers and corsairs. Here a Barbary ruler amuses himself by torturing a Christian prisoner or slave by dripping burning tar onto the soles of his feet.

This copy of an early
17th-century painting by the
Dutch maritime artist Andries
van Eertvelt shows a Barbary
pirate galley attempting to
board a Spanish galleon. It
depicts the crowded deck of
the galley, with musket-armed
janissaries stationed in her
bow.

A contemporary depiction of
a late 16th-century Barbary
galley, with a smaller galliot
behind her. Christian accounts
of this period mention that
pirate galleys were often
festooned with silk and taffeta
banners.

were forced to recognize that the region was officially part of the Ottoman Empire. Peace with the Turks therefore meant peace with the corsairs, as long as they didn't attack Spanish ships. This changed in 1659, when Turkish rule collapsed. The beys then ruled over their own city-state, answerable to nobody save the corsairs who kept them in power.

By that stage the Barbary corsairs had plenty of other victims. The mercantile growth of England and Holland meant that their ships now came under attack from the corsairs in the Mediterranean. However, these countries also possessed powerful fleets. Consequently, the English and Dutch navies inflicted a string of defeats upon the Barbary corsairs during the 17th century, and by its end the power of the Barbary States had been broken.

In Europe the Barbary corsairs were often depicted as fanatical Muslims, who waged an undeclared war against their religious enemies. Their reputation for slave trading was well known, and humanitarian organizations frequently raised money to purchase the release of Christian slaves on the Barbary coast. Surprisingly, renegade Christians made up a substantial portion of corsair numbers. This did not alter the fact that for much of the early modern period, the Barbary corsairs were the bogeymen of the Christians of Western Europe. Their rapacity was widely recognized, and therefore they instilled fear – a useful tool for any pirate, who always preferred a victim to surrender than to fight. While some of this unsavoury reputation was Christian propaganda, much of it was well deserved.

ARUJ 'BARBAROSSA': THE FIRST CORSAIR

The first major corsairs of the Barbary coast were Aruj and Hızır, the Barbarossa brothers. Aruj (or Oruç) and his younger brother Hızır (or Khızır) were born on the Aegean island of Lesbos during the 1470s. Their father was a Muslim potter and former Turkish soldier, and their mother was a Greek Christian. By the end of the 15th century Aruj was serving on a pirate galley operating in the northern Aegean. At that time Lesbos was a haven for both Greek and Muslim pirates. There, religions mixed freely, and pirates found a ready market for plunder. However, Aruj's pirate galley was captured by the Knights of St John, and he served as a galley slave until his release following a treaty between the Knights and the Egyptian Emir. Once freed, Aruj was granted a privateering licence by the bey of Antalya, and he operated from there until his patron fled to Egypt following a political dispute. By the time they arrived in Alexandria Aruj had been joined by his brother Hızır. Both siblings were gifted corsairs, and they gradually expanded their force until they commanded a small fleet of

The 'Barbarossa brothers' Aruj and Hızır, who, in the early 16th century, developed the Barbary coast into a thriving pirate haven and a Muslim bastion which limited Spanish Christian expansion in the western Mediterranean. The brothers' name derived from their red beards.

pirate galleys. Peace between the Egyptians and the Knights of St John forced the brothers to move their operation and in 1505 they arrived in Djerba, a small island port off the coast of Tunisia. The brothers obtained a privateering licence from the bey of Tunis, and were soon cruising the Tyrrhenian Sea in search of prey.

Then off Elba they ran into two galleys flying the colours of Pope Julius II. The papal ships turned out to be a rich trading galley and an escorting warship, both of which were boarded and captured. The advantage the corsairs enjoyed was that their crewmen were all free, and therefore available to fight. Their opponents relied on galley slaves. The brothers returned to the Tunisian port of La Goulette in triumph, and their reputation was assured. The Spanish historian Diego Haedo wrote: 'the wonder and astonishment that this notable exploit caused in Tunis is not to be expressed, nor how celebrated the name of Aruj Rais was to become from that very moment'. He added: 'By reason his beard was extremely red, from thenceforward he was generally called Barbarossa, which in Italian signifies Red Beard'. In a Mediterranean world filled with black hair, the two red-headed men stood out, and so their nickname was born.

The next victim was the *Cavalleria*, a Sardinian sailing warship bound for Naples, which the corsairs seized off the Lipari Islands. The advantage of a galley over a sailing ship was its ability to operate regardless of the wind. So the becalmed *Cavalleria* was completely defenceless. The result of this lucrative capture in 1509 was that hundreds flocked to join their band, including their remaining brother Ishak. Soon their new base of La Goulette outside Tunis was filled with pirate galleys and prizes.

The galleys and galliots used by the Barbary corsairs resembled the galleys of their Ottoman Turkish or Christian contemporaries, although by relying on volunteer oarsmen they could draw on a larger crew when it came to boarding an enemy ship.

In 1511 a disagreement between the brothers and the bey of Tunis led to another change of base – this time further west along the coast to Djidjelli (now Jijel), between Tunis and Algiers. The emir of Algiers who ruled the port had asked for their help fighting the Spanish who were threatening to attack him. The Spanish had captured Oran in 1509 and Bougie (now Béjaïa) the following year, so with the Spanish on either side of them the Algerians knew their city would be next.

At first the corsairs enjoyed some degree of success. Then they over-reached themselves. The brothers attacked Bougie, and were bloodily repulsed, with Aruj even losing an arm in the fight. The brothers had to content themselves by wreaking havoc on Spanish shipping. Meanwhile the bey of Algiers seemed happy enough to let them fight his battles for him, doing nothing to help them. Worse still, after the Spanish established a foothold at Peñón on the far side of the Bay of Algiers, he let them fortify it without trying to drive them into the sea. Finally, in 1516 the Algerians rose up in revolt. Aruj joined them, killed the bey, and seized control of the city. The Turkish Sultan not only approved the move, but named Aruj his beylerbey (governor of all the beys), making him the *de facto* ruler of the Barbary coast.

Aruj's private war with the Spanish reached a head three years later. First, in early 1519, a surprise Spanish attack on Algiers from Peñón was repulsed. Then in May the emperor Charles V arrived in Oran at the head of a large army. He planned to attack Algiers, but it was Aruj who struck first, landing behind Oran to destroy a force of Arab mercenaries who were marching to join the Spanish. However, the Spanish countered this with an attack of their own, and Aruj and his brother Ishak were trapped in the town of Tlemcen. After a siege lasting 20 days the Spanish assaulted the town, and Aruj and Ishak were both killed. It was the end of an era, but not the end of the fight. Hızır would continue the struggle, and would eventually prove an even greater threat to the Spanish than his elder brother.

This plan of Algiers was drawn up by the English cartographer Robert Norton in 1620. Under the rule of the Barbarossas, the port's defences were strengthened and a fortified harbour built to protect the galley fleet based there.

KHAIR-ED-DIN

As the new beylerbey, Hızır 'Barbarossa' became the head of the Barbary corsairs. In December 1518 he threatened Oran and recaptured Tlemcen, then stormed and took Bône (now Annaba), a Spanish-held port between Bougie and Tunis. The following year he defeated another expedition sent to capture Algiers. As a reward he was named as the emir (pasha) of Algiers. With his base secure, he was then able to resume his own attacks. Over the next few years Hızır raided the southern coast of France and Spain, and in 1522 he helped the

Hızır Barbarossa (c.1478–1576) was one of the most formidable of all the Barbary leaders, as well being a highly successful Turkish admiral. He was often referred to as either Hayreddin or Khair-ed-Din, both terms meaning 'Gift of God'.

sultan capture Rhodes, bastion of the Knights of St John. As a result the corsair was named 'Khair-ed-Din' (or Hayreddin) by the sultan, meaning 'Gift of God'. He had come a long way. More commonly, though, as the last of the red-headed brothers, he was known simply as 'Barbarossa'.

After returning to Barbary he led raids on the Italian coast before being driven away by the Genoese fleet. This pattern would continue for six years, from 1525 until 1531, by which time he had achieved an even

The galley fleet of Hızır Barbarossa shown anchored off the French port of Toulon during the winter of 1543/44. A temporary alliance with the French allowed the Barbary leader to use the port as a base for attacks against the Spanish, who at the time were at war with France.

more important victory at home. In May 1529 he captured the Spanish stronghold of Peñón in the Bay of Algiers, thereby ensuring the safety of his home base. In 1531 he also launched a major assault on Tripoli, which had been captured by the Spanish in 1510 and handed over to the Knights of St John. This time Khair-ed-Din was repulsed, and the city remained in Christian hands until 1551.

The following year, in 1532, the sultan needed his help to counter a Venetian offensive in the Adriatic. Not only did Barbarossa recapture several key islands lost to the Christians, but he even caused the church bells of Rome to ring in alarm as he cruised off the mouth of the river Tiber. Meanwhile, it was clear that a major clash was coming. It began when Barbarossa seized Tunis from a pro-Spanish bey, only to lose the city again to an overwhelmingly powerful Spanish expedition. Unable to tackle the Spanish head on, he led an Ottoman force against Naples, which captured the Spanish-held port in 1537. This prompted Pope Paul III to form a 'Holy League' of Christian powers to fight the Turks.

In 1538 Andrea Doria led a powerful Holy League fleet into the Aegean to destroy Barbarossa, consisting of galleys from Spain, Genoa, Venice and the papacy. The two fleets met at Prevesa on 28 September 1538 and the result was a victory for Barbarossa, who captured or destroyed 51 enemy vessels. This stunning victory meant that Turkish naval supremacy in the Mediterranean would remain unchallenged for another three decades. Meanwhile, the war between Spain and the Barbary corsairs would continue.

ABOVE A Barbary galliot, or small galley, from a 16th-century German woodcut depicting the tactics and techniques of naval warfare. On its prow, janissary archers engage the enemy, while behind them a piece from the galliot's bow gun battery also opens fire.

ABOVE RIGHT This depiction of a Barbary corsair galley is found in a 17th-century painting by the Dutch artist Lieve Pietersz Verschuir. While he might have exaggerated the rake of the bow and stern, the proportions of the vessel he shows are similar to those provided by contemporary accounts.

In 1540 Charles V tried and failed to capture Algiers again, while Barbarossa cruised the Mediterranean at will, operating in support of his new French allies. The following year he arrived off Genoa to negotiate the release of the Barbary corsair Turgut Rais. It was the old corsair's last cruise. In 1545 he was called to Istanbul, and he left Algiers in the hands of his son Hasan Pasha I. The following year Barbarossa died peacefully in the sultan's court. During their lives the two Barbarossa brothers had saved the Barbary coast from the Spanish invaders and ensured that these fragile semi-independent city-states would survive long after their passing. In the process, they established a fearsome reputation for the Barbary corsairs they commanded.

THE SULTAN'S CORSAIRS

The Barbarossa brothers were only the first of many Barbary corsairs who divided their time between privateering and service in the Ottoman navy. A deputy of Khair-ed-Din, Turgut Rais was born in Bodrum, on the coast of Turkey. He eventually joined a band of corsairs, becoming a master gunner. He soon rose to command his own galley, operating in the Aegean. In 1520 he joined Khair-ed-Din in Algiers, and was rapidly promoted to command a corsair squadron. As a naval commander he developed a reputation for skill and daring.

Turgut Rais took part in the battle of Prevesa (1538), where he commanded one wing of the Turkish fleet. The following year he fought his way up the Adriatic, defeating Venetian squadrons sent to fight him, and conquering a string of islands and fortresses in the name of the sultan. His next challenge was as the bey of Djerba, taking command of one of the most notorious corsair havens on the Barbary coast. He seemed born to the job, leading raids on Malta, Sicily and Corsica. However, it then went badly wrong. In 1541 he was cornered by a Genoese squadron while repairing his ships in a Corsican bay. The corsair and his men were captured, and he spent three years as a galley slave before he was finally released when Khair-ed-Din paid a hefty ransom. Back at the helm, Turgut spent the next three years preying on Genoese shipping. Following Khair-ed-Din's death in 1546, he became the new commander of the Ottoman fleet, and two years later he replaced his former commander's son as the bey of Algiers and the beylerbey, which made him the new corsair leader. He continued his attacks, and that August he captured a Maltese galley carrying a fortune of 70,000 ducats, the richest prize ever seen in Algiers. Then, though, the Christians launched a fresh assault on the Barbary bases. In 1550 Turgut found himself blockaded in Djerba by a powerful Christian fleet. Although he and his corsairs escaped, the port fell to the enemy, who held on to it for a decade. After summoning up Turkish reinforcements, he returned to the Barbary coast in August 1551 and recaptured Tripoli from the Knights of St John. This gave the corsairs a secure new base. His galleys defeated his Genoese rival Andrea Doria at the battle of Ponza (1552), which opened up the Italian coast to a fresh wave of corsair raids. Doria made another attempt to defeat Turgut, but this ended in a second humiliation for the Christians at the battle of Djerba (1560). From then until his death five years later during the Siege of Malta, Turgut was able to continue his raiding unhindered.

The Italian fisherman Giovanni Dionigi was captured by Barbary corsairs in 1536, and became a slave. When he could he converted to Islam and joined the corsairs of Tripoli. By 1560 he was known as Uluj Ali, a corsair captain serving under Turgut Rais. He rose to prominence during the fighting off Djerba and the Siege of Malta, and duly became the new bey of Tripoli after Turgut's death. Within three years he was named as beylerbey. For the next decade he led his galleys against the Spanish and the Knights of Malta, and in 1570 he captured a powerful Maltese squadron in a battle that earned him a post as an Ottoman naval commander.

Like several of his contemporaries the Barbary leader Turgut Rais (1485–1565) worked his way up from a volunteer corsair to become the beylerbey of the Barbary Coast, and an admiral in the Turkish navy. He was finally killed during the Siege of Malta.

TURGUT AND MURAT RAIS

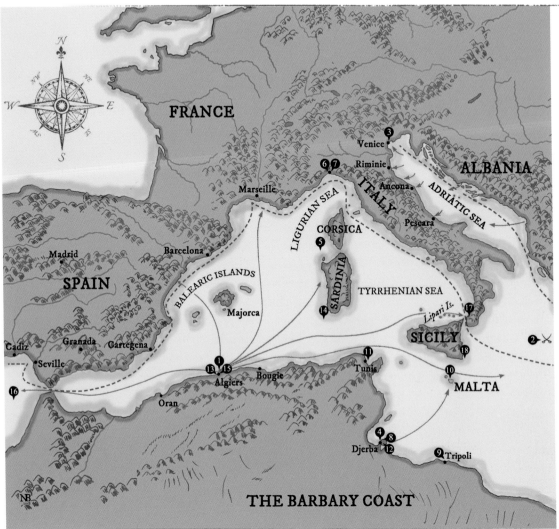

He took part in the disastrous battle of Lepanto in 1571, and in the aftermath of the defeat he took command of the battered Turkish fleet and rebuilt it as a fighting force. However, he was a corsair at heart, and he was soon allowed to return to Algiers. His next triumph came in June 1574, when he masterminded the recapture of Tunis from the Spanish. Uluj Ali made the most of his victory, consolidating his control of the Barbary coast from Tripoli to Oran and strengthening the ports under his command. Eventually the Spanish signed a truce, ending the six decades of threat to the Barbary coast.

KEY

- - - - Trade routes   ◄— Pirate raids   ✗ Battle

Turgut Rais

1. 1520: Turgut Rais joins the fleet of Barbarossa, based in Algiers.
2. 1538: Turgut becomes an admiral in the Turkish fleet and takes part in the battle of Preveza, fought off the western coast of Greece. He and Barbarossa win a spectacular victory.
3. 1539: Turgut is given his first independent command, harassing Venetian shipping in the Adriatic. He even ventures within sight of Venice itself.
4. 1540: Turgut establishes a corsair base at Djerba. He uses it to launch a major raid on Malta.
5. 1540: Turgut follows his Malta raid with further attacks on Corsica and Sardinia.
6. 1541: Turgut's raids come to an abrupt end when he is captured by the Genoese. He spends the next three years as a galley slave.
7. 1544: Barbarossa threatens to attack Genoa and raze the port to the ground unless Turgut is released. The Genoese duly hand over their prisoner.
8. 1550: Djerba is attacked and captured by a Christian force, and Turgut and his men are forced to flee to Tunis.
9. 1551: Turgut recaptures Tripoli from the Knights of St John.
10. 1565: Turgut assists the Turks in the Siege of Malta and is killed before the walls of Valletta.

Murat Rais

11. 1565: Murat Rais becomes the commander of a Barbary corsair galley, based in Tunis.
12. 1568: Murat, now operating from Djerba, falls into disfavour with his superior, Uluj Ali, and so is denied promotion to command a corsair squadron.
13. 1574: Finally, after proving himself, Murat is given command of a powerful corsair squadron based in Algiers.
14. 1574: Murat captures the Spanish viceroy after attacking his well-armed ship off the southern tip of Sardinia.
15. 1564: Murat becomes the beylerbey, based in Algiers. He now has titular command of all Barbary corsairs.
16. 1586: He leads a raid on the Canary Islands.
17. 1594: He is made a Turkish admiral and leads a large Ottoman fleet in raids on the coast of southern Italy.
18. 1595: Murat defeats a powerful Christian fleet off the southern-eastern tip of Sicily.

Tripoli, as depicted by the 17th-century Dutch artist Reiner Nooms. It shows several Dutch trading ships anchored outside the port, as at the time the Dutch enjoyed a trading agreement with the local bey, and so their ships were safe from attack.

That left Uluj Ali free to pursue his naval duties to the sultan until his death in 1586.

Probably the last great Barbary corsair was Murat Rais, who rose to prominence during the second half of the 16th century. He was probably born in Albania around 1534, and in 1546 he was captured by a roving band of corsairs and elected to convert to Islam and to join their crew. By 1565 he had command of his own galley, and he gained a reputation as a successful corsair but also as a maverick. This reputation meant it took two decades for him to be chosen to command an Ottoman fleet.

However, he was steadily gaining influence among the corsairs. In 1578 he captured the Spanish viceroy of Sicily, who was returning home to Spain in two powerful galleys. This enraged King Philip II of Spain, almost prompting a full-scale expedition to raze Algiers. For the next decade he fought an undeclared war against the Spanish, raiding their coastline, preying on their ships, and filling Algiers with Spanish slaves. He was now regarded as the most notorious corsair in the Mediterranean.

In 1594 he finally became an Ottoman Turkish admiral, and in 1595 he fought off a superior force of galleys and sailing warships off Sicily. For the next four decades until his death in 1609 he was the sultan's commander in the eastern Mediterranean. He finally met his death at Vlorë (Valona) in Albania, so ending his long corsairing career within miles of his birthplace.

This depiction of a 16th-century Turkish or Barbary galley comes from a contemporary Turkish depiction of the Siege of Famagusta (1570–71). The janissaries who serve as marines on board are shown on the shore, forming up for an attack on the Christian-held port.

THE DECLINE OF THE BARBARY PIRATES

By the time Murat Rais died in 1609, the heyday of the Barbary corsairs was over. It probably didn't seem so at the time, however, and some historians have even referred to the early 17th century as a golden age for the Barbary States. After all, the slave markets had never been busier. Under Islamic law a Muslim could not be fettered or be forced to row a galley, so some slaves converted to Islam to improve their lot. Not all got the chance: the richest captives were held for ransom, while most of the rest were condemned to a life of servitude.

Miguel de Cervantes, the Spanish author of *Don Quixote*, was captured by the corsairs in 1575. He remained their slave for five years, and described the constant fear of punishment. By the start of the 17th century, slavery rather than piracy

CORSAIR GALLEYS

In the rest of Europe the sailing ship reigned supreme, but in the Mediterranean the oared galley was the region's principal type of warship. Renaissance galleys were similar to those used by the Romans, but by the 16th century most carried guns, mounted in a gun platform in the bow. Indeed, the only offensive part of the vessel otherwise was the bow, especially as galleys were usually fitted with a ram.

Most galleys relied on galley slaves for propulsion, although the Barbary corsairs were all free men. Galleys also carried masts fitted with lateen sails, allowing them to take advantage of the wind. A typical war galley of the 16th century would carry 20–30 oars a side, each manned by three or more oarsmen.

The Barbary corsairs avoided using their ram or artillery except in a crisis, as damage to a potential prize lowered its value. Instead, their galleys carried swordsmen and musketeers. A preferred tactic was to manoeuvre behind an enemy ship, then swarm aboard it, overpowering its crew in hand-to-hand combat.

In fact most Barbary corsair galleys weren't true galleys at all, but were smaller, faster vessels known as galliots. A typical galliot was flush-decked with a single mast. Between six and 12 oars per side were manned by an average of two oarsmen apiece. Larger galleys were often used as command vessels, or to support the smaller galliots in battle. The advantage of a galley was that it was not reliant on the wind. In light airs the corsairs could outmanoeuvre their opponents, but if a sailing warship fired a broadside at close range, the effect was devastating. So a good Barbary corsair knew when to attack, and when to keep away.

ULUJ ALI: THE SULTAN'S PIRATE

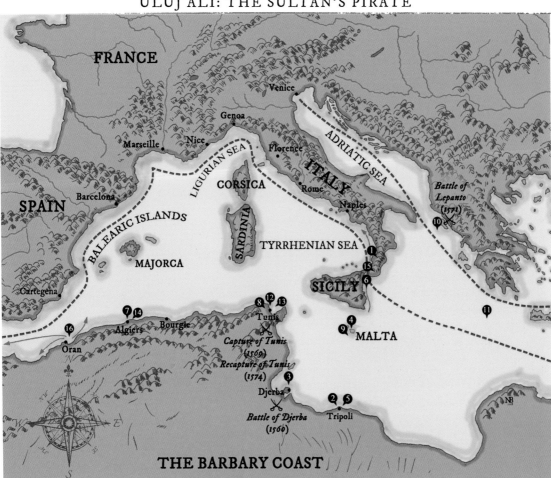

was the main source of income for the Barbary States. Peace treaties with the Europeans meant that these slave raiders were no longer privateering 'corsairs', but rather 'pirates' or 'slave traders'.

To keep these slave markets stocked the corsairs usually raided in the western Mediterranean, but sometimes they ventured further afield. For instance, in 1627 a Flemish convert to Islam called Murat the Younger led a force into the Atlantic. He raided his way up the Atlantic coasts from Spain to England. Reputedly he even ventured into the North Atlantic, where he harried Icelandic fishermen.

KEY

---- Trade routes   ◀— Pirate raids   ✕ Battle

1. 1536: Uluj Ali is born as Giovanni Dionigi of Calabria, the son of a fisherman.

2. After being captured, Dionigi converts to Islam and becomes Uluj Ali. By the late 1550s he has become the captain of a corsair galley based in Tripoli – part of the fleet of Turgut Rais.

3. 1560: Uluj Ali distinguishes himself at the Battle of Djerba.

4. 1565: He participates in the Turkish Siege of Malta.

5. 1566: He succeeds Turgut Rais as the bey of Tripoli.

6. 1567: He leads raids by the Tripoli fleet on Sicily and southern Italy, causing widespread devastation.

7. 1568: He becomes the beylerbey of Algiers, the ruler of the whole Barbary Coast.

8. 1569: He leads a major assault on Tunis and recaptures the city from the Spanish.

9. 1570: He defeats a squadron of galleys operated by the Malta-based Knights of St John.

10. 1571: As an admiral in the Turkish navy, Uluj Ali takes part in the battle of Lepanto, which ends in defeat at the hands of the Christian League.

11. 1572: Uluj Ali is given command of the Turkish fleet and rebuilds it after the disaster of Lepanto. He regains control over Greek waters.

12. 1573: Tunis is captured by Don Juan of Austria, at the head of a Spanish army.

13. 1574: Uluj Ali recaptures Tunis from the Spanish.

14. 1574: He strengthens the defences of Algiers and Morocco, which are threatened by Spanish invasion.

15. 1576: He leads a major raid on Calabria in southern Italy.

16. During the late 1570s, Uluj Ali leads raids against Spanish enclaves along the Barbary coast.

Murat the Younger was not unusual in being a Christian renegade. Around the same time many Christians were accepted into the ranks of the corsairs without renouncing their religion, particularly if they brought with them a knowledge of maritime technology. One was John Ward, an Elizabethan seaman who entered the service of the bey of Tunis, and rose to command a Barbary squadron. These renegades seemed to have no reservations when it came to enslaving their fellow Christians.

A typical slave raid of this period was the assault of Murat Rais the Younger and his pirates on the Irish village of Baltimore in County Cork, in which the entire population was rounded up, then carried off. Only two of the captives ever returned to Ireland. One of Rais' Icelandic captives wrote an account of his experience, as did the Frenchman Jean Marteille de Bernac, giving us useful first-hand accounts of life on the Barbary coast.

The only hope for many of the poorer captives was that some Christian religious order would buy their freedom. One of these groups – the Redemptionists – organized the purchase and freedom of some 15,500 Christian slaves of all nationalities between 1575 and 1769. Sometimes governments

OPPOSITE The Redemptionist Fathers negotiating with Barbary officials and slave owners for the release of Christian slaves. The order was funded by donations from throughout Europe, and during the 17th century it purchased the freedom of hundreds of captives.

In this illustration from a 17th-century Dutch book promoting the work of the Redemptionist Fathers, members of the order barter with a local janissary officer for the release of Christian slaves.

took a hand in the business of raising money. For example, in 1643, seven women petitioned the English Parliament to allow churches to take up collections because 'Their husbands and others were taken by Turkish pirates, carried to Algiers, and there now remain in miserable captivity'.

Another source of income was protection money. Merchants whose ships passed through the Mediterranean frequently paid a fee, which secured immunity from attack. In fact, some Dutch and English merchants actually welcomed the payment of these bribes as a means of limiting the effectiveness of less affluent competitors.

It has been argued that when the English and the Dutch began a long-running series of punitive actions against the Barbary pirates from the mid-17th century on, these actions were undertaken more to ensure a good deal for their merchants than as a serious attempt to end piracy. For instance, in April 1655 the English admiral Robert Blake arrived off the Barbary coast with orders to extract compensation from the beys for attacks on English shipping. From his letters, it seems his real aim was to negotiate a favourable deal for his countrymen. When the bey of Tunis refused to negotiate, Blake sent his fleet into Porto Farina (now Ghar al

While the Barbary corsairs continued to use galleys throughout the 17th and 18th centuries, they increasingly employed sailing vessels too. In this copy of a painting by the 17th-century Dutch artist Andries van Eertvelt, a Barbary sailing privateer is shown at anchor off a Barbary port.

Milh). The bey promptly began negotiating. The French also pulled the same trick, and in 1682 and 1683 they bombarded Algiers when trade negotiations failed. Of course, the Barbary rulers could be just as ruthless. When the French reappeared in 1683, the Algerian beylerbey seized the French consul, loaded him into an over-sized mortar, then fired him back at the French fleet.

By the 18th century, the extortion of protection money had replaced slavery as the region's main source of income. However, as a newcomer to

In this painting by an unknown early 17th-century Spanish artist, two small Barbary galliots are shown attacking a well-armed Spanish merchant ship. In fact, the corsairs would usually avoid the broadside guns of their prey.

The ruthless image of the Barbary rulers continued long after the heyday of the corsairs. Here, Ali Khoja, the bey of Algiers (ruled 1817–18), is shown amid a carpet of his dead soldiers, whom he had slaughtered when he suspected they were plotting to overthrow him.

maritime trade, the United States of America were less willing to pay for protection, which they rightly saw as a tool that benefited their European competitors. Consequently, American ships became prime targets, and American captives began to appear in the slave markets.

The American response was to send in their fledgling navy. In 1801 an American squadron arrived off Tripoli and blockaded the port. During this operation the USS *Philadelphia* was lost when she ran aground in the harbour, and the US Marines achieved fame by taking the fight 'to the shores of Tripoli'. The bey eventually signed a peace deal.

A second conflict (known as the Algerine War) erupted in 1815, and this time the British and French allied themselves with the Americans. The conflict ended with the allied bombardment of Algiers (1816), and the promise by the beylerbey that he would no longer enslave Christians. This was really the end of the Barbary States. Within two decades Algiers became a French colony, while Tunis followed suit later in 1881. The long history of privateering, slave trading and piracy ended more with a whimper than with a bang, the result of a fast-changing world.

The threat posed by the Barbary pirates continued long after their heyday. In this 19th-century painting, corsairs watch as another corsair galley attacks a European sailing ship.

ABOVE This early 19th-century watercolour shows a large Barbary privateer flying the flag of Algiers. By this time the majority of Barbary corsairs relied on sailing ships like this rather than galleys.

LEFT An early 19th-century engraving showing British sailors boarding an Algerine corsair. During the 18th and 19th centuries, the naval power of Britain in the Mediterranean ensured that any attack on its ships was met by swift punitive action.

Chapter Five

THE BUCCANEERS

DUTCH COURAGE

By the end of the 16th century the long-running war between England and Spain had run out of steam. In 1604 the Treaty of London brought the conflict to an end, and all letters-of-marque were cancelled. This just left the Dutch to continue the war. Since 1574 Dutch 'sea beggars' had been fighting the Spanish in their own home waters, but by the start of the new century they had the ability to carry out privateering attacks much further afield. The Spanish, though, had their own privateering fleet. The port of Dunkirk was already an established pirate haven when the Spanish captured it in 1585. They duly issued their own letters-of-marque, and over the next half century they captured hundreds of Dutch ships, ranging from fishing boats to East Indiamen. The Dunkirkers, however, were unable to halt the steady expansion of Dutch maritime power.

By the late 1580s Dutch privateers were operating alongside the English, and by the 1590s fleets of them were cruising as far

The Chagres River, which empties into the Caribbean, ran through much of the isthmus of Panama. It was along this river in 1669 that Henry Morgan and his buccaneers travelled by canoes such as this, during their attack on Panama. (Photo by Veronique DURRUTY/Gamma-Rapho via Getty Images)

afield as the Azores. In 1599 a Dutch squadron even rounded Cape Horn and attacked Spanish shipping off the coast of Chile. While these expeditions yielded little in the way of plunder, they showed just how far the Dutch Republic had come as a maritime power.

The Twelve Years' Truce (1609–21) brought a temporary halt to the conflict, and wisely the Dutch used this time to increase their naval strength. When the truce ended the Dutch were ready to take the fight to their enemy. In 1623 they even founded a West India Company to challenge the Spanish monopoly in the Caribbean. While a few small raids were launched directly against the Spanish Main, the main Dutch assault fell on the Portuguese colony of Brazil. In March 1624 a Dutch fleet arrived off Bahia (San Salvador), and claimed the port in the name of the Dutch Republic. The response was swift. A joint Spanish and Portuguese fleet arrived there in May 1625, only to find that by then the Dutch were in the Caribbean, sacking San Juan in Puerto Rico. Although this attack was spectacular, little was really achieved by this daring operation.

However, the next Dutch raid was very different. The second-in-command of the Brazil venture was Piet Heyn, a former privateer who in 1623 became a vice-admiral in the West India Company. In 1626 he led a small expedition back to Bahia, and plundered the town. It seemed that the Dutch had found their own Drake. Late the following year Piet Heyn returned to the Spanish Main at the head of a powerful fleet. By August 1628 he was off Havana, and when the New Spain *flota* appeared he was ready and waiting for it. Cut off from Havana, the Spaniards were driven into Matanzas Bay to the east of the city. On 8 September the Dutch captured the entire *flota*. The plunder was valued at 11.5 million ducats, the equivalent of several billion dollars today. Historians have argued that Spain's rapid economic, military and political decline was a direct result of this huge financial loss. Meanwhile, the Spanish were about to face an even more serious threat.

In 1628 a Dutch fleet commanded by Admiral Piet Heyn cornered and captured a Spanish treasure *flota* at Matanzas Bay, on the northern coast of Cuba. It has been claimed that Spain never fully recovered from the huge financial loss of this action.

The French corsair Jean Bart (1650–1702) was one of the greatest of the Dunkirk privateers, but he actually learned his trade sailing with the Dutch. From 1672, though, he preyed on his former employees and their English allies, and rose to command a French privateering squadron. (Photo by The Print Collector/Getty Images)

TROUBLE ON HISPANIOLA

Philip III of Spain (ruled 1598–1621) regarded illegal trade with his overseas colonies as a serious problem – it encouraged smuggling and even piracy, and led to a loss of royal revenue. So a programme of fortification building was begun, concentrating on the main ports in the Spanish Main. A small guard fleet, the Armada de Barlovento (Windward Fleet), was also created, with squadrons based in Havana and Cartagena. Then someone dreamed up the idea of depopulation.

The Spanish authorities had long known that the northern side of Hispaniola was a lawless place. The island lacked the resources of nearby Cuba, and its hinterland was never fully developed by Spanish colonists. The one successful economic development on the island was the introduction of cattle, and by the early 17th century beef and leather production became the mainstay of the island's economy. Away from the cattle ranches of the hinterland, small and impoverished settlements clung to the northern coast. Fraternization between Spanish colonists and 'interlopers' had always gone on in northern Hispaniola, but during Philip III's reign the region became notorious as a haven for smugglers. So, in 1604, the governor of Hispaniola gave orders to forcibly depopulate the north of the island. His men destroyed a string of settlements, and moved their inhabitants to new colonies established closer to Santo Domingo.

On paper the operation was a success. However, many colonists fled into the hinterland, and became *renegados* (renegades), existing outside the authority of the Spanish crown. With no legitimate income, they took to cattle rustling in order to survive. In effect the northern part of the island became a political vacuum, and while the Spanish might have benefited from this in the short term, by the 1620s they were beginning to reap the ill effects of their policy. Only a portion of the cattle herds was successfully moved to the ranches near Santo Domingo. The rest simply roamed wild. Legitimate cattle ranching on Hispaniola never really recovered from the relocation, and these wild cattle provided the *renegados* with a livelihood. In effect they became *boucaniers*, a French term meaning those who smoked meat, or *boucan*.

The Spanish were certainly aware of the problem. Patrols tried to round up stray cattle and hunt down *renegados* hiding in the forest. Invariably both the cattle and the *boucaniers* melted into the trees. Then the cattle hunting and meat smoking would continue as before. The process of smoking involved laying the carcass out on a green wood frame over an open fire. The native Arawak called the process *barbicoa*, but today we call it a barbecue.

The earliest buccaneers were French backwoodsmen from Hispaniola, making a living from hunting wild cattle and selling *boucan*, or smoked meat, to passing ships.

A French observer described these early *boucaniers* as looking like 'the butcher's vilest servants who have been eight days in the slaughterhouse without washing themselves'. They lived, worked and slept in rough leather hunting shirts, coarse homespun shirts, and boots made of pigskin. Animal fat was smeared over the skin to repel insects, which accounts for the repugnance shown by the Frenchman. Their barbecued meat and hides were transported to the coast, where they were sold to 'interlopers'. In exchange the *boucaniers* would buy weapons, powder and shot. They operated in small groups, developing their own complex codes of behaviour which would later develop into the buccaneering codes.

A 19th-century depiction of a buccaneer on Hispaniola, cautiously watching the landing of a longboat's crew. These frontiersmen made their living by trading with the crew of passing ships, if they proved to be friendly.

During the first decades of the 17th century other European powers began establishing small settlements in the West Indies. In 1600 the Dutch colonized St Eustatius, and both St Croix and Martin were established as colonies during the 1620s, while in 1622 the English settled St Kitts, and the French joined them there in 1625. Barbados was colonized three years later. Other colonies would follow throughout the Lesser Antilles, an area that had never been settled by the Spanish. The Spanish response was predictable. In 1627, after reclaiming Brazil from the Dutch, a Spanish force invaded St Kitts and razed the English and French settlements. Many of the surviving settlers simply founded new colonies on neighbouring islands. A number of French refugees from St Kitts headed west, seeking out a new home somewhere along the northern shore of Hispaniola. They selected the island of La Tortuga, off the north-west corner of the island, which seemed to offer everything they needed. Within a few years a thriving tobacco crop was being harvested there, while the island also attracted local *boucaniers* and other refugee 'interlopers'. It was the Dutch who gave this new settlement some degree of legitimacy, as the Dutch West India Company offered to protect the fledgling colony in exchange for leather hides. In other words, this pirate den began as a backwater trading post.

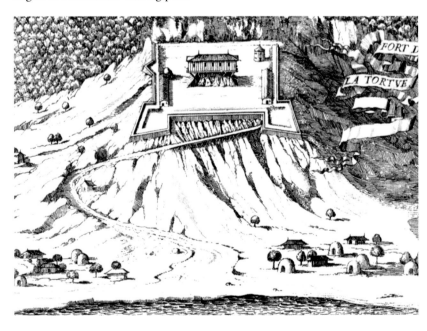

The French buccaneers of Tortuga defended their small island by means of shore batteries and this small fort, established on high ground some distance from the main settlement. It was captured by the Spanish, but later re-occupied by the French.

TORTUGA: THE BUCCANEERS' HAVEN

The island settlement of Tortuga had a rocky history. The first Europeans to settle there were the Spanish, who arrived in 1598. They soon discovered that the island was unsuitable for sugar production, but it could support a tobacco crop. Then came the forcible resettlement, which meant that any Spaniards who remained in Tortuga did so as *renegados*. By the time the first wave of French settlers arrived in 1627, they found that the island already supported a small but thriving business, where the locals ran a trading post, selling *boucan* to passing ships, and thus serving as a link between the *boucaniers* and 'interlopers'.

Tortuga was small, just 40 miles (64km) in circumference, and shaped like the turtle which gave it the name of Isle de la Tortue ('Turtle Island'). The soil was poor and rocky, while the hinterland was covered in forest. The northern coast of the island was fringed with cliffs, and the only suitable harbour lay on the southern shore. The best tobacco-growing area was on the western side. The French called this area La Ringot, and established their own settlement called Basseterre, which co-existed beside the *renagado* trading post of Cayonne.

The Dutch offer of protection never materialized, but their ships began trading with the island. Soon an English trading organization, the Providence Island Company, also appeared, and sent colonists to augment the settlers already there. Their agent Anthony Hilton was duly given titular control of the

After seizing a town, the buccaneers plundered what they could find. Then, they turned on any townspeople they captured, forcing them through intimidation or torture to reveal their hidden caches of valuables.

THE BUCCANEERS OF TORTUGA

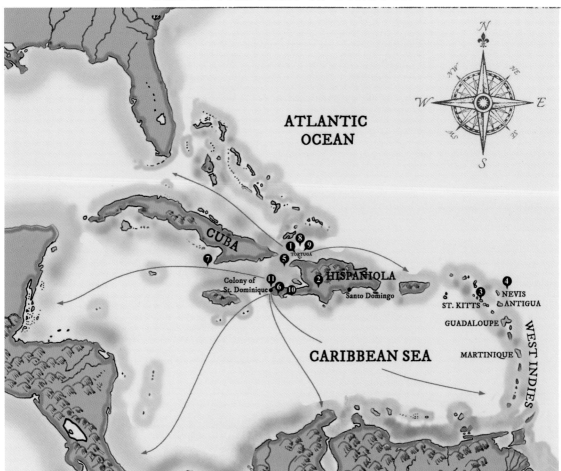

island. The French, English and *renagados* co-existed, although following the death of Hilton in 1634 the English left to join another colony on Providence (Santa Catalina), off the coast of Central America. This left the French in sole control of Tortuga, although they still enjoyed the protection of the Dutch. However, the Dutch were nowhere to be seen in 1635 when the Spanish attacked the island.

That January, a Spanish expedition destroyed the settlement and captured 240 colonists. All but 30 Spaniards and a few French Catholics were summarily executed. The settlers who fled to Hispaniola eventually returned, however, and by 1638 the Spanish were forced to launch another expedition. Once again they managed to disperse or capture the colonists, but the surviving islanders simply

The First Buccaneers

1. The island of Tortuga ('Turtle Island') is first discovered by Columbus in 1493, who names it after its distinctive turtle-backed shape.

2. The first 'buccaneers' are Spanish *renegados*, roaming Hispaniola in search of wild cattle. They are soon joined by other European 'interlopers'.

3. 1624: English settlers form a colony on Tortuga and begin trading with the *renegados*. The French send settlers, too. Over the next decade other English and French settlements are founded in Nevis, Antigua, Martinique and Guadeloupe. The Tortuga settlement thrives.

4. 1636: After the English move elsewhere, Tortuga becomes a French colony. English privateers from Nevis raid it, forcing the French to improve the island's defences.

The Brethren of the Coast

5. 1640: Pierre le Grand arrives in Tortuga, and uses it as a base for carrying out small-scale attacks on Spanish shipping in the Windward Passage.

6. 1642: The French establish the first of several settlements in western Hispaniola.

7. 1648: The Spanish report that buccaneering attacks on Spanish shipping have become commonplace, particularly off the southern coasts of Cuba and Hispaniola. Some buccaneers even venture as far as the coast of Central America.

8. 1650: Tortuga has become a bustling haven for the buccaneers, and a thorn in Spain's side.

9. 1654: The Spanish attack and capture Tortuga and take the inhabitants prisoner. They soon withdraw from the island after destroying its defences and buildings.

10. 1660: The French colonies in Hispaniola are formally recognized by the Spanish, who lack the resources to recapture the western part of the island.

11. 1670: Tortuga is deemed a backwater. Most of the buccaneers have either moved to the French colony of Saint Dominique or to Jamaica. Saint Dominique is now the main haven for French buccaneers.

---

returned as soon as the Spanish left. In 1640 the French Huguenot Jean le Vasseur arrived as the new governor, and he immediately set about improving the island's defences. He built Fort du Rocher (La Rocca), overlooking Cayonne harbour, and then called on the original settlers to join him in protecting the island as a Protestant enclave in the heart of the Spanish Main. This marked a new phase in the history of Tortuga. Until the arrival of le Vasseur the islanders had busied themselves with growing tobacco, trading with the *boucaniers* and acting as a trading post. However, under his leadership Tortuga became a haven for any fugitives nursing a hatred of the Spanish authorities. From 1640 on, these settlers began to attack passing Spanish ships. The era of the seagoing buccaneers had begun. Tortuga lay at the north-eastern end of the Windward Passage between Cuba and Hispaniola, and this busy shipping lane became the new hunting ground for le Vasseur's pirates.

The pirates used small sailing or rowing boats (known as flyboats or pinnaces), and attacked at night. Their aim was to creep up astern of larger Spanish ships, then board them before a lookout could sound the alarm. While

The Spanish galleon was primarily designed to transport specie from the New World to Spain. Treasure galleons were not only large and well armed, but they also sailed as part of a fleet (*flota*), which was too powerful for buccaneers to attack.

marksmen shot the helmsmen and officers, others wedged the ship's rudder to prevent their prey escaping. They then swarmed up the side and overpowered the Spanish crew. These pirates soon developed a reputation for cruelty, whether deserved or not, and this worked in their favour. It was often enough to encourage the Spanish to surrender without firing a shot, in the hope that their lives would be spared.

In his book *Buccaneers of America*, published in 1678, Alexandre Oliver Exquemelin claims that the first of these attacks was carried out by a Frenchman called Pierre le Grand (Peter the Great). According to his account, Pierre was from Dieppe, and arrived in Tortuga soon after 1640. Gathering a group of followers together, he began cruising the waters off Tortuga in a small canoe, hoping to intercept a Spanish trading ship. According to Exquemelin he managed to capture a small Spanish pinnace, and then used it to hunt for larger prey. After months of fruitless searching he finally stumbled across one of the most lucrative prizes on the Spanish Main – a straggler from a Spanish treasure fleet. He brought his boat up behind the Spanish ship, then boarded her before the Spanish realized they were being attacked. To encourage his followers to attack, he scuttled his own craft. The Spanish ship was duly captured, and, rather than take her back to Tortuga, Pierre sailed her home to Dieppe, where he retired on the proceeds.

If Exquemelin is to be believed, Pierre le Grand was the first real 'pirate of the Caribbean', and his exploits served to encourage others to follow in his stead. However, the story lacks any real corroborative evidence, and we are probably expected to see the tale as symbolic rather than to accept it as a straightforward account. Still, it shows how these French pirates operated. It suggests a trend in the waters off Tortuga – small canoes being used to prey on coastal shipping, and then these small Spanish vessels being turned into pirate ships in their own right.

Exquemelin's account is supported by a letter written by the Spanish governor of Santo Domingo in 1646, which stated that Tortuga had become a pirate haven, populated by Englishmen, Dutchmen and French Huguenots. According to Exquemelin, two important events took place around this time. First, the Tortugans began collectively to refer to themselves as 'buccaneers'. Secondly, they also started calling themselves the 'Brethren of the Coast'. In effect the Tortugan incomers had adopted the name and collective identity of the *boucaniers* of Hispaniola, which suggests that by the 1640s the two groups had become so intermingled as to become one body.

THE BRETHREN OF THE COAST

Our understanding of buccaneering society comes from Exquemelin. He claims that the buccaneers of Hispaniola operated in hunting parties of six to eight men, pooling their resources and making decisions by consensus. He also suggests that a pairing of buccaneers was common – a male union known as *matelotage*, a term which essentially meant 'bunk mate', but which has been more commonly linked to the French word *matelot*, meaning a sailor. This union – essentially a single-sex marriage – was recognized in the self-administered

Much of what we know about the buccaneers comes from this book, Alexandre Exquemelin's *Buccaneers of America*, first published in Amsterdam in 1678. Exquemelin was a French buccaneer who participated in many of the raids he described so vividly in his book.

buccaneering laws or guidelines known as 'the way of the coast'. A *matelot* stood to inherit the possessions of his partner on his death, and may well have had other rights that have gone unrecorded. The Brethren of the Coast was no tightly knit brotherhood, but more a loose confederation built up of these smaller partnerships and hunting groups.

The suggestion is that by the time Tortuga became established as a pirate haven, the *boucaniers* formed the core of the island population. In the process they brought their own ways with them. What these men shared with the incomers from Europe was a strong antipathy to Spanish authority. The Brethren of the Coast would soon grow from an island brotherhood into a maritime force capable of terrorizing the whole of the Spanish Main.

Calling Tortuga a pirate den is something of a misnomer. It was a gathering place, a trading centre, and a place where crews could be

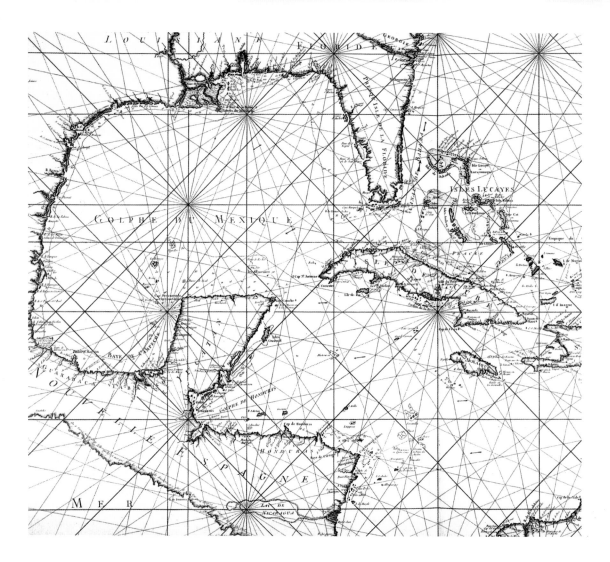

This late 17th-century French chart of the Western Caribbean shows just how much of this region was controlled by the Spanish, whose coast is highlighted in red. In the midst of this Spanish-controlled area lay the buccaneering bases of Tortuga and Port Royal.

recruited. It was not, however, a safe haven. On three occasions the Spanish assaulted and captured the island. Each time many of the inhabitants fled to the safety of the Hispaniola coast (which they called the 'Tierra Grande'). After the assassination of Jean le Vasseur by discontented buccaneers in 1653, the Chevalier de Fontenay, a Catholic, became the new governor. The following January the Spanish landed a powerful expeditionary force on the island, then marched on the Fort du Rocher. They carried the stronghold by a direct assault and crushed any resistance. The majority of the buccaneers had fled from Tortuga before the Spanish arrived, but 330 were still captured, along with artillery from the fort and 160,000 pieces-of-eight.

When the Spanish left the island the buccaneers returned, and Tortuga was soon back in business as a buccaneering haven. However, by then a new buccaneering den had become established on Jamaica, one that would soon develop into one of the most bustling and best-defended ports in the Spanish Main. The days of Tortuga were numbered, although the French government's encouragement of privateering meant that the island would enjoy one last hurrah when Tortuga briefly became a major buccaneering haven again.

In 1664 the French West India Company took over the administration of Tortuga and introduced new colonists. Their governor still needed the buccaneers, though, for both income and protection, and so letters-of-marque were issued, regardless of whether France was at war with Spain or not. This merely reflected a policy also adopted by English and Dutch governors in the Caribbean. Wars might come and go, but 'beyond the line' Spain always remained the enemy. If these three nations happened to be at war with each other, this rarely had an impact on their mutual co-operation in the Americas. In other words, Dutch, English and French buccaneers tended to work together, regardless of the political situation at home.

In Tortuga the heyday of buccaneering continued well into the 1670s. What brought it to an end was not the activities of the buccaneers themselves, but the interference of national governments, who had been trying to control the buccaneers since the 1640s. The final death knell was the Treaty of Ratisborn (Regensburg) of 1684, a Franco-Spanish peace treaty that ended the days of freely issued letters-of-marque. The French buccaneers began to drift away. By the mid-1680s at the latest the island had become little more than it had been when the buccaneering phenomenon first began: a trading post built on the declining trade in wild Hispaniola beef.

As for the Brethren of the Coast, it was never a united confederation – a true piratical force to be reckoned with. Throughout the 1660s and 1670s it remained what it had always been – a loose alliance of individuals, pairs, groups and crews of buccaneers, unified by a common temporary goal rather than by any larger political union. As such they were willing to join forces under the leadership of a dynamic buccaneering captain such as François L'Olonnais or Henry Morgan – Morgan even styled himself the 'Admiral of the Coast', suggesting that at least for a while he was the top dog in what was otherwise a society of equals – but as soon as the expedition returned to Port Royal or Tortuga, any allegiance became null and void. By the 1670s the term was mainly used to refer to the English buccaneers based in Port Royal.

THE WESTERN DESIGN

Although the English colonized several of the Windward Islands during the early 17th century, these lay far from the heart of the Spanish Main. During the 1650s England's Lord Protector, Oliver Cromwell, decided that now the Civil War was won, England was free to embark on a war with Spain. The reason for it was largely economic; English merchants wanted free access to Spanish ports, and by striking at Spain's overseas empire Cromwell hoped to secure his own national stake in the New World. The centrepiece of Cromwell's plan was his 'Western Design', an assault on the very heart of the Spanish Main.

The American artist Howard Pyle (1853–1911) almost single-handedly created the pirate 'look', as typified in this spirited portrayal of a buccaneer. Unfortunately, lacking hard historic references, Pyle based this 'look' on 19th-century Spanish bandits rather than 17th-century European seamen.

He decided to raise a special force and use it to assault Hispaniola, which an intelligence source claimed was only lightly defended. This force consisted of raw troops, adventurers in search of a new life in the Caribbean, augmented by the sweepings of the regular army. The experienced general Richard Venables was placed in command of the expedition, supported by General-at-Sea William Penn. The fleet arrived off Santo Domingo on 13 April 1655. Sickness amongst the troops meant that morale was low. Nevertheless, Venables landed his army and marched on the city. However, finding the defences too formidable, he withdrew again, and fell back to the ships.

Hoping to salvage something from the disaster, Venables and Penn decided to attack Jamaica, which was reportedly held by a negligible Spanish force. On 11 May the fleet arrived off the island, and this time the main settlement of Santiago de la Vega was captured with ease, and the Spanish colonists fled to nearby Cuba. Although thwarted on Hispaniola, the English now had a useful consolation prize, as Jamaica lay at the very centre of the Spanish Main. When the expedition returned home a garrison was left behind to build Fort Cromwell, on the tip of the sand spit known as the Palisadoes, which closed off the entrance to the island's main anchorage – now Kingston harbour. The fort was later renamed Passage Fort, and a small settlement known as Cagway was built up on the spit beneath its walls.

Santiago de la Vega (renamed Spanish Town) became the main agricultural centre of the island, while Cagway became the maritime hub, attracting buccaneers and merchants. However, the island's economy was slow to develop, despite the influx of

A TALE OF TWO BIOGRAPHIES

In 1678, the Amsterdam publisher Jan ten Horn began selling copies of a new book, *De Americaensche Zee-Rovers*, written by Alexandre Exquemelin (c.1645–1707). It proved an instant success, and it was soon reprinted in several other languages, including Spanish, French and English (where it appeared as *The Buccaneers of America*). Exquemelin was a French doctor employed by the French West India Company and participated in the French buccaneering raids of the 1660s and early 1670s. He had first-hand experience of these men, and would have talked to others who sailed with Christopher Myngs and Henry Morgan.

The next pirate biography was even more successful. In 1724 the London publisher Charles Rivington began selling a small book by an unknown author, Captain Charles Johnson. *A General History of the Robberies and Murders of the Most Notorious Pyrates* proved so popular that Rivington was forced to reprint a new expanded edition of the book within months. The book contained a series of pirate biographies, all of British-born swashbucklers, and is still in print today.

We know next to nothing about Captain Charles Johnson, except that his writing demonstrates an intimate knowledge of seamanship and maritime life, and that much of what he wrote about the pirates of the 'Golden Age of Piracy' was substantially accurate. Captain Johnson was probably a pseudonym, concealing a piratical past, or simply a literary *nom-de-plume*. Several candidates have been proposed, including Rivington himself, the playwright Charles Johnson, and the political journalist Nathaniel Mist. None of these had the necessary maritime experience, though, to write it alone. However, of the three, Mist is the only likely contender.

Another strong candidate is Daniel Defoe (1660–1748), the author of *Robinson Crusoe* (1719) and *Captain Singleton* (1720). Defoe was widely travelled, and could have gathered enough nautical knowledge to write such a salty tale.

While the identity of the author remains a mystery, there is no escaping the contribution Johnson's book made to pirate history. Like Exquemelin before him, his writing forms the cornerstone of all subsequent pirate histories, and remains one of the most useful tools for the pirate historian.

1,600 settlers in late 1656. Captain Christopher Myngs (1625–66) was one of the first to realize that the buccaneers were the island's best form of defence. The Norfolk-born sailor commanded the powerful 44-gun warship *Marston Moor*,

While a few buccaneering vessels were large three-masted ships, they were a rarity. For the most part the buccaneers operated in smaller vessels like this English pinnace. It was fast, manoeuvrable and had a shallow draft, making it an ideal craft for coastal raiding or to evade larger pursuers.

which arrived off Cagway in early 1656. As the deputy naval commander in Jamaica, Myngs enlisted the help of the buccaneers in defending the island. While some of them were French, Dutch or even Spanish *renegados*, most were English, many of whom had served as soldiers in the Western Expedition. The Jamaican governor, Edward d'Oyley, fully supported Myngs' scheme, and issued dozens of letters-of-marque to the leaders of these men.

In early 1656 Myngs led raids on Santa Marta and Rio de la Hacha on the Tierra Firme, and when his superior was recalled to England the following January, Myngs assumed command of the squadron of three Commonwealth frigates. He also became the *de facto* leader of a buccaneering fleet. The success of these first raids attracted more buccaneers from Tortuga to Cagway. In May 1658 the Spanish responded by invading Jamaica, but after Myngs destroyed their transports, Governor d'Oyley defeated the invaders on land.

In retaliation Myngs led another expedition to Santa Marta, and off Coro he intercepted a ship carrying silver on behalf of the Spanish crown. Unfortunately, on his return to Cagway he discovered that the crew had stolen the bulk of this plunder, although Governor d'Oyley was not convinced by this excuse and sent Myngs home to face charges of embezzlement. However, by then Cromwell had died, and Charles II had reclaimed his father's throne. Charles II not only accepted Myngs' protestations of loyalty, but he also removed d'Oyley from office. Myngs returned to Jamaica in August 1662 as a free man, and a powerful one.

PORT ROYAL: THE WICKEDEST CITY ON EARTH

In the spirit of the Restoration, Fort Cromwell was renamed Fort Charles, while Cagway became Port Royal. A new wave of settlers arrived in Jamaica, and they transformed the island's fragile economy. In fact, the only thing that remained the same was the policy of encouraging privateering. In the process Cagway – now Port Royal – developed into a boisterous haven for buccaneers. As the re-appointed commander of the Jamaica squadron, Myngs flew his flag in the 46-gun man-of-war HMS *Centurion*, although his real naval strength lay with the buccaneers. Spain and England might now be at peace, but the Spanish refused to recognize the English claim to Jamaica, and barred her merchants from trading with Spanish ports. So the buccaneers were still vital to Jamaica's survival.

In September 1662 the governor Lord Windsor signed new letters-of-marque 'in order to subdue our enemies on land and at sea, along the entire coast of America'. By the end of the month Myngs had raised a force of some 1,300 men. On 1 October he put to sea and only then did he tell his followers their target was Santiago, the second-largest city in Cuba. Two weeks later Myngs landed his men at the mouth of the San Juan River, and by dawn the following day they were outside the city.

Governor Pedro Morales knew the English were coming, but he never expected them to attack so quickly. He had just 750 men under his command, and, bribed by Myngs, half of them accompanied their deputy commander as

Santiago de Cuba was the second-largest city on the island and was well defended by city walls and this substantial fort, though this didn't stop Sir Christopher Myngs and his buccaneers from capturing the city in 1662. (Art Marie/Getty Images)

This evocative Howard Pyle painting shows how the early buccaneers used small craft such as canoes (or *piraguas*) to prey on larger Spanish ships, hoping to sneak up on them unobserved.

he fell back and abandoned the city's defences. The city quickly fell to the attackers, as did several ships in the harbour. The plunder was disappointing, but Myngs' aim was to hurt the Spanish, and so, before he left, his men destroyed most of the city's defences and major buildings, including the cathedral. It was said that it took the city a whole decade to recover from the damage caused by Myngs' raid.

The following year Myngs led his buccaneers to New Spain (Mexico). This time his force included Dutch and French buccaneers, making it a truly international body. He headed to Campeche on the Yucatán Peninsula, but his fleet was dispersed by storms, and so by the time the *Centurion* made landfall only two-thirds of the force remained. Myngs decided to attack anyway. The defenders were unable to halt the dawn onslaught, and within an hour most of Campeche was in English hands. The buccaneers remained in Campeche for two weeks, then in April 1663 they returned to Port Royal with their spoils. In all some 150,000 pieces-of-eight were plundered in the raid. However, by then Charles II had yielded to Spanish diplomatic pressure and forbade further attacks. In 1665 a fresh war with the Dutch saw Myngs promoted and recalled to England. Myngs proved himself a gifted admiral, and was knighted for his services in the Four Days' Battle (1666). However, just weeks later he was killed during the battle of North Foreland. England had lost a valuable naval commander and a highly successful buccaneer. In Jamaica Myngs had almost single-handedly turned Port Royal into the largest buccaneering haven in the Caribbean, and his example would be followed by others – men like Henry Morgan – who would lead Myngs' buccaneers on larger and more daring raids, and in the process wreak havoc in the very heart of the Spanish Main.

As for Port Royal, the town prospered. Merchants followed in the wake of the buccaneers, ensuring Port Royal provided a ready market for plunder. Warehouses were built to hold this merchandise, and by the late 1660s Port Royal was a thriving but lawless boom town of some 6,000 people. Many of Jamaica's leading landowners and merchants had a stake in buccaneering, and consequently they grew rich from their share of Spanish plunder. During its heyday Port Royal was larger and more prosperous than any other city in the Americas, apart from Boston. These landowners did not restrict themselves to merchant ventures. Taverns, brothels and gambling dens sprang up by the score, all vying with each other to deprive the buccaneers of their money. In fact it was said in a letter of complaint by disapproving visiting clerics that a fifth of the town's buildings were 'brothels, gaming houses, taverns and grog shops'. It was the perfect party town – a sailor's dream. However, others were less impressed. A visiting English clergyman said of Port Royal: 'This town is the Sodom of the New World … its population consists of pirates, cutthroats, whores and some of the vilest persons in the whole of the world'.

More accurately, he probably took exception to the population's *laissez-faire* attitude towards religion. Port Royal provided a welcome haven for people of all religious persuasions. However, it was still a rough and often violent place. No wonder another unnamed visitor from puritan New England called Port Royal 'the wickedest city on earth'.

What finally killed Port Royal as a pirate den was the same thing that ended Tortuga's glory days – good government. Henry Morgan's great raid on Panama took place between 1670 and 1671, three years after a peace treaty had been

Today, Port Royal in south-western Jamaica is little more than a small village. Once, though, before much of the town slipped into the harbour in 1692, it was the most bustling port in the Americas, and a major haven for buccaneers such as Henry Morgan. Little now remains of that lost buccaneering port. (Education Images/UIG/Getty Images)

signed with the Spanish. The same treaty allowed English merchants to trade with Spanish colonies, and meant that the island was no longer threatened by a Spanish invasion. In 1671 the governor, Sir Thomas Lynch, threatened to take legal action against buccaneers who continued to attack the Spanish. After all, with no war going on, these privateers had effectively become pirates.

As a pragmatist, Lynch also saw the need to pardon some of the worst (and most powerful) offenders, as part of a 'carrot and stick' approach to illegal buccaneering. In 1675 Sir Henry Morgan became deputy governor, and he served as acting governor twice – in 1678, then again from 1680–82. Ironically, under his leadership an anti-piracy law was passed by the Jamaican legislature (1681), and the following year Sir Thomas Lynch resumed control of the island and continued his policy of discouraging buccaneering. The result of all this was that by the early 1680s at the latest, buccaneering was no longer considered a viable business in Port Royal. Merchants turned to more legitimate pursuits, and as the selling of plundered goods became harder, sailors were forced to operate elsewhere; for instance, many ventured into the Pacific.

The final blow came in 1692, at exactly 11.40am on 7 June, when the first tremors of an earthquake hit Port Royal. The first shock was followed by other stronger ones, and within minutes buildings throughout the town had collapsed, while the northern section of Port Royal slid into the sea, taking most of the docks with it. Thousands were trapped in the rubble, or drowned in the tsunami-like tidal wave that followed. Some 2,000 townspeople died that day, and many more perished later from disease or injury. The town never recovered, and a fire in 1702 destroyed much of what had been rebuilt amidst its ruins. Following another earthquake in 1722 the town was abandoned, and the sands slowly covered over what ruins were left. There were those who saw this as a final divine judgement on what was once described as 'that wicked and rebellious place, Port Royal'.

LOW-LIFES OF THE CARIBBEAN

It is inevitable that any account of buccaneers will be dominated by the most successful. However, for every Henry Morgan, there were dozens of less successful buccaneers – men who barely scraped a living from their activities. A quick survey of a couple whose careers were recorded by Exquemelin also reveals a little about the type of men who turned to buccaneering.

Roche (or Rock) Braziliano was one of the Dutchmen who settled in Brazil, as part of the Dutch West India Company's venture. In 1630 the Dutch company captured Recife (Pernambuco) from the Portuguese and renamed the town New Holland. It was besieged intermittently by the Portuguese until it finally capitulated in 1654. In 1665 one of these Dutchmen, 'Rock the Brazilian', turned up in Port Royal, where he became a seaman. However, he eventually quarrelled with the captain of his ship and he deserted, taking a small group of followers with him.

According to Exquemelin, Braziliano succeeded in capturing a small Spanish vessel, probably by using the techniques adopted by Pierre le Grand. He therefore returned to Port Royal as a buccaneering captain, and continued to operate out of Jamaica during the mid-1660s. His big break came in 1666 when he captured a Spanish galleon outward bound from Vera Cruz in Mexico. However, his successes were tempered by spells of wild behaviour. On his return to Port Royal he and his followers 'wasted in a few days in taverns all they had gained'. After a bout of heavy drinking, 'he would run up and down the street, beating and wounding whom he met, no person daring to oppose him or make any resistance'. Many buccaneers were hard-bitten volatile characters, but Braziliano embraced violence so readily that he set himself apart from the rest.

During an expedition to Campeche in 1667, he was captured by the Spanish and thrown into the port's jail. While in prison Braziliano forged a letter, supposedly written by accomplices outside the city, who threatened to sack Campeche and slaughter its inhabitants if the captives were executed. The governor felt intimidated enough to cancel the planned execution, and instead he shipped Braziliano and his crew onto the next ship bound for Spain. Once there Braziliano managed to escape, and made his way back to Jamaica.

Exquemelin's account of Braziliano lacks dates or corroborative evidence. However, he places him back in Port Royal at the time the buccaneering captain L'Olonnais was active there around 1668, and he suggests that Braziliano served under him. Like his leader, the Dutchman gained an unsavoury reputation for the torture of Spanish prisoners. Exquemelin said: 'He perpetrated the greatest atrocities possible against the Spaniards. Some of them he tied or spitted on wooden stakes and roasted them alive between two fires, like killing a pig.'

By 1669 Braziliano was back in the Gulf of Campeche, where he wrecked his ship by running her aground. He knew that buccaneers frequently used the far side of the Yucatán Peninsula as a watering place, and so he led his men across country, fighting off Spanish patrols as they went. On reaching the coast, he stumbled upon a logwood camp. The harvesting of logwood – valuable for the dye it produced – was a lucrative industry in Central America. The

LESSER BUCCANEERS OF PORT ROYAL

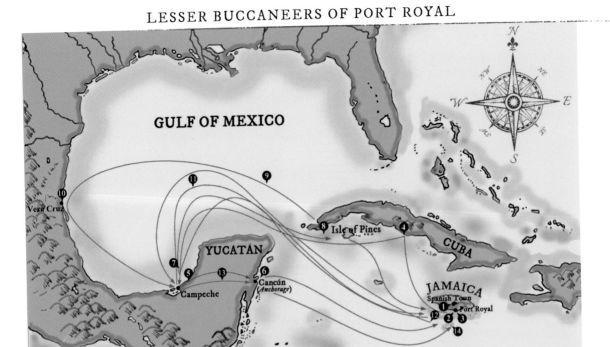

buccaneers drove off the loggers, then stole their boat, using it to make their way back to Port Royal. After that Braziliano fades from the record, which suggests he probably died in Port Royal soon after his return in or around 1670.

A buccaneer who was even less successful was Bartolomeo el Portugues. Exquemelin places the Portuguese buccaneer in Jamaica soon after the island's capture by the English. At first he served as a buccaneering crewman, participating in Myngs' raids on the Spanish Main in 1657 and 1658. However, within a few years Bartolomeo had his own small vessel, crewed by 30 men. He used her to cruise off the southern coast of Cuba, but in his first attack in 1662 he was repulsed, losing half his crew. Undeterred, he attacked again, and this time he captured the prize, which contained a chest of coins. Bartolomeo abandoned his own small vessel as he lacked enough crew. However, before he could escape he ran into a Spanish patrol off the western tip of Cuba, and the buccaneers were captured. The Spanish put in to Campeche but before they

KEY

◄——— Bartolomeo's voyages   ◄——— Roche's raids

Port Royal

1. 1655: Cromwell's Western Expedition invades Jamaica and captures the island.
2. 1662: The island's main harbour of Cagway – now Port Royal – becomes a thriving buccaneer haven. It is soon regarded as the richest and most debauched city in the Americas.
3. 7 June 1692: Port Royal is hit by an earthquake and tidal wave. Much of the town is destroyed, and its inhabitants killed. A third of the buildings slip into the sea.

Bartolomeo el Portugues

4. 1662: Bartolomeo el Portugues captures a Spanish ship off Cuba, but is captured in turn by a Spanish warship.
5. He is taken to Campeche to be executed, but he and some of his men manage to escape.
6. He reaches the coast near Cancún, where he finds a ship willing to take him back to Jamaica.
7. 1663: He returns to Campeche and cuts a ship out from its harbour.
8. He runs the prize aground on the Isle of Pines, but makes it back to Jamaica in the ship's boat. He is deemed unlucky and ends his days begging on the streets of Port Royal.

Roche Braziliano

9. 1665: Roche Braziliano arrives in Port Royal and begins attacking Spanish ships off the Cuban coast.
10. 1666: He captures a Spanish prize off Vera Cruz.
11. 1667: He and his men are captured near Campeche, but they escape in a small boat and return to Jamaica.
12. 1669: He returns to Campeche, but runs his ship aground as he approaches the harbour.
13. He leads his crew across the Yucatán Peninsula, fighting off the Spanish as he goes. On reaching the coast he steals two small boats, and sails them back to Jamaica.
14. 1670: Braziliano dies shortly after his return to Port Royal.

could hang the prisoners, Bartolomeo and several of his men escaped and swam for the shore. They hacked their way through the Yucatán jungle and made it to the coast, where a passing ship took them to Jamaica.

Bartolomeo was hell-bent on revenge, so as soon as he could he returned to Campeche with 20 men in a canoe. He seized a ship anchored in the harbour and made off in her, only to run her aground off the Isle of Pines. He took to the boats, and made his

Bartolomeo el Portugues, as depicted in the original edition of Exquemelin's *Buccaneers of America.* This Portuguese buccaneer had a largely unsuccessful career, and according to Exquemelin he died 'in the greatest wretchedness'.

ignominious way back to Port Royal. During the years that followed Bartolomeo remained a buccaneer captain, which suggests he acquired another ship. However, as Exquemelin put it, Bartolomeo made 'many violent attacks on the Spaniards without gaining much profit from marauding, for I saw him dying in the greatest wretchedness in the world'.

What is particularly interesting about these characters is that they highlight two things. First, buccaneering was a risky business, and while the profits could be huge, so too were the inherent dangers. Secondly, both buccaneers shared the same trait – an intense drive that let them continue on in the face of often severe setbacks. Buccaneers might have been united by their hatred of the Spanish, but they also showed a remarkable collective determination.

L'OLONNAIS: THE FLAIL OF THE SPANIARDS

In a violent age, the French buccaneer François L'Olonnais earned an especially notorious reputation for cruelty. In this engraving he is shown cutting the tongue from a Spanish prisoner and forcibly feeding it to another captive.

'The flail of the Spaniards' hailed from the fishing town of Les Sables d'Olonne near La Rochelle, on the French Atlantic coast. It was this birthplace that gave him his nickname 'L'Olonnais', the man from Olonne. Exquemelin also provided a name for the buccaneer, François Nau – although it might have originally been Jean-David Nau. Around 1660 the teenage Nau arrived in Martinique as an indentured servant. After three years he was freed from his obligations, and drifted to Hispaniola, where he spent time hunting with the *boucaniers* before turning to piracy. On Tortuga he bought a small sloop, a former prize, and Governor d'Ogeron issued him with a letter-of-marque. After recruiting 20 men, L'Olonnais set off in search of Spanish prey.

He was lucky. Off the eastern coast of Hispaniola he captured a Spanish merchantman, and then another ship carrying a military payroll. After these successes others joined him, and his force of ships and men grew. Then, in 1666–67, he suffered a setback. During a raid on Campeche he was shipwrecked near the port, then hounded by Spanish patrols until he and his men managed to escape by stealing a small boat. Exquemelin claims he was repulsed during an attack on the city, but there is no historical evidence for this. On his way back to Tortuga he was near the southern coast of Cuba when he encountered a Spanish patrol ship, out hunting for them. L'Olonnais and his men boarded the Spanish sloop as she lay at anchor, her crew asleep. The buccaneers massacred their prisoners, leaving one man to take a message back to the governor in Havana. According to Exquemelin, it read: 'I shall never henceforward give quarter to any Spaniard whatsoever'. In other words, L'Olonnais was now fighting his own personal war against the Spanish. From that point on he would give no quarter.

Despite this unsuccessful venture, by mid-1667 L'Olonnais commanded a squadron of eight ships. He was now a force to be reckoned with, and was able to contemplate more ambitious raids. So, in September 1667, he appeared in the Gulf of Venezuela, off the entrance to the lagoon known as the Lago de Maracaibo. Once he stormed the battery guarding the entrance, the lagoon lay at his mercy. They found that the town of Maracaibo had been abandoned, but the buccaneers spent two weeks there, searching for hidden loot. Then, L'Olonnais crossed the lagoon to Gibraltar (now Bobures), which was not only still occupied, but was also defended by a Spanish garrison. He captured the town after a short but bloody fight. This time he held the place until a 10,000-piece-of-eight ransom was paid. Before leaving he returned to Maracaibo to extort another ransom. Then L'Olonnais returned to Tortuga, with plunder estimated at 260,000 pieces-of-eight.

The psychopathic French buccaneer François L'Olonnais, as pictured in Exquemelin's *Buccaneers of America* (1678). He was eventually captured and killed by cannibals after being ambushed by them on the Honduran Coast.

Another account of his activities suggests that in 1668 L'Olonnais led a major raid on the Mosquito Coast – now Nicaragua. Contrary winds prevented him from making a landfall there, so instead he attacked Puerto Cabellos (now Puerto Cortés) on the coast of Honduras. He captured the port and then led his men inland to San Pedro, the regional capital. The town was stormed, and the defenders fled into the jungle. After plundering San Pedro the buccaneers razed it to the ground, and then returned to their ships. By then, though, L'Olonnais had an even greater prize in his sights. From prisoners he captured in Puerto Cabellos he learned that the annual Honduras treasure galleon was due, so he decided to intercept it. It finally showed up three months late, and was captured in a particularly bloody action. However, L'Olonnais discovered it had already unloaded its cargo, so the buccaneers found nothing left to plunder.

FRANÇOIS L'OLONNAIS

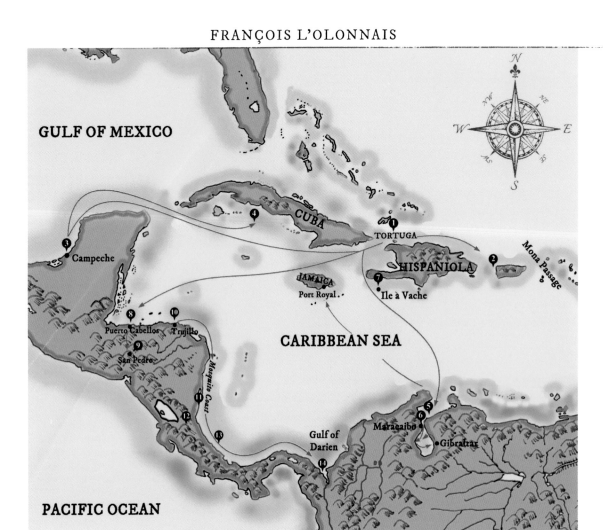

L'Olonnais had developed a reputation for barbarity. In a way this played against him, as Spanish captains such as the commander of the galleon would prefer to fight to the end rather than surrender to him. After all, as Exquemelin put it, 'it was the custom of L'Olonnais that, having tormented any persons and they not confessing, he would instantly cut them to pieces with his hanger (sword) and pull on their tongues'. That was when he was feeling magnanimous. On other occasions he would resort to 'burning with matches and suchlike torments, to cut a man to pieces, first some flesh, then a hand, then an arm, a leg, sometimes tying a cord about his head and with a stick twisting it till his eyes shoot out, which is called woolding'.

1. Spring 1667: The French governor of Tortuga gives L'Olonnais a buccaneering letter-of-marque.
2. L'Olonnais captures his first prize in the Mona Passage.
3. Summer: He is shipwrecked near Campeche, but escapes from his Spanish pursuers.
4. L'Olonnais and his men capture a Spanish vessel off Cuba, which they sail back to Tortuga.
5. September: He enters the Gulf of Maracaibo and captures the Spanish battery guarding it.
6. He sacks the settlements of Maracaibo and Gibraltar, then escapes with his plunder.
7. The French divide their plunder at the Île à Vache, a favoured rendezvous for buccaneers. L'Olonnais also sends ships to Port Royal to convert plundered goods into cash. He then returns to Tortuga.
8. Spring 1668: L'Olonnais sails for Honduras and captures Puerto Cabellos.
9. He marches inland and sacks the regional capital of San Pedro. Both raids, though, yield little plunder.
10. L'Olonnais captures a Honduran treasure galleon off Trujillo but finds it has already unloaded its cargo. At this point most of his men desert, leaving him with one ship and 400 men.
11. L'Olonnais heads to the Mosquito Coast, but is shipwrecked again, this time off Punta Mono.
12. He leads the survivors on a raid up the San Juan River, but is ambushed by the Spanish, and forced to withdraw.
13. The buccaneers build a boat, and L'Olonnais sails it south to the Gulf of Darien.
14. The buccaneers go ashore in search of food, but are attacked by native villagers, and L'Olonnais is killed.

As an example, during his march on San Pedro L'Olonnais used two Spanish prisoners as guides, but suspected they were leading him into a trap. So he 'ripped open one of the prisoners with his cutlass, tore the living heart out of his body, and gnawed at it'. After that the remaining prisoner was fully co-operative.

It was just after the attack on the galleon that L'Olonnais' expedition fell apart. Most of his men refused to continue following him and returned to Tortuga with their ships. L'Olonnais was left with just his own ship and 400 men. His problems were soon compounded when he ran her aground near Punta Mono ('Monkey Point') on the Mosquito Coast. The survivors established a camp on the shore, salvaged what they could, and built a small boat from the wreckage. L'Olonnais then used this boat to lead his remaining men south towards the comparative safety of the Gulf of Darien.

However, the area was full of hostile natives. Half-starved, the buccaneers attacked a native village, hoping to find stocks of food. Instead, they were surrounded and killed. According to Exquemelin there was only one survivor, who recounted that, along with his men, L'Olonnais was hacked to pieces, then eaten by the cannibalistic natives. It seems that the most brutal of all the buccaneers met a fate that he richly deserved.

THE RISE OF HENRY MORGAN

Henry Morgan is generally seen as a Falstaff figure, a bluff, plump and somewhat comic character. Such is the legacy of pirate fiction. Certainly he would have appeared larger than life to his contemporaries. However, Morgan was so much more – a born leader, a skilled tactician and a consummate politician. He was also a more complex person than history gives him credit for. For that matter, if he was ever seen as a comic figure during his lifetime, the Spanish failed to get the joke.

Henry Morgan was born into a genteel Welsh farming family in 1635, although he never spoke of his early life. He arrived in Jamaica with the expedition that seized the island in 1655. For the next few years little or nothing is heard of him, although he may have participated in a buccaneering raid as early as 1659. In 1662 he was appointed as a captain in the Jamaican militia, which suggests some military experience. Later that year he was granted a letter-of-marque, empowering him to conduct his own raids against the Spanish.

Morgan took part in Myngs' attacks on Santiago de Cuba in 1662, and in his subsequent assault on Campeche the following year. Exquemelin suggests that Morgan owned a small sloop, and consequently was a bit player in these early buccaneering dramas. However, by February 1665 his stock had risen sufficiently for him to serve as one of three co-commanders in a raid. Together with the English buccaneer John Morris and the Dutchman David Martien, Morgan landed on the Mexican coast near Santa Maria de la Frontera, at the mouth of the Grijalva River. The buccaneers made their way up river and fell upon the regional capital of Villahermosa, taking the town by surprise. Two coastal vessels were commandeered to carry the plunder and captured supplies back to the coast.

The raiders retraced their steps, only to find that in their absence three Spanish frigates had captured the buccaneers' ships, leaving the raiders with nothing but their little coasters. Undaunted, they sailed up the coast in search of a larger ship. However, the Spanish tracked them down while taking on water, and Spanish militia were landed to capture them. The Spanish attack was repulsed, and the buccaneers went on to capture the two Spanish ships the militia had landed from. The buccaneers were therefore able to sail off with their plunder. Before heading home, though, they raided Trujillo on the Gulf of Honduras, then cut south again to the Mosquito Coast. In early June 1665 they anchored off the mouth of the San Juan River, and used canoes to reach the Lago de Nicaragua. There on 29 June they fell on the regional capital of Granada and sacked it. By the end of August the buccaneers were safely back in Port Royal.

The Welsh-born buccaneering leader Henry Morgan is often portrayed as a Falstaff figure, but his corpulence developed after his buccaneering days were over. By contrast, this engraving shows him as he looked at the height of his fame, during his attack on Panama.

In early 1668, Henry Morgan landed a force in Cuba and attacked the town of Puerto Principe. He captured the place after a brief fight, but found that the townspeople had fled, taking most of their valuables with them.

Morgan used his share of the plunder wisely, buying the first of several Jamaican plantations, then courting and marrying his cousin Mary, the daughter of his soldier uncle Sir Edward Morgan, deputy governor of the island. Henry Morgan also cultivated a friendship with the new governor, Thomas Modyford. As governor Modyford was reluctant to turn his buccaneers on the Dutch, with whom the English were currently at war, but, bowing to pressure from London, he finally authorized two expeditions.

The first, led by Sir Edward Morgan in 1665, was directed against the island of St Eustatius, one of the Leeward Islands. Although the raid was a success, Sir Edward died of a stroke during the attack. Another expedition against Curaçao was abandoned when the buccaneers refused to fight their fellow Protestants.

Back in Jamaica, Henry Morgan missed out on these raids, but he spent the time consolidating his social and political standing in Jamaica. Then in January 1668 Modyford ordered Henry Morgan 'to draw together the English privateers and take prisoners of the Spanish nation, whereby you may gain information of that enemy'. Officially this was a reconnaissance mission, and Morgan's letter-of-marque said nothing about conducting raids. Morgan's subsequent actions pushed the boundaries of what he and Modyford could legally get away with.

Morgan assembled a force of ten ships and 500 men, and rendezvoused with a force of French buccaneers from Tortuga. On 28 March 1668 they landed on the south-eastern coast of Cuba, and marched on the provincial capital of Puerto Principe (now Camaguey). The buccaneers captured the city, but found there was little there to plunder. According to Exquemelin, the raiders locked the inhabitants in a church. Morgan agreed not to burn the building down in return for a ransom of 50,000 pieces-of-eight – a meagre reward for such a substantial raid. Once the buccaneers returned to their ships, the French sailed back to Tortuga, but the English elected to attack a more lucrative target: Porto Bello, the treasure port on the isthmus of Panama. It was a bold decision – the port was guarded by three forts, although Morgan's sources told him they were under-manned. In addition, the governor of Panama could call on a sizeable force of troops, meaning the raiders could easily be outnumbered.

On reaching the coast Morgan transferred his men into canoes, then crept up the coast towards the port. By the afternoon of 10 July Morgan was just a few miles from his objective. His force disembarked that evening, and, using the darkness as cover, Morgan marched along the coast. The port lay on one side of a bay, with a fort on either side of the harbour, and a third unfinished fort covering the beach. Capturing the city would require a combination of speed, surprise and luck. The buccaneers reached Porto Bello's western outskirts just before dawn on 11 July, and Morgan launched an immediate attack. Within minutes his men were in the town, firing their muskets at everything they could. Then, with the place secure, Morgan decided to assault Fort Santiago, guarding the west side of the harbour. For this he had his men gather up a 'human shield' of nuns, friars and prominent townspeople. Understandably the fort's defenders were unwilling to fire on their own people, so the buccaneers reached the walls unscathed, and within minutes the fort was taken and the garrison overwhelmed.

The unfinished fort had already been abandoned, which just left Castillo San Felipe, covering the eastern side of the harbour. The following morning Morgan led 200 men across the bay and landed beneath the walls of the fort. The outnumbered defenders meekly surrendered after a token resistance. With Porto Bello in Morgan's hands, the buccaneer recalled his ships, which entered the

In 1668, Henry Morgan led a daring raid on Porto Bello, the treasure port on the isthmus of Panama. It was guarded by three forts, all of which either surrendered to the buccaneers, or were stormed by them. This one, Fort Santiago, was taken by Morgan after he used the townspeople as a human shield during his assault. (Gary Weathers/Getty Images)

The Île à Vache (Cow Island), 6 miles (9km) off the south-western coast of Hispaniola, was used as a rendezvous by buccaneers. It was there in 1669 that Henry Morgan's flagship HMS *Oxford* blew up during just such a meeting. This anchorage is now called Port Morgan, in honour of the buccaneer. (John Seaton Callahan/Getty Images)

harbour a week later. Meanwhile Morgan wrote to the governor of Panama, telling him that he planned to destroy the town and its defences. To avoid this, the governor had to pay a ransom of 350,000 pieces-of-eight. The governor wrote back, saying that 'vassals of the King of Spain do not make treaties with inferior persons'. Morgan replied: 'We are waiting for you with great pleasure, and we have powder and ball with which to receive you.' It was all stirring stuff, but the real test would come when the troops the governor sent from Panama reached Porto Bello.

On 24 July, the attack finally came, but it was easily repulsed, and the Spanish troops fled back to Panama. Having run out of options, the thoroughly humiliated Spanish governor agreed to pay a ransom of 100,000 pieces-of-eight. In return the undamaged but now impoverished port was returned to him. Once it was made, Morgan honoured his agreement and sailed back to Port Royal. The ransom money brought the Porto Bello plunder up to a respectable total of 250,000 pieces-of-eight. That summer Henry Morgan was the toast of the Caribbean, and hundreds of fresh volunteers flocked to join his band of buccaneers.

'HARRY MORGAN'S WAY'

Within a few months Morgan put to sea again, this time at the head of a powerful buccaneering force that included the frigate HMS *Oxford* on loan from Modyford. As before, in early January 1669 Morgan rendezvoused with the French buccaneers from Tortuga, meeting them at the Île à Vache (Cow Island), off south-western Hispaniola. Morgan and his captains sat down to dinner in the great cabin on board the *Oxford* and the rum flowed freely. Then disaster struck. A spark ignited a powder barrel, and the explosion ignited the forward powder magazine. The *Oxford* was ripped apart. Amazingly, Morgan and many of his guests survived the disaster, unlike most of the *Oxford*'s crew.

Morgan held a council of war with his surviving captains. By then, most of the French had abandoned the enterprise. Before the disaster, the plan was to attack Cartagena, but with just eight ships and 500 men that was now

impossible. Finally, they decided to repeat L'Olonnais' raid on the Lago de Maracaibo. Morgan set sail, and his fleet arrived off the Maracaibo Bar on 9 March. The battery there had been rebuilt since L'Olonnais' visit, but it was poorly manned and was taken without loss. Morgan was free to enter the now defenceless lagoon. On reaching Maracaibo, the buccaneers found the town had been abandoned, so they spent the next three weeks searching it for hidden valuables. They then sailed across the lagoon to Gibraltar, which was also abandoned before the buccaneers arrived. Altogether a relatively modest haul of 100,000 pieces-of-eight was gathered from the two towns.

By 17 April Morgan was back at Maracaibo, having captured a large Spanish merchantman on his way across the lagoon. It was from her crew that Morgan discovered that the lagoon had become a trap. While the buccaneers were sacking Gibraltar, Admiral Alonso de Campo had arrived with a squadron of four warships from the Armada de Barlovento. Admiral Campo's first move was to re-occupy the Maracaibo battery, and lead his ships over the bar to help defend it. Morgan responded by sailing up the lagoon and anchoring his larger

After raiding the towns around the Maracaibo lagoon, Morgan's buccaneers found their exit to the open sea blocked by a powerful Spanish squadron. Morgan relied on a fireship attack to scatter this Spanish force and so avoid being entrapped.

THE VOYAGES OF HENRY MORGAN

but less powerful force just outside gun range of the enemy. For the next two days the two squadrons faced each other. Then, on the morning of 27 April, Morgan made his move.

Led by the captured merchantman, the buccaneers bore down on the Spanish ships, whose crews hurriedly prepared for battle. The merchantman headed straight for Campo's flagship. The Spaniards grappled her and swarmed on board. Then the flames appeared, licking out of the merchant ship's hold. Morgan had converted her into a fireship, and the flames soon spread to the Spanish flagship. Unable to stem the inferno, Campo and his men abandoned ship just before the flames reached the magazine. Minutes later the two ships blew up in a shattering explosion.

KEY

✕ Battle

1. April 1668: Morgan sacks Puerto Principe (now Camaguey) in Cuba.

2. July: Morgan seizes Porto Bello and holds the port to ransom. He leaves with 250,000 pieces-of-eight.

3. January 1669: Morgan's flagship HMS *Oxford* blows up in an accidental explosion off the Île à Vache during a rendezvous between English and French buccaneers.

4. March: Morgan captures the fort guarding the entrance to the Gulf of Maracaibo. He then sacks the towns of Maracaibo and Gibraltar.

5. April: Finding a Spanish squadron blocking his way, Morgan uses a fireship to scatter his opponents, and after a ruse to distract the fort there he reaches the open sea and returns to Port Royal.

6. June: Peace is declared between England and Spain, and the Jamaican buccaneers are forced to disband.

7. January 1670: A Spanish privateering raid on Jamaica provides the English with an excuse to ignore the peace treaty.

8. August: Morgan puts to sea with a fleet of 11 ships.

9. September: At the Île à Vache he is reinforced by a large French contingent.

10. December: Morgan captures Santa Catalina, then continues on to the isthmus of Panama.

11. January 1671: An advance guard captures the fort guarding the mouth of the Chagres River. Morgan and his men continue up the river and advance on Panama.

12. 27 January: In a battle outside Panama, Morgan's buccaneers defeat the Spanish army defending the city. Panama is captured, looted and partially destroyed.

13. March: Morgan divides the plunder among his men, then returns to Port Royal.

Eager to avoid the other buccaneer ships, which were following astern of the deadly fireship, two of the Spanish warships were deliberately beached under the guns of the fort, where their crews then set fire to them. The buccaneers managed to salvage the smaller warship and towed her to safety, but her companion was burned to the waterline. Of Campo's squadron, only one warship survived, having fled over the bar when the flagship blew up. However, the Spanish still controlled the battery, and so, despite all their efforts, the buccaneers remained trapped. Morgan ordered his ships back to Maracaibo while he worked out what to do next.

Admiral Campo survived the loss of his flagship, and so he took direct command of the battery. He and Morgan continued to exchange messages, but Campo was not prepared to strike a deal. The impasse lasted a week, and then Morgan made his next move. Prisoners reported that only six of the fort's guns were mounted and these covered the bar, not the landward side of the battery. Morgan moved his ships up and then began ferrying troops ashore, within sight of the fort. To the Spaniards it looked like the buccaneers were planning to launch an assault from the land. So Admiral Campo ordered his six guns transferred to cover the landward approach to his walls.

The isthmus of Panama lay between the Caribbean and the Pacific, and so formed a vital part of the Spanish operation to move silver from Peru to Spain. By attacking Panama, Morgan hoped to seize much of this annual haul of specie for himself.

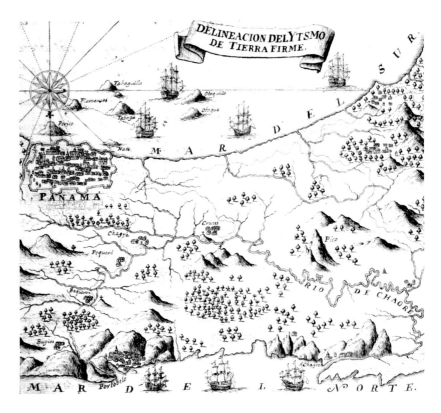

In fact Morgan's landing was a ruse – each group of longboats contained the same men, who simply hid from view each time the boats returned to the fleet. To the Spanish it looked like a steady stream of men being landed, while in fact the buccaneers remained on their ships. That night the Spanish stood ready, expecting Morgan to launch a nocturnal assault. Instead, his ships spent the night working their way over the bar, and by dawn they were safely riding at anchor on its seaward side. Morgan had outfoxed Admiral Campo, who was unable to redeploy his guns to stop him. The buccaneers returned home on 27 May with their plunder. This haul ensured that the taverns and brothels of Port Royal were kept busy for months.

However, the political climate had now changed. Modyford had been ordered to revoke all privateering licences. Then, on 24 June he was forced to issue a proclamation stating that 'the subjects of His Catholic Majesty be from now until further order treated and used as good friends and neighbours'. It seemed as if Henry Morgan had led his last raid. However, he and his buccaneers would soon be given one last great opportunity to enrich themselves with Spanish plunder.

THE SACK OF PANAMA

Henry Morgan's return to buccaneering came about thanks to poor communications. As a response to Morgan's raid on Porto Bello, the Spanish crown decided to allow its colonial governors to commission their own privateers. However, bureaucratic delays meant that it was early 1670 before any letters-of-marque were issued, six months after Modyford's declaration of peace 'beyond the line'. The Spanish saw the raids that followed as an opportunity for revenge. The Jamaicans saw them as a betrayal.

The most successful of these Spanish privateers was a Portuguese captain called Manoel Rivero Pardal, who operated out of Cartagena in his ship the *San Pedro y la Fama*. In late January 1670 he raided an English fishing settlement in the Cayman Islands, then attacked and captured an English privateer off Manzanillo in south-eastern Cuba. This prize turned out to be the *Mary and Jane*, commanded by the Dutch privateer Bernard Claesen Speirdyke, known as 'Captain Bart', who was killed in the battle. At the time Speirdyke was sailing under a flag of truce, delivering a notification of Modyford's peaceful intentions to the local Cuban governor. The Jamaicans were outraged. In May Pardal returned to Jamaica, attacking a sloop and burning coastal villages. He even issued a challenge to Morgan, offering to meet the buccaneer in an equal fight. That way Morgan 'might see the valour of the Spaniards'. This provided Modyford with the excuse he needed to unleash Morgan and his buccaneers. Morgan never accepted Pardal's challenge, however. He was planning a much more dramatic response. On 9 July 1670, Modyford proclaimed Morgan 'Admiral and Commander-in-Chief of all the ships of war belonging to this

Providence Island (called Santa Catalina by the Spanish) off the Caribbean coast of Central America was the site of an English colony, which was subsequently captured by the Spanish. In December 1670 Morgan landed there on his way to attack Panama, and he captured the island to use as a secure base.

The Castello of San Lorenzo on the eastern coast of the isthmus of Panama guarded the mouth of the Chagres River. It was attacked by Henry Morgan's buccaneers in 1670 and captured after a particularly bloody assault. (Photo by: MyLoupe/UIG via Getty Images)

harbour', and gave him a letter-of-marque. Within a month Morgan had 11 ships and 600 men at his disposal. On 11 August he led his fleet out to sea. Henry Morgan was back.

His target was Panama, the richest prize in the Americas. Morgan had arranged to rendezvous with the French buccaneers at the Île à Vache, which brought his strength up to 32 ships and approximately 1,800 men. At the rendezvous, Morgan also appointed the veteran Dutch buccaneer Captain Laurens Prins as his deputy. Morgan now commanded just about every buccaneer on the Spanish Main. One of his most welcome recruits was Captain John Morris and his privateer *Dolphin*, who arrived at the rendezvous in late October, followed by the *San Pedro y la Fama*. He had run into the Spanish privateer off the eastern tip of Cuba. Morris attacked, and in the brief fight that followed Pardal was killed and his ship captured.

On 18 December the fleet got under way, setting a course for the coast of Panama. On the way, Morgan visited Providence Island off the Honduran coast, only to find the small English settlement had been captured by the Spanish. By reclaiming the island Morgan had a secure base to fall back to if things went wrong in Panama. Next, he sent three ships and 470 men under Captain Joseph Bradley on ahead to capture the Castello San Lorenzo, which guarded the mouth of the Chagres River. Morgan followed a few days behind him. On 6 January 1671 Bradley landed a few miles from the fort, then advanced 'with flags and trumpets'. The buccaneers were confident of an easy victory, but instead they were met by a storm of musketry. The commander Pedro de Elizalde was in no mood to capitulate. His men repulsed two attacks, holding the buccaneers at bay until nightfall.

Then Bradley decided to change tactics. He sent a small group forward in the dark, who crept up to the wooden outer walls and then hurled incendiary *grenadoes* (grenades) over the palisade. The defences caught fire, and by morning the palisade had been destroyed and half of the garrison had fled. The remaining

defenders managed to repulse Bradley's dawn attack, but the fort was carried in the next assault. Having suffered heavy casualties, including Bradley himself, the buccaneers were in no mood to give quarter. Still, the way now lay open for an advance up the river to Panama, the city that had eluded Sir Francis Drake some seven decades before.

On 19 January Morgan and 1,500 buccaneers began making their way upriver by canoe. It was a bold move, as Panama lay 70 miles (113km) away across the isthmus, and thanks to Elizalde's sacrifice the governor Juan Perez de Guzman had been given time to organize his defences. If Morgan failed, then his men would be hard-pressed to make it back to their ships. Actually, the whole operation went smoothly. The canoes were abandoned at Venta de Cruces, halfway to their destination, and from there the buccaneers marched down the Royal Road, which ran between Panama and Porto Bello. Finally, on the morning of 27 January, they reached the crest of a hill overlooking Panama.

The closest thing to a full-scale battle fought between the Spanish and the buccaneers came when Henry Morgan appeared in front of the walls of Panama. The battle fought there decided the fate of the city, and secured Morgan's standing as the greatest buccaneer of them all.

This Howard Pyle drawing depicts Morgan's buccaneers plundering and looting their way through the smoking ruins of Panama, after capturing the city the day before.

Their great prize lay before them. In the meantime, Guzman marshalled his Spanish defenders out onto the plain and formed his battle line. He had some 1,200 infantry and 400 cavalry, but his army lacked artillery and experience.

Morgan's buccaneers divided into three groups, each of 500 men, with Captain Prins and his vanguard advancing on the left and the other two groups echeloned to the right of him.

As Prins' men contacted the enemy, Guzman unleashed a herd of cattle hidden behind his centre, which stampeded towards the buccaneer ranks. He hoped the cattle would disrupt the buccaneers. However, one volley was enough to make the cattle stampede the other way, into the Spanish troops. Meanwhile, Prins defeated the Spanish right and repelled a cavalry charge with musket fire. At that point Morgan's other men stormed forward, heading towards the Spanish soldiers who were still reeling from the cattle stampede. Within minutes the terrified defenders were running back into the city.

The buccaneers flooded into Panama and made their way down to the harbour – arriving in time to see the governor sail out into the Pacific, one of hundreds of refugees who were spirited to safety by the ships in the harbour. Unfortunately for Morgan, the warships also carried away the bulk of the city's treasury. That night much of Panama burned to the ground, and the following morning the buccaneers began sifting through the ruins, looking for hidden plunder. Morgan and his men remained there for a month, torturing prisoners to find where they had stashed their possessions and ransoming others. Finally, on 24 February Morgan began the return march, taking 750,000 pieces-of-eight back to the ships. That was when the arguments began. The English and French contingents fell out, as the Tortugans suspected that Morgan planned to cheat them of their share. The bickering would continue long after the buccaneers returned to Port Royal. The real problem was that the booty had to be divided among the remaining 1,600 men. This meant that most buccaneers received little reward for all their efforts. Back in Port Royal, Morgan discovered that Thomas Modyford had fallen out of favour in London, and that any further attacks against the Spanish would be seen as open acts of piracy.

The climate cooled even further in June when Modyford was relieved by Sir Thomas Lynch, who promptly arrested his predecessor and Morgan, and shipped them both home to answer charges. However, on Morgan's arrival in London he found that England was at war with the Dutch, and privateers were back in demand. When Spain sided with Holland, the charges against Morgan were dropped. In January 1674 Governor Lynch was recalled, and Morgan found himself appointed as the new deputy governor, with orders to advise Lynch's replacement Lord Vaughan on Jamaican matters. In effect it was a full exoneration, and Morgan's reversal of fortune was completed when he was knighted by Charles II.

Here, Henry Morgan is shown interrogating a black slave, while his followers torture Spanish townspeople in an effort to find hidden caches of valuables buried amid the ruins of Panama.

Morgan returned to Jamaica and spent his last years drinking with old comrades, tending his plantations, and, rather bizarrely, prosecuting pirates – former buccaneers who had stepped over the line from privateering into piracy. He was to live another 13 years, growing fatter all the while, until he finally died of dropsy (now called oedema) in 1688, brought on, according to Morgan's physician, by 'drinking and sitting up late'. His passing marked the end of an era. Already the days of the buccaneers had gone, replaced by smaller and highly regulated groups of privateers. However, a few last English buccaneers ventured further afield, and in the process they created a whole new chapter in the history of piracy.

Following the attack on Panama, a new city was built a short distance away, and the remains of Panamá Viejo (Old Panama) look much as they did when the buccaneers left the city and returned to their ships. (Maximilian Müller/ Getty Images)

In his latter years, Henry Morgan turned his back on buccaneering and devoted his energies to the running of his substantial estates in Jamaica. In fact, as the island's deputy governor, he actively suppressed the activities of his former supporters, as raids against Spanish towns were now considered illegal.

THE BUCCANEERS OF THE PACIFIC

In early 1679, William Dampier arrived in Port Royal from London. Born in Somerset in 1651, he first went to sea in 1669. For the next ten years he served in privateers and warships before working as a logwood cutter in Central America. As an experienced seaman, Dampier was recruited by a group of die-hard buccaneers, who continued to wage their own unofficial war against the Spanish. This group included the experienced buccaneering captains Bartholomew Sharp, John Coxon and John Cook. In December 1679 they sacked Porto Bello, yielding some 36,000 pieces-of-eight. They then worked their way across the isthmus of Panama, but on reaching the Pacific coast they were unsure what to do next. The expedition split up, with Coxon returning home, and others remaining on the isthmus.

The rest elected Sharp as their leader, and Dampier joined them as they headed down the Pacific coast in a captured ship. Sharp was both unlucky and unpopular, and his crew mutinied twice, while others led by John Cook returned home by way of Cape Horn. Dampier went with them, and eventually Cook reached Virginia in April 1683. Meanwhile, in a reversal of fortune Sharp struck it rich, capturing two prizes and 37,000 pieces-of-eight. He also captured a detailed set of charts of the Pacific coast, yielding information that would benefit those who followed them. He then headed for home too, and arrived in Barbados in February 1682. On his return to England Sharp was arrested and tried for piracy, but the charts saved him, and the trial was conveniently abandoned after he presented them to the Admiralty.

As for Cook, in August 1683 he decided to return to the Pacific, and William Dampier accompanied him. After renaming a captured Danish ship *Bachelor's Delight*, Cook rounded Cape Horn and entered the Pacific in March 1684. There he encountered Captain John Eaton in his privateer the *Nicholas*, who had sailed from London six months before. Together they headed north to the Juan Fernández Islands, then on to the Galapagos. They captured a few ships, but none of their prizes yielded much in the way of plunder. At that

In this illustration from John Seller's artillery treatise *The Sea Gunner* (1691), a naval gunner is shown operating a typical naval piece of the period, mounted on a four-wheeled truck carriage.

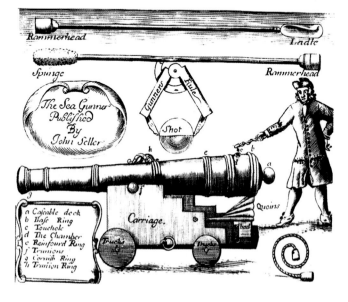

This mural by Frank Schoonover shows the buccaneer Captain Swan and his men enjoying the delights of Mindanao in the Philippines, having crossed the Pacific after raiding the western coast of the Spanish Americas.

point they decided to sail back east to search for Spanish ships off the South American coast. Cook died before the buccaneers made landfall, so Edward Davis assumed command of the *Bachelor's Delight* and led the buccaneers on a largely unprofitable raid on the nearby town of Paita. However, their luck changed in October when they ran into another buccaneer, Charles Swan.

Swan, who had sailed with Henry Morgan, left London in October 1683, bound for the Pacific. The following spring he reached the Pacific coast of Panama, where he spent several months trying to intercept a treasure galleon. In July he teamed up with Peter Harris, a buccaneer who had crossed the isthmus six months before. On the Pacific coast Harris stole a ship, then used it to capture several Spanish prizes. They met Davis off the coast of Chile, at which point Swan, Harris and Davis decided to make an attempt on the treasure galleons that were due to sail from Lima to Panama the following summer. The fourth captain at the gathering was John Eaton, who had been sailing in consort with Davis. He declined to join them, and instead elected to return home.

The rest were soon joined by three other privateering ships, two of which were French. All of these newcomers had crossed the isthmus and captured ships on the Pacific coast. In all some 1,000 buccaneers joined forces that winter, when they made the Isla del Rey in the Gulf of Panama into their temporary haven. However, when the galleons finally arrived off Panama in June 1685, the buccaneers discovered that they were extremely well-defended, and that they were badly outnumbered. They attacked anyway, but were driven off.

At that point Dampier jumped ship, signing on with Captain Swan, who planned to sail home via the Far East. They crossed the Pacific to the Philippines, where Swan spent six months dallying with a local woman. Eventually, his crew sailed on without him. They headed south past the East Indies to make landfall on the western coast of New Holland (now Australia) in January 1688. Meanwhile, Dampier's old skippers Edward Davis and Peter Harris moved on to Nicaragua, where they launched a few more unsuccessful raids. Harris eventually went his own way and was never heard of again. During 1686 Davis and another captain led two successful raids on the coast of Peru, garnering 60,000 pieces-of-eight. They split up in the Juan Fernández Islands that November, and by the summer of 1688 Davis and his men returned to Virginia, where they were unsuccessfully charged with piracy.

On his voyage home Dampier jumped ship again, this time in the Nicobar Islands. He spent the next two years serving aboard a local trading vessel before returning home in 1691, some 12 years after leaving London. Dampier duly wrote about his travels, and his book *A New Voyage Around the World* proved a runaway success. He made two other voyages, one of them as the unsuccessful

In this map of the Western Caribbean by the Dutch cartographer Danckerts, dated 1696, a lot of useful new information has been included, showing hitherto unmarked reefs and shoals, particularly around the shallow waters of the Bahamas and the Gulf of Honduras. For the most part this information was gathered by buccaneers operating in those waters.

A 19th-century depiction of Michel de Grammont, one of the most successful of the later French buccaneers. For a decade from 1678 he led a series of raids against the Spanish Main until his ship foundered in a hurricane in 1686, somewhere off the north coast of Cuba.

commander of a privateer. Then in 1708 he was asked to join a new buccaneering expedition into the Pacific, led by the experienced Bristol seaman Captain Woodes Rogers. What followed would make pirate history and would inspire a semi-fictional bestseller.

The expedition set sail from Bristol in August 1708, and reached the coast of Brazil in mid-November. By January they had safely rounded Cape Horn, and on 2 February 1709 Rogers' two ships *Duke* and *Duchess* reached the Juan Fernández Islands. Rogers sent a boat ashore to investigate a light they had seen during the night, and when the landing party returned it was accompanied by a strange-looking man, clothed in goatskins. He turned out to be Alexander Selkirk, the former master of the privateer *Cinque Ports*, who had been left behind on the island five years before. Selkirk soon became the mate of the *Duke*, and was later given command of one of Rogers' prizes. The story would inspire Daniel Defoe to write *Robinson Crusoe* (1719).

Next, Rogers headed for the Peruvian coast, where he captured a large merchantman. Then he raided the Ecuadorian port of Guayaquil, which yielded a substantial haul of plunder. To avoid any Spanish pursuit Rogers headed back into the Pacific, and in May he reached the Galapagos Islands. By that time half his crew were stricken by scurvy, so he spent two months there while his men recovered. During this sojourn he decided to end his cruise by trying to intercept that year's Manila galleons, the treasure ships that made the annual trip from the Philippines to Acapulco.

Rogers was in luck. Following Dampier's advice, he headed north-east towards the coast of what is now Mexico's Baja California. It was there that the galleons made landfall after their voyage from Manila. He lingered for a month, and finally, in mid-December 1709, when he had almost given up the search, a lookout spotted the galleon *Nuestra Señora de la Encarnación y Desengaño*. The *Duke* and *Duchess* gave chase, and captured the treasure ship after a hard-fought engagement, during which Rogers was wounded in the jaw. His prisoners told him that a second galleon was following them, so, leaving a prize crew on board, Rogers went off in search of her. On Christmas Day he found the *Nuestra Señora de Begoña*, but she fought well, and this time the buccaneers were driven off. However, Woodes Rogers still had their first prize. It yielded a fortune in specie, porcelain, spices and Chinese silks, enough to delight Rogers, his crew and their English backers. Renamed the *Bachelor*, the galleon was added to Rogers' squadron. On 10 January 1709 the three ships set course for Guam, then continued on to Batavia in the East Indies, then across the Indian Ocean to the Cape of Good Hope. By October 1711 they were back in London, with plunder valued by some contemporaries at 1,600,000 pieces-of-eight. Dampier's own share was 3,000 pesos. It wasn't a bad haul for a writer, even a bestselling one.

Woodes Rogers was acclaimed as one of the most successful privateers of all time – and as the last of the buccaneers. Actually, the days of the buccaneers were long gone, and Dampier alone remained the last link with that swashbuckling past. He went on to write a fresh account of his voyages, while Woodes Rogers is now best remembered as the 'poacher-turned-gamekeeper' who cleared pirates such as Blackbeard out of the Bahamas.

THE FRENCH FILIBUSTERS

As English buccaneering was passing into history, the French were just getting into their swashbuckling stride. Part of this impetus came from colonization, as during the 1660s a string of French settlements were established on the western part of Hispaniola. In 1664 the French government officially claimed the area as their own, naming the region Saint Dominique (now Haiti), although the Spanish still insisted they controlled the whole of Hispaniola, a claim they only dropped in 1697. Tortuga continued as a buccaneer haven until the early 1670s, but Petit Goâve in Saint Dominique overtook it in importance. As the 17th century drew to a close Tortuga became a backwater, a lingering reminder of a violent past.

This change of base also led to the creation of a new breed of French buccaneer. One of the most prominent of these was Michel de Grammont. Exquemelin claims he was born in Paris, and then served in the French navy. By early 1672, de Grammont commanded a French privateer in the Caribbean. However, he crossed the line from privateering into piracy and was therefore unable to return to the more established French colonies. Instead he based himself in Saint Dominique, where fewer questions were asked. He soon became one of the colony's most successful privateers, although the men themselves preferred the term 'filibusters' (or *flibustiers* in French), which itself was derived from the Dutch term for 'freebooter'. They were prepared to operate against the perceived enemies of France, regardless of whether these countries

Another dramatic but largely inaccurate depiction of buccaneers by Howard Pyle, in this case questioning a captive about the whereabouts of hidden valuables.

were at war with the French or not. By 1678 de Grammont was accepted as the *de facto* leader of the Saint Dominique filibusters, and he adopted the title of Chevalier, as a form of unofficial acknowledgement of his status.

In May 1678 de Grammont sailed out on a raid against the Dutch island of Curaçao. First, though, he rendezvoused with a French naval squadron sent from Martinique, commanded by Jean, the Comte d'Estrées. However, the expedition was caught by a hurricane, and many of the ships were wrecked. Once the tempest passed, d'Estrées limped back to Martinique, leaving the filibusters to salvage what they could from the wreckage. With just six ships and 700 men de Grammont was too weak to assault Curaçao, so he decided to pick on the Spanish instead. In June 1678 he arrived off the Maracaibo Bar.

Confronted by a newly built fort there, de Grammont landed a battery of ships' guns and bombarded the Spanish into submission. He left some of his ships behind to guard the lagoon entrance, and then pressed on. Once inside the Lago de Maracaibo, he discovered that Maracaibo and Gibraltar had not really recovered from the raids a decade before. However, de Grammont used captured horses to move his raiders inland, capturing Trujillo on 1 September. He razed Trujillo and Gibraltar, then returned to Maracaibo, where he lingered until early December, trying to find hidden caches of valuables. Then he returned to Saint Dominique, his ships laden with plunder.

A year and a half later, in May 1680, de Grammont led another raid against the Venezuelan coast, this time attacking La Guaira, the harbour that served Caracas, the provincial capital. The port was captured, but the following day a Spanish relief column arrived and besieged the place. The Spanish launched several assaults but the Frenchmen held on, despite mounting losses. De Grammont himself was badly wounded in one of these desperate attacks. Finally, at dusk he gave the order to retreat back to the ships. The filibusters managed to escape, but they returned home empty-handed.

It was another three years before de Grammont managed to organize another large-scale raid. In May 1683, he joined forces with the Dutch buccaneer Laurens de Graaf, and together they decided to assault Vera Cruz, the principal harbour of New Spain (Mexico). In all, the Franco-Dutch raiding force consisted of 13 ships and 1,300 men. First of all, de Grammont made sure that the annual treasure *flota* was not in port. That meant that if they attacked, the buccaneers would probably outnumber the port's defenders. That night the buccaneers sneaked ashore, and at dawn on 18 May they assaulted the town from two directions, the Dutch from the north and the French from the south. It was all over in minutes, and the raiders set about plundering the city. Although a Spanish garrison still held out on the fortress island of San Juan de Ulúa, they could only watch impotently as the port they were there to protect was comprehensively looted. To augment his haul, de Grammont stranded the city's inhabitants to a nearby island, where they were held until they were ransomed. Once again, the buccaneers sailed home, their ships laden with plunder. What was particularly striking was that the three nations – France, Holland and Spain – were at peace at the time, so de Grammont's actions amounted to nothing more than piracy. Still, there was no peace beyond the line.

In the summer of 1685 de Grammont and de Graaf joined forces again for another attack on New Spain, this time assaulting Campeche, the scene of so many attacks a decade earlier. On 6 July some 30 buccaneer ships anchored off

Beque, a fishing village just outside Campeche, but Spanish troops managed to prevent the raiders from landing. The following morning the buccaneers tried again, and this time the milita were routed, and de Graaf led a column of buccaneers northwards towards the city, leaving de Grammont to circle behind it to prevent any escape. The town fell within a few hours. Two days later a Spanish counter-attacking relief column was defeated, leaving the buccaneers the undisputed masters of the region. After that, de Grammont sent men mounted on captured horses to plunder the hinterland. The buccaneers finally returned home in early September. Although the haul had been relatively poor, the reputation of the 'Chevalier' was now at its height. The governor of Saint Dominique, Jean du Casse, even offered him the post of his lieutenant-general, defending the French colony from attack. Instead de Grammont elected to continue raiding, but in May 1686 his flagship was lost at sea somewhere off the west coast of Florida, during a reconnaissance of the Spanish settlement of St Augustine.

The rich port of Cartagena was defended by formidable city walls and by forts that guarded its outer and inner harbours. Here a chain boom is stretched across the entrance of the outer harbour, which in turn is guarded by a fort.

THE LAST GREAT RAID

In 1688, the French became embroiled in the War of the League of Augsburg (1688–97), a conflict that simultaneously pitted them against the English, the Spanish and the Dutch. This conflict, and the War of the Spanish Succession (1701–14) that followed, made the French government view the filibusters as a strategic asset rather than a national embarrassment.

As this first war began to draw to a close, French strategists looked for the opportunity to launch an attack on Spain's overseas empire, so it would influence the forthcoming peace talks. As the richest city on the Spanish Main, Cartagena was deemed the perfect target. So far its formidable defences had deterred the buccaneers. However, this time the French planned to combine the enterprise of the filibusters with the professionalism of the French army and navy. The result was a sort of government-sponsored business opportunity involving private investors, royal troops and privateers. In March 1695 the French admiral Bernard, Baron de Pointis, arrived in Petit Goâve to take command of the expedition. He brought with him a squadron of ten French warships and transports carrying 3,000 troops. The filibusters supplied 11 ships and 1,200 men, led personally by Governor Jean du Casse, the governor of Petit Goâve. Unfortunately, the arrogant French admiral soon fell out with the filibusters, who feared that he planned to trick them out of any plunder. Placated by written contracts, the filibusters finally agreed to sail under the admiral's orders. On 13 April the fleet arrived off Cartagena. Baron de Pointis was all for an immediate attack, but du Casse counselled for a reconnaissance first. It was just as well, as the seaward side of the city was protected by a reef, which would have prevented the assault boats from reaching the shore. In the end Baron de Pointis and du Casse followed Drake's plan of 1586. The fleet would force the entrance to Cartagena Bay, then assault the city by way of La Caletta, the coastal spur that ran westwards from the city. The only problem was that the entrance to the bay was now guarded by the imposing Fort San Luis, at the western tip of La Caletta. On 15 April, 1,200 men were landed on La Caletta, just out of range of the fort's guns. The following day its walls were stormed, and San Luis surrendered after a brief resistance.

The French could now enter Cartagena Bay, but the inner harbour with the city was still protected by two more forts, Santa Cruz on a spur of La Caletta, and Manzanillo on the opposite side of the harbour entrance. De Pointis ordered an advance up La Caletta, and Fort Santa Cruz was abandoned minutes before the French troops arrived at its walls. The admiral then ordered the filibusters to land on the north-eastern side of Cartagena Bay, then skirt round Fort Manzanillo to occupy La Popa, a hill overlooking the landward approaches to Cartagena.

In 1697 a French expedition led by the Baron de Pointis at Cartagena on the Spanish Main laid siege to the port. The city was briefly besieged, but was soon captured following daring assaults on the city's walls, spearheaded by French buccaneers.

It was with some misgivings that the filibusters did what they were asked, but by 20 April they had seized the high ground, and so had sealed Cartagena off from its hinterland. The city was now besieged. Next, heavy guns were landed from the fleet and a siege got under way, supported by the warships lying off the seaward side of the city. After two days a breach had been made in the landward defences, and de Pointis ordered an assault. It was launched at dawn on 1 May, but was repulsed with heavy losses, thanks to enfilading fire from Fort Manzanillo. Still, the French attacked again the next day, and on the evening of 2 May, the garrison surrendered. Cartagena had been captured.

That was when the deceit began. Claiming that a relief column was approaching the city, de Pointis ordered the filibusters to block their approach, supported by French troops. The attack never materialized, and by the time the filibusters returned to Cartagena the city gates were shut in their faces. Then they discovered that the admiral had spirited the bulk of the plunder onto his ships, leaving the filibusters with just 40,000 pieces-of-eight. So, on 30 May when the French garrison withdrew, the filibusters stormed the city and occupied it for themselves. They soon resorted to their traditional methods of

extorting money from the Spanish, and within three days they raised another million pieces-of-eight. The result was that on 3 June when the filibusters sailed home to Petit Goâve, each man had around 1,000 pieces-of-eight in his pocket.

That, though, wasn't the end of the matter. On 4 June de Pointis' squadron was intercepted by an Anglo-Dutch squadron commanded by Vice-Admiral Neville. The allies chased de Pointis for a week before he managed to evade them. Turning back towards Cartagena, Neville's ships ran into the filibusters on their way home. Four of the 11 French privateers were captured or driven ashore, and those who reached Petit Goâve were in no mood for further forays, or partnerships with the French crown. The majority of the filibusters became low-level privateers, while several quit the Caribbean in search of more lucrative prey in the Indian Ocean.

Cartagena marked the last great hurrah of the buccaneers, the end of an era. By the turn of the century the age of the buccaneers was over, and a new phase, in which privateers hunted on their own, would take its place. It was also inevitable that some of these men would reject the tight controls imposed on privateers, and would become fully-fledged pirates.

Chapter Six

THE GOLDEN
AGE OF PIRACY

A GOLDEN AGE?

In recent years the period of piratical history from the start of the 18th century until about 1730 has been dubbed the 'Golden Age of Piracy'. Some historians have narrowed it even further. For instance, maritime historian David Cordingly established it as starting in 1698, when the privateer-turned-pirate Captain Kidd captured the *Quedah Merchant*. He dated its end as 1722, when the surviving members of 'Black Bart' Roberts' pirate crew were executed in a mass hanging at Cape Coast Castle in West Africa. In my biography *Blackbeard: America's Most Notorious Pirate* (2006), I argued for an even tighter historical span – from 1714 until 1725. In the end it's all subjective, as the parameters we use are a matter of personal opinion. What everyone agrees on is that during the first decades of the 18th century there was a marked increase of piratical activity in the waters of the Americas, off the

This spirited painting by the 19th-century artist Jean Leon Gerome Ferris captures the ferocious nature of Blackbeard's last fight off Ocracoke Island in November 1718. It shows the infamous pirate engaged in his duel to the death with Lieutenant Maynard of the Royal Navy. (SuperStock/Getty Images)

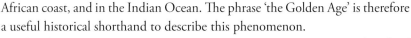

African coast, and in the Indian Ocean. The phrase 'the Golden Age' is therefore a useful historical shorthand to describe this phenomenon.

The phase never appears in any contemporary newspapers, court records, official letters, pirate biographies or any other correspondence of the time. That means that it was invented after the 'Golden Age' came to an end. Modern pirate historians have all used the phrase, but none of us invented it. Instead, it was first coined by Rafael Sabatini (1875–1950), the British author who penned pirate novels such as *Captain Blood* (1922) and *The Black Swan* (1932), both of which were transformed into Hollywood swashbucklers. The origin of the decidedly ironic phrase is immaterial, though, as its importance today is to help define an era.

In a way, both the pirates and their victims were the product of official policy back in Europe. We have seen how the buccaneers were gradually brought under government control. By the 1670s it was no longer considered acceptable to prey on the Spanish unless there was a war on. The English managed to establish a firm grip on their buccaneers after Morgan's raid on Panama in 1670–71, and Morgan himself was involved in the introduction of legislation designed to prevent illegal forays. The French took longer to establish control over their buccaneers, but did so before the end of the century. This meant that when the War of the Spanish Succession (1701–14) began, all of the leading maritime powers had managed to control the way in which privateers operated, making sure they kept within the bounds of the law.

This conflict – also known as Queen Anne's War – pitted the French against the other three powers. Although neither the Dutch nor the Spanish operated many privateers in Caribbean waters, the French and the English (or rather the British after 1707) both made great use of them. In Europe, ports such as Dunkirk for the French and Bristol for the British turned into privateering havens, while in the Caribbean, Fort-de-France in Martinique, Bridgetown in Barbados, Petit Goâve in Saint Dominique and Port Royal in Jamaica were all filled with captains bearing letters-of-marque.

In this detail of a larger engraving, the pirate Bartholomew Roberts or 'Black Bart' is shown wearing the elegant outfit he donned for his last fight against the crew of HMS *Swallow*, fought off the West Coast of Africa in 1722.

During these years privateering was a highly lucrative business, and places like Port Royal attracted seamen in their hundreds, all eager for the chance to earn big money. Port Royal became a boom town again, and everyone benefited, apart of course from those ship owners whose vessels were captured. However, in 1711, as the war was winding down, the British government opened secret peace talks with the French. The result was the Treaty of Utrecht, signed in April 1713, which put an end to the hostilities between all of the major maritime powers.

Peace revealed the full extent of the problem Britain had created for herself. When the war ended, all outstanding letters-of-marque were immediately cancelled. As many as 6,000 former privateersmen now found themselves unemployed, and ports were soon filled with seamen looking for work. Many were lucky, as when the war ended the British merchant fleet expanded dramatically. With more merchant ships at sea the demand for sailors

The majority of pirates came from large and bustling port cities, where a life as a sailor allowed them to escape the poverty and cruelty of their birthplace, as epitomized in this Hogarth print of London's 'Gin Lane'.

gradually increased, and many former privateers were more than happy to accept the poor conditions and pay they were offered. Others, though, decided to use their privateering skills by continuing as if the peace had never happened. In other words, they turned to piracy, but tried to cover their actions by maintaining a fiction of legitimacy. While these former privateers-turned-pirates limited their attacks to their old French or Spanish enemies, other men, such as Blackbeard and Bartholomew Roberts, had no such scruples. They simply attacked whoever they wanted.

So the end of the war meant an increase in both pirates and potential victims, particularly British pirates and British (or Colonial American) merchantmen. Although the worst affected areas were the Caribbean and the Atlantic seaboard of America, this new breed of pirate ranged further afield, and both the West African coast and the Indian Ocean became pirate 'hot-spots'. In other words, although these pirates did not operate in large fleets like the 17th-century buccaneers, their attacks were not confined to the Caribbean. This meant they had a noticeable impact on international trade, reflected in a markedly sharp rise in insurance costs.

Another factor was the lack of authority. Piracy tends to develop in areas where governments lack the power or the will to deal with the problem. The paucity of strong government in many of the American colonies during the period made the Atlantic seaboard an attractive area for pirates, at least until governments took firm action. Often this action came about when the benefits of illicit trade between pirates and colonists were outweighed by the disruption of shipping and rising insurance prices. The 'Golden Age of Piracy' came to an end when one by one these pirates were hunted down and killed. High-profile pirate executions also tended to discourage other seamen from choosing a piratical career. By 1730 at the latest, the 'age' had passed.

During their careers, pirates attracted the full attention of the press, as pirate trials and executions all helped to sell newspapers and broadsheets. This contributed to the creation of a somewhat glamorous image of piracy that was largely undeserved, and which completely failed to account for the brutal realities of pirate life. This 'Golden Age' produced some of the most famous pirates in history, men who now seem almost improbably larger than life after centuries of romanticized accounts of their activities. Even the phrase 'the Golden Age of Piracy' is a misleading one, as it suggests a romantic movement rather than a decade of brutal attacks and economic disruption. The truth of this 'Golden Age' is often far removed from the depiction of it by those writing about it long after the pirate scourge had faded into history.

The Leeward Islands of the West Indies were a popular hunting ground during the 'Golden Age of Piracy'. Captains like Bellamy, Roberts and Teach preyed on ships sailing down the chain of islands, and often lurked in secluded bays such as this one on Guadeloupe, once used by Roberts as a hiding place. (John Burcham/Getty Images)

NEW PROVIDENCE

One of the many drawbacks of being a pirate was that the plunder captured usually did not come in the form of coins, which could easily be divided up amongst the crew. The merchant ships that were the victims of pirate attacks were usually small craft – often brigs or sloops. Larger vessels might be slavers bound for Jamaica from the West African coast, ships carrying rum or sugar from the Caribbean to Europe or colonial America, or else vessels that brought manufactured goods to the American colonies and returned home laden with tobacco, cotton, furs, timber or tar. Even the fishing fleets that operated off Newfoundland and the Grand Banks were targeted.

While Howard Pyle's depictions of pirates may not always have been historically accurate, they served to capture the age, and fuelled the romantic aura that developed around the pirates of this period.

For the most part the pirates simply drank the rum, although other cargoes were sometimes destroyed in an orgy of wanton destruction. Like any criminals, in order to turn anything into money the pirates needed to find someone willing to buy stolen property. Most ports were barred to them thanks to an increasingly tough line on piracy and illegal trade. This left the smaller settlements and islands. Of course it was much better if the pirates could have their own town filled with shady merchants, brothels, taverns and gambling dens. In 1715 they got it.

The pirate haven on the island of New Providence in the Bahamas came about because of a Spanish maritime disaster. On 30 June 1715 the annual Spanish treasure *flota* was homeward bound, heading north up the Bahamas Channel between Florida and Grand Bahama. The winds had risen steadily, and that evening the fleet ran into a hurricane. Eleven ships were dashed against the Florida coast, and by morning only one ship of the *flota* remained afloat. It sped back to Havana with the news, and the Spanish governor immediately sent an expedition to rescue the survivors and recover the lost silver.

Others had the same idea. In late November 300 raiders attacked the salvage camp, driving off its small garrison and capturing the salvaged treasure. These men, former privateers from Port Royal, made off with at least 60,000 pieces-of-eight. For many it must have been just like the old days. Earlier that month the governor of Jamaica had sent the privateer Captain Henry Jennings to Florida to see if anything could be salvaged. Jennings took that as an excuse to raid the salvage camp. Jennings returned to the Florida coast in January 1716, and attacked

The entrance to Havana, from a less than accurate 17th-century print. This large and well-defended port was the last gathering place for the Spanish treasure fleets before they headed home to Spain.

the camp again, this time capturing 120,000 pieces-of-eight. However, that was the last of the raids, as the Spanish soon turned their salvage camp into a heavily armed fortress. That summer two galleons carried the salvaged treasure home to Spain, and the camp was abandoned. However, some 250,000 pieces-of-eight still lay scattered amongst the wreckage. That was when treasure fever swept the Caribbean. Within weeks Henry Jennings and other salvors returned, and began picking over the wreckage. Florida was Spanish territory, so, bowing to diplomatic pressure, the Jamaican authorities disowned the salvors.

This denied them the opportunity to spend their gains in Port Royal. However, they now had an alternative. In early 1716 a handful of shady Jamaican merchants established themselves in the struggling British settlement of New Providence in the Bahamas. They willingly provided a marketplace for stolen goods, and so Jennings and the other salvors began trading with them. By the summer, New Providence had grown into a bustling den of pirates, treasure hunters, smugglers and illicit traders. In June 1716 the governor of Virginia wrote to London complaining that pirates had taken over the Bahamas, which means that the new pirate den was already well established.

New Providence was ideal. It was close to major trade routes and to the Florida wreck sites, and favourable winds allowed an easy passage to these pirate hunting grounds. Its natural harbour of Nassau was large enough to hold a hundred ships or more. The island had a good supply of food, water and timber, vantage points for lookouts, and even a small fort, built by the island's original and now outnumbered settlers. Above all, New Providence contained a thriving shanty town that provided for the pirates' every need. The island was about 60 square miles (97 sq km) in size, barely large enough to support a settlement. Although it was nominally a British colony and the capital of the British Bahamas, there was no governor to impose the authority of the crown. In other words, there was nothing that could prevent the takeover of the island by the pirates.

By the summer of 1717 over 500 pirates were reportedly using the island as a base, serving in at least a dozen small vessels. Men such as Benjamin Hornigold, Charles Vane, Henry Jennings, 'Calico Jack' Rackam, Edward Teach ('Blackbeard') and Sam Bellamy all passed through New Providence during these few heady years. Merchants traded with these men, and then smuggled the goods into the established markets of colonial America and the Caribbean. Captured ships were bought, then sold on elsewhere. Meanwhile shipwrights earned a living repairing pirate ships or mending prizes, while blacksmiths repaired guns and weapons. New Providence must have been a robust and bustling place, where the only form of government stemmed from the collective wishes of the leading pirate captains.

Then the party came to an end. As complaints about all this piratical activity reached London, it was decided that something needed to be done. Consequently, on 5 September 1717 King George I signed *A Proclamation for Suppressing Pyrates*. If the pirates surrendered by 5 September 1718, they would be granted a full pardon, but only for crimes committed before that January. Those who

Modern Nassau, on New Providence Island in the Bahamas, is a thriving tourist destination, and it is hard to imagine the small settlement that existed there in the early 18th century, which then grew into a pirate haven. Virtually no traces of this older pirate community have survived. (Adermark Media/ Getty Images)

THE VOYAGES OF BENJAMIN HORNIGOLD

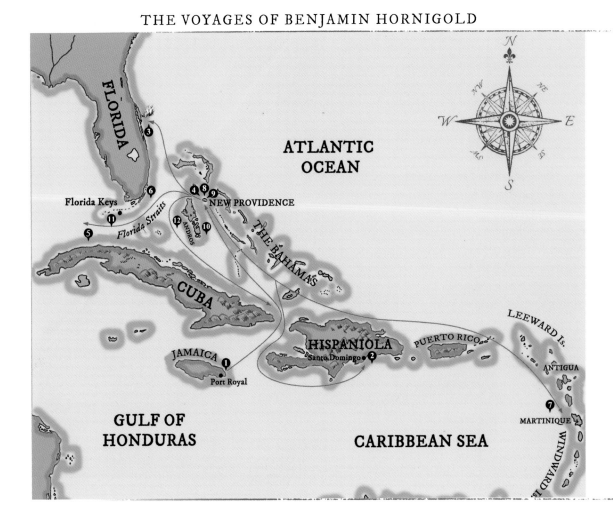

OPPOSITE In 1718 Woodes
Rogers arrived in the Bahamas
as the island's new British
governor. However, he was no
stranger to piracy – this
engraving shows him as a
privateer in 1704, looting
jewellery from the Spanish
women of Guyaquil in what is
now Ecuador.

refused the pardon would be hunted down. It was a classic 'carrot and stick'
policy, based on the notion that many pirates would change their ways if given
a second chance. A copy of the proclamation reached New Providence in
December 1717. The effect was to create two political groups: the first, headed
by Hornigold and Jennings, favoured accepting the offer. The 'die-hards' led by
Charles Vane refused to countenance any surrender. In March 1718 HMS
Phoenix arrived, her captain eager to discover how the pirates had reacted to the
offer. Captain Pearce received a surprisingly cordial welcome, and he left with a
list of more than 200 pirates who had accepted a provisional pardon. The list
included both Hornigold and Jennings. Pearce told the pirates that the
authorities would be sending out a governor, who would formally approve the

KEY
Spanish shipwrecks

1. 1713: News of a peace treaty between Britain and Spain reaches Jamaica, and so Benjamin Hornigold's privateering letter-of-marque is cancelled.
2. June 1714: The Spanish report that Hornigold is attacking Spanish shipping off Santo Domingo.
3. November 1715: Hornigold is associated with the plundering of the Spanish salvage camp on the Florida coast, erected following the shipwrecking of the 1715 Spanish treasure fleet.
4. February 1716: Hornigold establishes himself in New Providence and helps develop it into a pirate haven.
5. June: He cruises off the Florida Straits, preying on Spanish ships.
6. August: He cruises the Bahamas channel, with Teach and Bellamy among his crew.
7. Summer 1717: Hornigold, now described as the leader of the New Providence pirates, cruises off the West Indies, preying on French ships.
8. December: News of a royal pardon reaches New Providence, and Hornigold encourages his fellow pirates to accept the offer.
9. July 1718: Hornigold signs the pardon and supports the new British governor, Woodes Rogers, who appoints Hornigold as a pirate hunter.
10. September: Hornigold hunts unsuccessfully for Charles Vane, but captures other pirates off the Bahamian island of Andros.
11. January 1719: He hunts for pirates in the Florida Keys.
12 Summer: Hornigold and his ship are lost in the Bahamas Channel after being overtaken by a hurricane.

The leader of the 'die-hard' pirates of New Providence who refused to accept a pardon, Charles Vane was eventually shipwrecked, then captured. He was tried, and was executed in the spring of 1721.

provisional pardons. The man the British government chose was Woodes Rogers, the former buccaneer who had once captured a Manila galleon. Rogers would be a poacher-turned-gamekeeper. Since his return to Bristol in early 1711, he had thrived in the slave-trading business. His acceptance of the governorship combined duty with a desire for further business opportunities. So, late on 26 July, Rogers appeared off New Providence with seven ships, including three warships and two troop transports. He anchored just outside the harbour for the night, planning to land with full ceremony the following morning. However, Charles Vane had other ideas.

That evening Vane and 90 'hard-liners' boarded his sloop *Ranger*, and together with a French prize Vane had converted into a fireship they set a course for the harbour entrance. Vane tucked the *Ranger* in behind the blazing fireship, and watched as the British crews cut their anchor cables and made sail to avoid the flames. In the confusion, the *Ranger* slipped out of the harbour and escaped into the darkness. It was a spectacular gesture on Vane's part, but it also left Jennings and Hornigold in firm control of the island. When Rogers stepped ashore the following morning the two captains escorted him to the fort, where Rogers raised the Union Jack. New Providence was now under British control. The majority of the pirates were true to their word, and while Jennings retired to Bermuda, Hornigold became Rogers' pirate hunter, tracking down those who returned to their old ways. The first test of Rogers' government came in December, when he hanged several 'die-hard' pirates caught by Hornigold. There was no uprising, and the hanging showed that both Rogers and the rule of law were there to stay. It was now clear that the days of New Providence as a pirate haven were over.

Unfortunately, without the economic impetus of piracy, the Bahamas quickly turned into an economic backwater. Rogers never managed to turn the islands into a profitable colony, and by 1721 his money had run out. He returned to Britain, where he was briefly imprisoned for debt. He eventually returned to New Providence, where he died in 1732. By that time the 'Golden Age of Piracy' was over, and Rogers was appropriately remembered as the man who struck the first blow against the pirate scourge.

CHARLES VANE AND HIS 'DIE-HARDS'

By the time Charles Vane made his dramatic exit from New Providence he was already seen as one of the toughest pirates of his day. He began his piratical career with Henry Jennings, attacking the Spanish treasure camps, but before that he was a privateer, based in Port Royal. By early 1718 he had his own pirate sloop, the *Ranger*, and that April he took her on his first independent cruise. He captured two Bermudan sloops, and one captain claimed that Vane had beaten him and then tortured one of the crew by jabbing burning matches into his eyes. On the other sloop Vane hanged one of the crew, then slashed at him with his cutlass. Charles Vane was quickly gaining a reputation for cruelty.

After his escape in July 1718, Charles Vane remained at large. Hornigold wasn't the only pirate hunter looking for him, though. The South Carolina colony despatched two ships to track him down. Although Vane avoided them, another pirate, Stede Bonnet, was less fortunate, and was cornered in the Cape Fear River. Bonnet and his men were taken back to Charles Town (now Charleston) where they were tried and executed.

The execution of the 'gentleman pirate' Stede Bonnet at Charles Town in the South Carolina colony, in late 1718. He is shown clutching a posy of nosegay, a sign of penitence for his crimes.

By September the *Ranger* was lying off Ocracoke Island in North Carolina's Outer Banks, a haven used by Blackbeard. The two pirate crews spent a week together and had a party, complete with rum and women shipped in from a nearby town. Then Blackbeard and Vane parted company, and Vane sailed north, bound for the waters off New York. By late October he was off Long Island, where he captured a brig. However, winter was approaching, so the pirates decided to return to the warmer waters of the Caribbean. This was a common practice for pirates. Like migrating birds, they tended to head south for the winter. By late November Charles Vane was cruising the Windward Passage between Hispaniola and Cuba, after a month-long voyage that brought no prizes or plunder.

Then, on 23 November, they sighted what they thought was a French merchantman. It seemed as if Vane's luck had returned. However, she turned out to be a French man-of-war, which had been trying to lure the pirates within range. Vane stood away and the French ship gave chase. As the pursuit continued, some of the crew led by the quartermaster Jack Rackam felt that Vane was running scared. Although the

THE VOYAGES OF CHARLES VANE

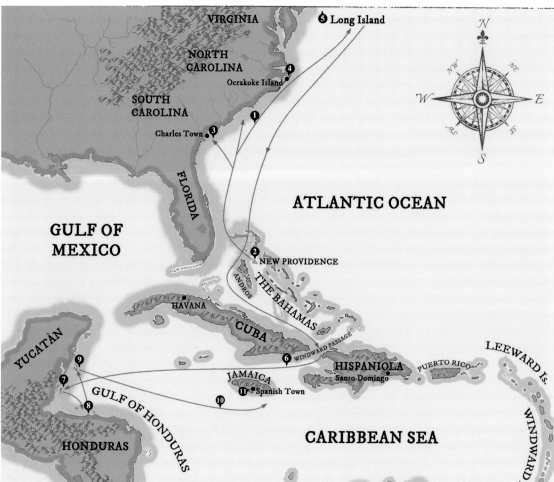

Ranger escaped, the taint of cowardice was left behind in her wake. Rackam called a vote, and a resolution was passed branding Vane a coward and removing him from his captaincy. Rackam replaced him as captain. At the time the *Ranger* was accompanied by the small prize captured off Long Island. Vane and 16 supporters were moved into her, and Rackam sailed off in the *Ranger*, leaving Vane to his fate.

Vane was undeterred. He headed south, capturing a sloop on the way. By January 1719 he had reached the Gulf of Honduras. He intended to prey on the logwood ships that operated there, but instead a violent storm struck them, and Vane and two other survivors were shipwrecked on a small island. The pirate

1. April 1718: Vane makes his first solo cruise in the sloop *Ranger*, capturing two ships off the Carolinas.
2. June: Vane fires at Governor Woodes Rogers as he arrives in New Providence, then escapes.
3. August: Vane captures several ships off Charles Town.
4. September: Vane encounters Blackbeard (Edward Teach) on Ocracoke, and the two pirate crews spend a week celebrating there.
5. October: Vane is cruising off Long Island when he captures another prize.
6. November: He heads south for the winter, but flees from a French warship in the Windward Passage. His crew replace Vane as captain, leaving him with a captured brig and 16 men.
7. December: Vane cruises off the coast of Belize, and heads towards the Gulf of Honduras.
8. January 1719: He establishes a base on an unidentified island called 'Barnacko', and captures several vessels in the area.
9. February: Vane is caught in a hurricane and shipwrecked on Lighthouse Reef off the coast of Belize. He and two of his crew survive.
10. April: Vane and his companions are rescued, but he is recognized and taken to Jamaica to stand trial.
11. November: Vane is tried for piracy in Spanish Town, and is condemned to death. He is eventually hanged in March 1721.

THE ROUTES OF 'CALICO JACK' RACKAM

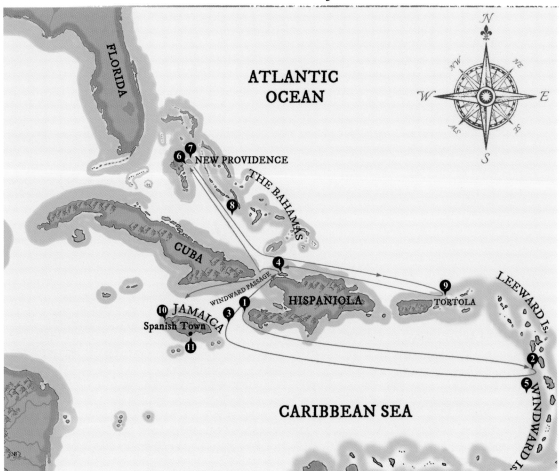

castaways survived for several weeks before a ship put in for water. Unfortunately for Vane, Captain Holford recognized him and refused to help him. The next ship was more obliging, and the marooned men were rescued. Then, in an unlikely twist of fate, their rescuers encountered Holford's ship, and one captain invited the other over for dinner. Holford spotted Vane and the game was up. The pirates were transferred to Holford's ship, put in irons, and taken to Jamaica.

By November 1719 Charles Vane was in Spanish Town jail. His trial began on 22 March 1721, and the result was a foregone conclusion. After all, Vane had refused the King's pardon and fired on Governor Rogers. The condemned pirate was taken to Gallows Point overlooking Port Royal, where he was hanged. Afterwards his body was displayed in a cage as a warning to others.

KEY
◀─── 1718–19 voyage   ◀─── 1720 voyage

1718–19

1. November: When Charles Vane flees from a French warship in the Windward Passage, the crew of his ship the *Ranger* depose him as captain, and elect Jack Rackam to the captaincy instead.
2. Early December: Rackam cruises the Leeward Islands and captures a few small prizes.
3. Mid December: The *Ranger* captures a ship carrying wine, and the crew drink the cargo dry.
4. Late December: The *Ranger* is careened on the north coast of Hispaniola.
5. Spring 1719: Rackam returns to the West Indies, but fails to capture any significant prizes.
6. May: He returns to New Providence and accepts a pardon from Woodes Rogers. For the next year he cruises as a legitimate privateer.

1720

7. 22 August: Rackam steals the sloop *William*, and with a crew of 13 he returns to piracy. His followers include the two women pirates Anne Bonny and Mary Read.
8. September: He plunders a fleet of fishing boats off the Bahamas, then heads east.
9. October: He captures two sloops off Tortola, then heads west again to escape any pursuit.
10. 15 November: Rackam anchors off the western tip of Jamaica. That night he is attacked by a pirate hunter, who captures the *William* after a brief one-sided fight. The pirates are taken to Spanish Town to stand trial.
11. 26 November: Rackam is found guilty, and hanged, along with most of his crew. The two women pirates escape the noose because they are found to be pregnant.

The second of Vane's two sloops – a prize that had parted from him in the storm – was commanded by Robert Deal, Vane's right-hand man. He was captured by a British warship just a few weeks after his captain, and he and his crew were hanged on Gallows Point while Vane was still marooned on his island. Vane of course was not the last of the 'die-hards'. His nemesis 'Calico Jack' Rackam still remained at large.

'CALICO JACK' RACKAM

The execution of Charles Vane served as a stern warning to any would-be pirates. As Captain Vernon, a naval officer based in Jamaica, put it: 'These punishments have made a wonderful reformation here'. However, Vane was merely a figurehead, and most of the 'die-hards' were still at sea. After the rebellion on the *Ranger* in November 1718, 'Calico Jack' Rackam became the new leader of her fifty-strong pirate crew. That made Rackam the new leader of the 'die-hards'.

'Calico Jack' Rackam was a fairly unsuccessful and low-level pirate, who accepted a pardon in New Providence but soon returned to his own ways. However, his fame was assured after his capture in 1720, when it was found that two of his dozen-strong pirate crew were women.

We know nothing of Rackam's life before he sailed with Vane, apart from his nickname – 'Calico Jack'. Calico is a textile made from unbleached cotton, less coarse than canvas, and far cheaper than processed cotton. In 1700 its import from India was banned in an attempt to protect the English cotton industry, and so Rackam may well have earned his nickname as a smuggler of cloth. However, this is speculation, and the real reason for his nickname may never be known. After parting with Vane, Rackam cruised off the Leeward Islands, where he captured a few prizes. Between Jamaica and Saint Dominique he took a ship laden with madeira, and his men spent two days drinking the cargo. Christmas was celebrated with a beach party on Hispaniola, but after that they cruised the Windward Passage without capturing anything more than a single convict ship, bound for the Jamaican plantations.

Then fate intervened. That December Britain declared war on Spain, and privateers were needed again. Woodes Rogers re-issued his offer of a pardon, and when they learned of this, Rackam and his 'die-hards' decided to accept the offer, so they could become legitimate privateers.

So the 'die-hards' hauled down their black flag, and the *Ranger* was sold off, the profit divided amongst her crew. Rackam and his shipmates signed on as privateers, but the war proved a brief one, and a peace treaty in February 1720 ended their lucrative spell of employment. It was during this period that Rackam met Anne Bonny, the first of two women who would scandalize polite society. On 22 August, Rackam and 13 followers, including Anne Bonny, stole the 12-gun Bahamian sloop *William* and escaped from New Providence before anyone could stop them. Strangely, one of the dozen men in his crew turned out to be another woman, Mary Read, who had disguised herself as a man. Woodes Rogers responded by naming them all as pirates, his list including the two women.

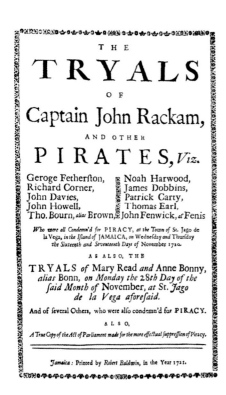

Rackam took the *William* south through the Windward Passage, and on 1 October he captured two sloops near Tortuga and a third vessel off Jamaica. The Jamaican authorities sent the pirate hunter Captain Jonathan Barnet out to find Rackam in the 12-gun sloop the *Eagle*, while Rackam continued along the northern Jamaican coast to Negril Point, the island's westerly tip. There, on 15 November, the pirates dropped anchor and uncorked the rum. A few hours later Barnet was approaching the Point from the south when he heard the sound of musket fire. He altered course to investigate, and came upon the *William*. The shot was probably fired off by a drunken pirate. Rackam cut his anchor cable and tried to escape, but the *Eagle* soon overhauled them. Evidently an excess of rum was not conducive to good seamanship. Barnet ordered the pirates to surrender, and was answered by a shot from a light swivel gun. He replied with a broadside, which splintered the *William*'s boom. The pirate sloop swung up into the wind, which allowed Barnet to come up and board her. Only Bonny and Read seemed to have been in a sober enough state to resist, cursing their drunken shipmates as they fought. As Captain Johnson put it, they 'called to those under deck to come up and fight like men'. These two firebrands were soon overpowered, and the pirates were taken back to Spanish Town in chains.

ABOVE As the governor of the Bahamas, Woodes Rogers ruled the island for three years and succeeded in turning it from a pirate haven into a law-abiding British colony. In this painting by Hogarth dated 1729, he is shown with his son, studying a map of New Providence island.

ABOVE LEFT The published report of the trial of 'Calico Jack' Rackam, Anne Bonny and Mary Read, along with ten of their shipmates, which was held in Jamaica in November 1720.

On 16 November 1720 the Vice-Admiralty Court tried and convicted Rackam and his male shipmates, and 'Calico Jack' and ten others were duly hanged on Gallows Point outside Kingston. As for the two women pirates, their arrest caused a storm. So began a public fascination with the lives of Bonny and Read that has never really gone away.

ANNE BONNY AND MARY READ

The capture of the two female pirates Anne Bonny and Mary Read in 1720 provoked the outrage of a society where women were simply not supposed to become seamen, or pirates, or fight. As a result, the pair became some of the best-known pirates of the 'Golden Age'.

On 28 November 1720 the two women pirates were tried in Spanish Town, and like their male shipmates they were sentenced to be hanged. However, they then both claimed they were pregnant. A doctor confirmed their claim, and their sentences were deferred. Exactly who the fathers were has never been explained. Suggestions include Rackam or even their jailers, coupled with in a bid to escape from the gallows. Mary Read died in prison five months later, still carrying her unborn child. As for Anne Bonny, 'she was continued in prison but what became of her since we cannot tell; only this we know, that she was not executed'.

Whatever the truth behind the lives of Anne Bonny and Mary Read, the two women seemed to scandalize and titillate society in equal measure. One of the most shocking revelations was that they both passed themselves off as men. In doing so they escaped the restrictions imposed on other women of the time. They had also turned to a life of crime, and fought like men. It was little wonder that the newspapers were full of the story, and what was not actually known was happily made up. The public was shocked that two women could turn to piracy. However, this was not exactly the first time that women had followed the black flag.

There was the 14th-century Breton noblewoman Jane de Belleville, who fitted out three privateers and led them on raids of the French coast. Then there was Charlotte de Berry, a 17th-century Englishwoman, who dressed as a man to follow her husband to sea. She was captured by a privateer, and after being raped by its captain she led a mutiny, which ended with the murder of her assailant. The trouble with these tales is they cannot be substantiated, unlike the account of the 16th-century Irish pirate Grace O'Malley, or even Lady Killigrew, who commanded a privateer in the English Channel around the same time. However, these were very isolated cases, and so female pirates were very much a novelty.

While this depiction of Anne Bonny is probably fairly accurate – she wears the standard clothing of a sailor from this period – the artist felt obliged to emphasise her gender by giving her a low-cut shirt.

Consequently, both of them warranted their own chapter in a revised edition of Captain Johnson's pirate biography. Unfortunately, despite all the contemporary newspaper coverage, we know very little about them. The biographer probably embroidered what was known from the stories that had circulated in the press. However, Johnson still remains our best source of information on Bonny and Read.

According to him, Anne Bonny was Irish, the illegitimate daughter of a lawyer and his maid. Johnson claims Anne was passed off as a boy, allowing her father to collect an allowance set aside for a son. Eventually Anne's father emigrated to the Carolinas, where his maid became his wife. It was hoped that Anne would marry well, but instead she ran off with a sailor who 'was not worth a groat'. By the end of 1719 the runaways had landed up in New Providence.

Johnson's description of her relationship with Rackam is revealing. 'Here [in New Providence] she became acquainted with Rackam the pirate, who making

Like the depiction of Anne Bonny by the same artist, Mary Read is shown wearing the outfit of a European sailor from the period.
A contemporary said of the two women that they 'wore men's jackets and long trousers, and handkerchiefs tied about their heads'.

courtship of her, soon found means of withdrawing her affections from her husband, so that she consented to elope with him, and go to sea with Rackam in men's clothes.' Johnson claimed this happened before Rackam accepted the renewed pardon, but it is more likely they met after his return to New Providence in early 1719. After Rackam returned to piracy, Johnson claims that 'nobody was more forward or courageous than she'. He added that when she visited Rackam in his cell on the morning of his execution, she told him that 'she was sorry to see him there, but if he had fought like a man, he need not have been hanged like a dog'. Johnson makes little mention of the pregnancy but hinted that her father might have had a hand in her reprieve. The implication is that she may have returned to her father's home after being released from prison.

Johnson provides even less information about Mary Read. She was English, and her mother's second child. The first, a son, was legitimate, but his sailor father never returned from the sea. The boy died shortly before his mother gave birth to Mary, who was illegitimate. Afterwards, Mary was passed off as her dead brother in order to claim an allowance from her late father's family. That story is too similar to that of Anne Bonny's childhood to be truly believable. Apparently, when she became a teenager Mary left home, and served for a time in the navy and then the army. Johnson drew this unlikely biography from the sensationalist newspaper stories written around the time of the trial.

The tale soon became even more unbelievable. While serving in the army Mary fell for a Flemish soldier. They both quit the service, married, and opened a restaurant in Breda. Then in 1697 her husband died. She boarded a vessel bound for the West Indies, but was captured by English pirates, who recruited her. She remained with them until they accepted the pardon in New Providence. There, she met Anne Bonny and Jack Rackam. Unfortunately, this does not hold up under scrutiny. No unknown pirate crew could have remained at large for two decades. According to Johnson, she would have been in her early 20s when her husband died, and mid-40s when she joined Rackam's crew. That makes her pregnancy a near impossibility.

If we accept a grain of truth in the account, it makes far more sense to suggest that her husband died around 1713, the end of the War of the Spanish Succession, and that afterwards she took passage to the West Indies. That fits in with a short piratical career, the granting of a pardon, and her meeting with Rackam and Bonny. However, there is also nothing to say that Johnson's account is any more than a complete fabrication, based on melodramatic newspaper stories.

Johnson goes on to describe how Read dressed as a sailor, and only revealed her real identity to Anne Bonny, possibly Rackam, and a young sailor she took a fancy to. Within three months of joining Rackam's crew, the young man was hanged as a pirate along with his captain, while the pregnant Mary Read remained in jail, where 'she was seized of a violent fever soon after the trial, of which she died in prison'. She was buried on 21 April 1721, still carrying her unborn child. A victim of Rackam said of the women that they 'wore men's jackets and long trousers, and handkerchiefs tied about their heads, and that each of them had a machete and pistol in their hands'. Another claimed of the women that 'they were both very profligate, cursing and swearing much'. It was a sensational image and one that guaranteed the inclusion of Bonny and Read in any account of piracy during the period. However, everything else we know about them before their capture is little more than supposition.

In this 19th-century illustration, Mary Read, having vanquished a fellow pirate in a duel, exposes her breast to reveal to her dying adversary that he was shot by a woman. After their capture it was said that she and Anne Bonny put up more of a fight than all the rest of Rackam's pirate crew.

THE RISE OF BLACKBEARD

These days, if most people want to imagine a real pirate, they'll think of Blackbeard. He owes his fame to Captain Johnson, whose vivid description of him captured the imagination:

> So our hero, Captain Teach, assumed the cognomen of Blackbeard from that large quantity of hair which, like a frightful meteor, covered his whole face and frightened America more than any comet that has appeared there a long time. The beard was black, which he suffered to grow of an extravagant length; as to breadth it came up to his eyes. He was accustomed to twist it with ribbons, in small tails, after the manner of our ramilies wigs, and turn them about his ears.
>
> In time of action, he wore a sling over his shoulders, with three brace of pistols, hanging from holsters like bandaliers, and stuck lighted matches under his hat, which, appearing on each side of his face, his eyes naturally looking fierce and wild, made him altogether such a figure, that imagination cannot form an idea of a fury, from hell, to look more frightful … If he had the look of a fury, his humours and passions were suitable to it.

Clearly Blackbeard, or Edward Teach, was careful to cultivate a fearsome image. He realized that intimidation was the key to piratical success. If your victim is terrified of you, then your task is made a lot easier. Blackbeard used his appearance as a weapon. Like many pirates, we know little about his life before he started his piratical career. Captain Johnson claims he was born in Bristol around 1680, but there is also evidence that he was born and raised in Jamaica. Johnson claims that Teach 'sailed some time out of Jamaica in privateers, in the late French war; yet though he had often distinguished himself for his uncommon boldness and personal courage, he was never raised to any command'. There is also evidence that he briefly served aboard the frigate HMS *Windsor*. This privateering background was shared by most of the New Providence pirates, and like them Teach soon turned to piracy. He began in 1716 as one of Benjamin Hornigold's crew. However, when he realized Blackbeard's potential, Hornigold 'put him into a sloop that he had made prize of, and with whom he continued in consortship till a little while before Hornigold surrendered'.

The first official mention of Teach came in March 1717, when a Captain Munthe ran his sloop aground on the western fringe of the Bahamas. While freeing his vessel he spoke to local fishermen, who told him a little about the

Blackbeard deliberately cultivated a ferocious appearance to intimidate his enemies. It was said that he stuck lengths of burning slowmatch under the rim of his hat to enhance his already demonic appearance. In this contemporary aquatint, his flagship *Queen Anne's Revenge* can be seen in the background.

ABOVE This contemporary depiction of Edward Teach, or Blackbeard, shows how his cognomen came about – his thick black beard was worn so long that it gave him a notably ferocious appearance.

TOP RIGHT Frank Schoonover's illustration 'Blackbeard in smoke and flame' reflected Captain Johnson's description of the pirate as 'altogether such a figure that imagination cannot form an idea of a fury from hell to look more frightful'.

pirates in New Providence. In a letter to officials in the Carolinas Munthe reported that 'Five pirates made ye harbour of Providence their place of rendevous vizt. Horngold, a sloop with 10 guns and about 80 men; Jennings, a sloop with 10 guns and 100 men; Burgiss, a sloop with 8 guns and about 80 men; White, in a small vessel with 30 men and small arms; Thatch, a sloop 6 guns and about 70 men'. That means that by the spring of 1717 at the latest, Blackbeard had his own command.

At the time Teach was still cruising in concert with Hornigold, but dissent was brewing. Hornigold always claimed he was a privateer rather than a pirate, a fiction he supported by limiting his attacks to French or Spanish ships. Blackbeard had no such scruples, and so that autumn, when Hornigold's crew deposed him as captain, Teach sided with them. Hornigold returned to New Providence, where he led the 'pro-pardon' group. Blackbeard then began operating on his own.

By late September 1717 Blackbeard was off Cape Charles in Virginia, where he captured and sank the sloop *Betty*. In mid-October the *Boston News Letter* reported from Philadelphia that a merchantman was captured in the mouth of the Delaware River 'by a pirate sloop called *Revenge* of 12 Guns, 150 men, commanded by one Teach, who formerly sail'd mate out of this port'. The enigmatic reference to Blackbeard's earlier association with Philadelphia may suggest that he spent some time as a merchant sailor. The newspaper reported three other attacks in the same area. Heading north, Teach captured three more prizes off the Virginia Capes, where he added a second sloop to his force.

The *Boston News Letter* explained what happened. After mentioning the *Revenge*, it said that 'On board the pirate sloop is Major Bennet, but has no command'. This is hardly surprising, as Bennet (actually Stede Bonnet) was the owner of the *Revenge*, a pirate sloop Blackbeard encountered, most likely in New Providence, but possibly at sea off the Carolinas. Teach suggested that the inexperienced Bonnet should let Teach's pirates run his ship for him, and so Bonnet became a prisoner in his own sloop. Blackbeard promptly turned Bonnet's *Revenge* into his own flagship.

By the end of October Blackbeard was off New Jersey. This was the usual time when pirates headed south for the winter. So Teach set a course for the Leeward Islands, and by 17 November his two sloops were 60 miles (97km) to the west of Martinique. On sighting a large merchantman, the pirates gave chase, and she surrendered after a token resistance. The prize was *La Concorde*, a well-built 200-ton French slave ship from Nantes, bound for Martinique. Teach led her into the secluded island anchorage of Bequia, where he set about converting her into his new flagship.

This unusual portrayal of Blackbeard shows him in a captain's coat, but rather than a tricorne, he is depicted wearing a fur hat – a typical form of winter headgear for early 18th-century mariners.

THE *QUEEN ANNE'S REVENGE*

Blackbeard had been storing captured guns in the holds of his sloops. These were used to transform his prize into the ultimate pirate ship. First, Teach cut down her stern structure and forecastle to make her more suitable for a fighting ship, and then added the extra guns. By the time he had finished, the prize, which he renamed the *Queen Anne's Revenge*, carried 40 guns, making her one of the most powerful ships in American waters. He kept the *Revenge*, but let his French prisoners sail to Martinique in his smaller unnamed sloop. *La Concorde's* human

This early 18th-century plan of Charles Town shows a bustling and well-defended port, but when Blackbeard arrived there in 1718 the city lacked adequate defences.

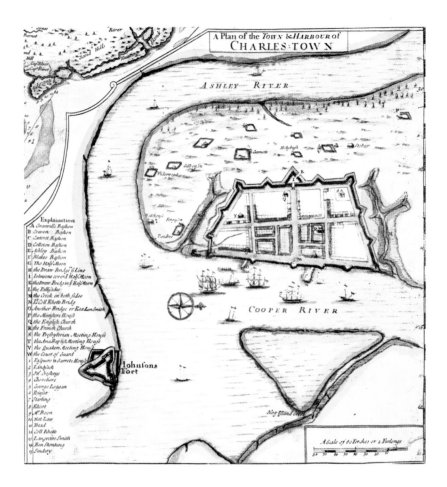

cargo were left behind on Bequia as Teach set off in search of another victim.

It was now late November 1717. His first prize was a small sloop, which he added to his fleet. Then off St Lucia he captured the Boston merchantman *Great Allen*, en route to Jamaica. The pirates kept her for a day, plundering her of anything they wanted, and then set fire to her. He went on to take three other smaller vessels before he encountered the sloop *Margaret* off Anguilla. The importance here was that her captain gave a detailed description of the pirate to the authorities. He described 'Capt. Tach' as 'a tall spare man with a very black beard which he wore very long'. This is the description that Captain Johnson used as the basis for his more exuberant version. It also gave rise to the pirate's nickname. From that point on he would be widely known as 'Blackbeard'.

Johnson describes a fight between the *Queen Anne's Revenge* and the frigate HMS *Scarborough* that never actually happened, although both ships were cruising in the same waters at the time. News of the warship was probably what prompted Teach to leave the West Indies. He spent Christmas in Semana Bay, on the eastern side of Hispaniola, and then led the *Queen Anne's Revenge* and the sloop *Revenge* to the Gulf of Honduras. Blackbeard spent a month attacking the logwood ships that frequented the Gulf. By late April he was heading north again, passing the western tip of Cuba, then sailing up through the Florida Straits. He captured a small Spanish sloop off Havana, then spent a few days lying off the wreck sites of the 1715 treasure *flota*. Off Florida he captured another brig, which he decided to keep.

That meant he now had four ships, including his 40-gun flagship, and 250 men. With all that power, he would have felt that the whole of the Atlantic seaboard lay at his mercy. He would take full advantage of it. On 22 May 1718, Blackbeard appeared off Charles Town (now Charleston), in the province of South Carolina. A string of sandbars separated Charles Town harbour from the ocean, and so, by guarding the only navigatable gap in the bar, Blackbeard managed to blockade the port. His first victim was the pilot boat escorting out the *Crowley*, a large merchantman bound for London, and Blackbeard captured both vessels. The pirates captured a few more prizes over the next few days. Then, when the prizes dried up, Blackbeard decided to be even more audacious.

Captain Johnson describes his next move:

> Teach detained all the ships and prisoners, and, being in want of medicines, resolved to demand a chest from the government of the province ... threatening that if they did not send immediately the chest of medicines and let the pirate ambassadors return without offering any violence to their persons, they would murder all their prisoners, send up their heads to the governor, and set the ships they had taken on fire.

Holding a town to ransom was something that had not been seen since the days of the buccaneers. While the South Carolina governor sent off for help, he knew that time was not on his side. The nearest Royal Navy warships were in Virginia's James River, and they would take a week to reach Charles Town. The port was reasonably well defended, but the local militia was of dubious military value. So:

This wonderfully atmospheric painting by Frank Schoonover captured the moment in 1718 when a detachment of Blackbeard's men landed on the waterfront of Charles Town to demand a ransom from the townspeople.

The [Carolina] government were not long in deliberating upon the message ... they complied with the necessity and sent aboard a chest valued at between £300 and £400, and the pirates went back safe to their ships.

Blackbeard had his medicine, but what he wanted it for has never been satisfactorily explained. A syringe used for treating venereal disease found on the wreck site of the *Queen Anne's Revenge* may provide an explanation; his crew may have caught the disease during their winter on Hispaniola. Then again, their recent visit to the Gulf of Honduras may have resulted in an outbreak of the flux (yellow fever). We can only speculate, but evidently the pirates considered the chest more important than plunder. Of course, they did not leave empty-handed: the passengers on the *Crowley* reported being robbed of £1,500 worth of silver coins.

True to his word, Blackbeard raised the blockade and sailed off, heading north. He realized that if he delayed, the chances of being caught by warships would increase. What he needed now was a place where he could lie low, divide the plunder and plan his next move. Although there was no chance of being offered a pardon by Woodes Rogers, and he had just infuriated the South Carolina colony's governor, he had other options. A pardon was still being

In May 1718, after his blockade of Charles Town, Blackbeard moved up the coast to the Outer Banks, and deliberately ran the *Queen Anne's Revenge* aground in Topsail Inlet, near the modern town of Beaufort NC. (Diane Cook and Len Jenshel/Getty Images)

HOISTING THE BLACK FLAG

In the 17th century buccaneers fought under either their national flag or a privateering standard. For this, red was the most common colour, signifying no quarter would be given. Some buccaneers embellished these flags with other symbols of death or threats. In French, such flags were known as '*La Jolie Rouge*', 'the pretty red'. The English translated this as the 'Jolly Roger'.

The first reported instance of a black flag being flown was in 1700, when the French pirate Emmanuelle Wynne flew one decorated with a skull, crossed bones and an hourglass. By the time of the 'Golden Age of Piracy' the colour was closely associated with piracy. Like their red predecessors, these black flags stood for the threat of violence, for no quarter being given, and for danger. Any sailor understood the implication when the black flag was hoisted. Nowadays pirate flags are expected to have a skull and crossbones on them. Other variants – a skull and crossed swords, a skeleton, an hourglass (representing time running out) and drinking cups (toasting death) – were all common during this period. These symbols of death reinforced the black flag's message, and all served to intimidate pirate victims.

The symbolism could be even more specific. 'Black Bart' Roberts designed a flag to show his hatred of two governors who challenged him from Barbados and Martinique. The flag showed a pirate standing on two skulls – one labelled ABH, the other AMH. These stood for 'A Barbadian's Head' and 'A Martiniquan's Head'.

Roberts' main flag showed a pirate holding an hourglass standing beside a skeleton holding a spear. Blackbeard flew a flag showing a skeleton holding an hourglass with a spear and a bleeding heart next to it, while 'Calico Jack' Rackam flew a black flag with a skull surmounting a pair of crossed swords. Stede Bonnet flew one with a skull, flanked by a heart, a dagger, and surmounting a single bone. In fact, the only pirate to fly anything akin to the skull and crossbones of pirate legend was Edward England.

offered by the colony of North Carolina. This small colony lacked the powerful mercantile lobby that made neighbouring Virginia a hotbed of anti-pirate feelings. However, Blackbeard had one small problem. His flagship was too large to operate in Carolina's sheltered waterways, and she also acted as an attractive challenge to the Royal Navy. Somehow he had to abandon her.

He hit upon the perfect plan. On 2 June Blackbeard appeared off Topsail Inlet, near the modern town of Beaufort, North Carolina, which in those days consisted of a few fishermen's huts. The channel was only 300 yards (274m)

In 1996 the wreck of a sailing
ship was found in Beaufort
Inlet, North Carolina. It has
subsequently been identified
as Blackbeard's *Queen Anne's
Revenge*, which ran aground
there in May 1718. This anchor
was recovered from the
wreck and is one of hundreds
of objects which have been
conserved, and which are now
displayed in the North
Carolina Maritime Museum in
Beaufort. (Robert Willett/
Raleigh News & Observer/
MCT via Getty Images)

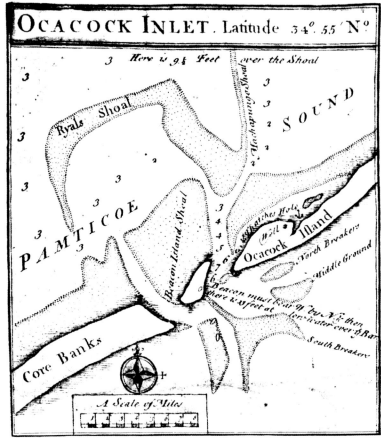

In November 1718,
Blackbeard's sloop lay at its
usual anchorage off the
western side of Ocracoke
Island, marked 'Thatches Hole'
on this chart. The only way to
reach it from the open sea
was through Ocracoke Inlet,
the narrow passage to the
south of the island.

wide, and a tricky passage. Halfway through it, Blackbeard's helmsman turned the *Queen Anne's Revenge* hard to starboard, and she ran aground. Teach called on Israel Hands, commanding the sloop *Adventure*, asking him to tow him off. In the process, Hands ran his sloop aground too. It is almost certain that Blackbeard and Hands had planned the whole thing. Although the *Adventure* might be repaired, the *Queen Anne's Revenge* was a complete loss – exactly what Blackbeard wanted.

In June 1996 the wreck of *Queen Anne's Revenge* was discovered off Beaufort, and since then the site has been surveyed and systematically excavated. A bronze bell dated 1705 was found, along with numerous cannons, weaponry, roundshot and a small venereal syringe. Was it part of the medicine chest Blackbeard demanded from the citizens of Charles Town? Flakes of gold dust were also recovered – the kind of thing often carried by the crew of slave ships who visited the West African coast. Since then the wreck has been conclusively identified as Blackbeard's lost flagship. Consequently, the North Carolina Maritime Museum in Beaufort is a treasure trove of pirate artefacts.

LORD OF THE OUTER BANKS

The next part Blackbeard's plan to legally retire with his plunder was to get rid of Bonnet. So Blackbeard sent him off to the colony's administrative seat in Bath Town (now Bath, NC) with instructions to obtain a provisional pardon for everybody. Meanwhile, Teach and his men salvaged what they could from the wrecks, and moved the plunder into a smaller sloop. Blackbeard then made his

Ocracoke is a barrier island, now part of North Carolina's Outer Banks. In 1718 it was used as a lair by Blackbeard, due to its easy access to the Atlantic, and its proximity to his legitimate base in nearby Bath Town (now Bath, NC). It was off here, in November 1718, that he was killed in a fight with the Royal Navy. (wbritten/Getty Images)

In late 1718 Alexander Spotswood (c.1676–1740), governor of the Virginia colony, was willing to invade neighbouring North Carolina rather than ignore evidence that Blackbeard had resumed his piratical activities.

move. He collected all of Bonnet's remaining men and marooned them on a nearby deserted island. After stripping the *Revenge* of her sails, he sailed off in the Spanish prize, taking just 30 chosen men with him. The other 200 pirates were left behind. When Bonnet returned, he was furious to discover that Blackbeard had pillaged his ship, stranded his crew and absconded with the loot. That's what comes of trusting a pirate.

Bonnet took a week to set the *Revenge* to rights, and then gave chase. He never caught up with Blackbeard, who by that time was safely hidden behind North Carolina's Outer Banks. After dividing his plunder, Teach made his own way to Bath Town, and in mid-June he accepted a pardon from Governor Charles Eden. A supposedly reformed character, Blackbeard gave every impression of having turned over a new leaf. This idyll would last for several months, during which time Blackbeard established another, more secure base on nearby Ocracoke Island in the Outer Banks. He rented a house in Bath Town, took a young mistress, and kept his crew occupied by sailing his sloop (which he renamed the *Adventure*) between the town and the island. In September he entertained Charles Vane and his men on Ocracoke. That was when Blackbeard returned to his own ways. He ventured further afield, and this time he captured two French merchantmen in Delaware Bay. However, according to the testimony he gave to Eden, he found them abandoned and came aboard merely to establish salvage rights. The pirate was walking a legal tightrope, as if word got out that he had engaged in piracy, then he would immediately lose all legal protection.

For Governor Alexander Spotswood of Virginia, this attack was the final straw. He decided that he would deal with Blackbeard before he could become more of a threat, regardless of the pirate's legal standing. Consequently, he organized a two-pronged assault. While Captain Brand of the Royal Navy led a force overland to Bath Town, a smaller naval expedition would seek out Blackbeard at Ocracoke. The man he entrusted with this naval enterprise was

Lieutenant Robert Maynard, Brand's second-in-command on board the frigate HMS *Pearl*. As the *Pearl* and her consort HMS *Lyme* were too big to pass through the Outer Banks, Spotswood hired the small sloops *Ranger* and *Jane*. Neither carried any guns, but they were crewed by 57 well-armed seamen from the two frigates. To encourage them, Spotswood offered a reward for each pirate killed or captured, and a bonus for Blackbeard himself.

The two sloops arrived off Ocracoke Island at dusk on 21 November. Maynard decided to anchor for the night, and to attack at dawn. That evening Blackbeard had company. A sloop arrived from the town that afternoon, and the 25 pirates spent the evening drinking. The rest of Blackbeard's crew, another 24 men, were in Bath Town. Before dawn on Friday 22 November 1718 Maynard got under way, his sloops being towed into the inlet by their longboats due to the lack of wind. The two sides were evenly matched. Although Maynard had twice as many men as Teach, the pirate sloop carried eight guns. A lookout on the *Adventure* spotted the longboats as they rounded the southern tip of the island. A gun was fired at the nearest longboat, and the boat crews hastily pulled back to their sloops. The battle had begun.

In this depiction of Edward Teach (or 'Blackbeard'), the artist has included a stylized version of his last battle off Ocracoke in the background, set against an incongruous backdrop of a tropical island, rather than part of the North Carolina colony's Outer Banks.

Maynard hoisted the Union flag and turned towards the pirates. Fortunately for Maynard, the pirates didn't fire their guns again as he approached. When they came within a hundred yards the two captains hailed each other. Maynard recorded the conversation: 'At our first salutation he [Blackbeard] drank Damnation to me and my Men, whom he stil'd Cowardly Puppies, saying, He would neither give nor take Quarter'. Both sides exchanged small-arms fire, but the pirates then fired one of their guns, and the *Jane* was badly hit, with her master killed and five crew wounded. She dropped astern, and only rejoined the battle in its closing moments. A broadside then ripped into the *Ranger*, killing six and wounding ten.

Maynard expected that the pirates would try to board him, so before his approach he hid most of his crew below decks. As the two sloops crashed into each other, Blackbeard's men threw *grenadoes* onto the *Ranger*'s deck, then they swarmed aboard. At that moment Maynard's men surged up from below decks. The fight was brutal, with no quarter given. In the swirling mêlée, Teach and Maynard singled each other out, and fought their own duel. 'Blackbeard and the lieutenant fired the first pistol at each other, by which the pirate received a wound. The pirate then drew a cutlass, which he swung at Maynard.'

THE VOYAGES OF THE NOTORIOUS BLACKBEARD

The *Boston News Letter* reported: 'Maynard and Teach themselves begun the fight with their swords, Maynard making a thrust, the point of his sword went against Teach's cartridge box, and bended it to the hilt. Teach broke the guard of it, and wounded Maynard's fingers but did not disable him, whereupon he jumped back and threw away his sword and fired his pistol, which wounded Teach.' The pirate had now been hit twice, but he still kept fighting. With Maynard's sword broken, Blackbeard moved in to deliver a killing blow. At that moment one of Maynard's men slashed at Blackbeard, cutting his throat. Blackbeard staggered and fell, and was dead by the time he hit the deck.

KEY

← 1717 voyage   ← 1718 voyage   🚢 Spanish shipwrecks

1717

1. March: Blackbeard parts company with Benjamin Hornigold and begins his own cruise in the Bahamas Channel.
2. September: He cruises off the Virginia Capes and Delaware Bay, and captures several prizes there.
3. October: Blackbeard encounters Stede Bonnet, and commandeers his sloop. They sail in consort as far north as New Jersey, before heading south for the winter.
4. 17 November: Off Martinique Blackbeard encounters the French slave ship *La Concord*. He captures her and converts her into a pirate flagship, which he calls the *Queen Anne's Revenge*.
5. December: He cruises the waters of the Leeward Islands, capturing four more prizes there.
6. Late December: Blackbeard puts in to Samana Bay on the north-eastern coast of Hispaniola to careen his ships.

1718

7. March: Blackbeard heads to the Gulf of Honduras, and spends a month there, capturing several prizes.
8. April: He returns north, and off Havana he captures a Spanish sloop. He then rifles the salvage camp of the Spanish treasure fleet before sailing on to the north.
9. 22 May: Blackbeard arrives off Charles Town, and blockades the port with the *Queen Anne's Revenge* and two sloops. He captures more ships there and demands a ransom from the town before sailing away.
10. June: In Topsail Inlet, the *Queen Anne's Revenge* is run aground. Bonnet is sent to Bath Town to ask the governor there for a pardon. Meanwhile Blackbeard sails away in a sloop, leaving most of his men behind and taking all the plunder with him.
11. July: Blackbeard accepts a pardon from Governor Eden, and rents a house in Bath Town, while maintaining a pirate base on nearby Ocracoke Island.
12. September: He captures two French ships off the Delaware coast.
13. November: Governor Spotswood of Virginia sends two sloops to hunt down Blackbeard, and also dispatches a land force to seize the pirates in Bath Town.
14. 22 November: Blackbeard is surprised while his sloop lies at anchor off Ocracoke Island. Lieutenant Maynard's two sloops attack him, and in the ensuing battle Blackbeard is killed, and the survivors of his crew are captured. They are duly taken to Williamsburg to stand trial.

The fight went out of the surviving pirates, or most of them. According to Captain Johnson, Blackbeard had 'posted a resolute fellow, a Negro who he had brought up, with a lighted match in the powder room with commands to blow up when he should give him orders'. Fortunately, he was overcome before he could light the fuse. By the time the fighting ended, eight pirates lay dead, and the rest were either badly wounded or were swimming to the island. They were rounded up later, as were the five pirates still on board the sloop *Adventure*.

The cost, however, had been high. Eleven of Maynard's men had been killed in the action and 22 wounded. The victorious Maynard remained off Ocracoke for

This Howard Pyle illustration shows the frenetic last moments of Blackbeard's piratical career, when he fell in his final battle with the Royal Navy. Lieutenant Maynard, with his back to us, can be seen holding off Teach and his crew.

three days, repairing the sloops, burying the dead, treating his wounded and capturing any escaped pirates. After putting in to Bath Town he sailed back to Virginia, with the severed head of Blackbeard hanging from his bowsprit.

In Bath Town Captain Brand rounded up the other pirates, and marched them back to Williamsburg. Governor Eden of North Carolina was furious – Brand's action was tantamount to an invasion of one colony by another. Although the lawsuits would fly around for years, Spotswood was delighted that the pirate threat on his doorstep had been eradicated. Their trial of the surviving pirates was held in Williamsburg on 12 March 1719. There was no doubt about the verdict. Only one man was given a reprieve – the remaining fifteen were condemned to death The exception was the Bath Town sloop owner, who had been in the wrong place at the wrong time. Just before the mass hanging, Quartermaster Israel Hands was also given a last-minute reprieve, having convinced the court that because he had been shot in the knee by his captain, he took no part in the attack on the French ships. He was allowed to walk free. Within days the rest were dangling from gibbets lining the road between Williamsburg and Jamestown.

The strange thing about Blackbeard is that for all his ferocious reputation, there is no evidence that he actually killed anybody. Captain Johnson built up his fearsome image with tales like the wounding of Israel Hands. Blackbeard and Hands had been playing cards with guests, when Teach shot Hands in the knee with a hidden pistol. According to Johnson, when asked why he did it, he was said to have replied: 'that if he did not now and then kill one of them, they would forget who he was'.

After defeating Blackbeard and rounding up what remained of his pirate crew, Lieutenant Maynard sailed back to Virginia, displaying the severed head of Blackbeard on the bowsprit of his sloop.

Today people remember Blackbeard for his appearance and his ferocity, not for his actions. More than most of the other pirates of his day he seemed to be a figure who developed a larger-than-life persona, whose image developed into something akin to a pirate caricature. In his biography of the pirate, this author shows that the dramatic reality of Edward Teach and his piratical career was much more fascinating than the modern legend.

STEDE BONNET,
THE GENTLEMAN PIRATE

In most cases, we know very little about pirates before they broke the law. Stede Bonnet is an exception, as he left a trail of evidence behind him. In fact, the details of Bonnet's background were so sensational that at the time of his trial the newspapers were filled with accounts of his life. The novelty was that he never needed to turn to piracy at all. He was a gentleman, and a prominent member of polite colonial society. At his trial the judge described him as 'a gentleman that has had the advantage of a liberal education, and being generally esteemed as a Man of Letters'. That was essentially correct. Bonnet was born in England, but moved to Barbados during the early 1700s. He bought and developed a sugar plantation outside Bridgetown, and by 1717 he was a prosperous plantation owner. He was highly respectable, having made a good marriage, and had become a major in the Barbados militia. Then he threw everything away to become a pirate.

Various reasons have all been suggested for this, including 'a disorder of the mind', but whatever the reason, Bonnet decided to become a criminal. He certainly set about it in a unique way. He bought a large 10-gun sloop, an ideal pirate vessel, which he renamed the *Revenge*. He then combed Bridgetown for a crew. While all other pirates called for volunteers, Bonnet hired them and paid them wages. The 70 crewmen of the *Revenge* were probably the only pirates in history to earn a regular income.

He avoided the West Indies, where he might be recognized, and instead he headed for the American colonies, which he reached during the early summer of 1717. He spent a month cruising off the Virginia Capes, where he captured four merchantmen including one from his home island of Barbados. To cover his tracks a little he burned this prize, the sloop *Turbet*, after pilfering her cargo and setting her crew ashore. He then headed north and captured a sloop off the Long Island. Then Bonnet took the *Revenge* back down to the Bahamas. It was there, or just possibly at sea off the Carolinas, that he ran into Blackbeard. The *Boston News Letter* carried a story filed in Philadelphia on 24 October that Teach was operating in Delaware Bay, and that his sloop was called the *Revenge*. It went on to say that:

Despite lacking maritime experience, in 1717 Stede Bonnet, a plantation owner from Barbados, decided to become a pirate. He soon fell in with Blackbeard, who virtually held him prisoner until the two parted company. Bonnet then had his own brief piratical career, until he was captured and executed in late 1718.

> On board the Pirate Sloop is Major Bennet, but has no Command, he walks about in his Morning Gown, and then to his Books, of which he has a good Library on Board, he was not well of his wounds that he received by attacking a Spanish Man of War, which kill'd and wounded thirty to forty men. After which putting into Providence, the place of Rendevouze for the Pirates, they put the afore said Capt. Teach on board for this Cruise.

Major Bennet was obviously Stede Bonnet, but the report of him fighting a Spanish warship is not borne out by the Spanish archives. He may well have sailed to New Providence, though, and either encountered Teach there, or shortly afterwards, when both pirates were at sea. The description of him in his 'morning gown' fits in with Johnson's account of the relationship between the two pirates:

> The major was no sailor as was said before, and therefore had been obliged to yield to many things that were imposed on him during their undertaking, for want of a competent knowledge of maritime affairs … To him [Blackbeard] Bonnet's crew joined in consortship, and Bonnet himself was laid aside, notwithstanding the sloop was his own.

Bonnet became little more than Blackbeard's prisoner for eight months, a confinement that ended in June 1718 when Bonnet sailed to Bath Town in the hope of securing a pardon from Governor Eden. This pardon excluded attacks made by Blackbeard (and therefore Bonnet) in the Gulf of Honduras or off

Today, Charleston, South Carolina is renowned for its charm and antebellum architecture, but in 1718, when it was known as Charles Town, it was blockaded by Blackbeard, and then became the setting for the trial of the pirate Stede Bonnet and his crew, who were hanged not far from this spot. (Photo by Visions of America/UIG via Getty Images)

Charles Town. However, provincial governors had the right to waive this clause if they saw fit. Blackbeard hoped that by sending Bonnet to see Eden first, the governor would be more amenable to clemency when it came to Blackbeard himself. The plan worked, and Bonnet sailed back to Topsail Inlet clutching a pardon. That was when he learned that Blackbeard had absconded with all the plunder.

After rescuing his men, Bonnet re-crewed the *Revenge* and prepared the sloop for sea. For once the name of Bonnet's sloop was completely appropriate. Bonnet was too angry to realize he was on a fool's errand. He had a chance to walk away from piracy, but once the *Revenge* put to sea that opportunity would be lost. However, when news came that Teach was at Ocracoke, there was no turning back. The *Revenge* set off in pursuit, but when he failed to find Blackbeard, his men headed north to Virginia to resume their pirate cruise. In fact, Blackbeard was in Bath Town, accepting his own pardon.

The first ship Bonnet captured was a sloop laden with rum, which his men drank. A string of four prizes followed. The *Revenge* continued towards Delaware Bay, where Bonnet captured another sloop carrying furs. It was all slim pickings, and hardly worth giving up a pardon for. However, in July he captured five more vessels off the mouth of the Delaware River, and Bonnet decided to keep two of the sloops. Expecting that his attacks would have attracted the attention of the navy, Bonnet then headed south again.

This illustration from an early 18th-century broadsheet depicted colonial America as a semi-clad Amazon, fighting off the piratical scourge caused to her commerce by capturing and executing the pirates, her actions aided by a fisherman's fair wind.

BATTLE IN THE CAPE FEAR RIVER

The sloop *Revenge* was in need of repair, so Bonnet put in to the Cape Fear River. He remained there for two months, but by mid-September she was ready, and bore a new name, the *Royal James*. However, after Teach's blockade of Charles Town, the colony's governor sent the armed sloops *Henry* and *Sea Nymph* to sea to hunt for him. They were commanded by Colonel William Rhett, whose main targets were Teach and Vane, but he was also on the lookout for Bonnet. On 26 September Rhett's two sloops entered the Cape Fear River,

The single-masted sloop was probably the most commonly encountered pirate vessel of this period. Fast and shallow-drafted, sloops made near-perfect pirate craft. This British sloop is shown lying off Boston Light in 1718.

and, as Johnson recounts, 'saw, over a point of land, three sloops at an anchor, which were Major Bonnet and his prizes'. Rhett decided to attack at dawn, on the incoming tide. Bonnet and his men spotted them too, and so that night both sides prepared for battle.

The two-masted brigantine was a common sight in the 18th century, as it was one of the most popular types of merchant vessel found in American waters. It could also be converted into a well-armed pirate ship.

PIRATE JUSTICE

The way the authorities combated the spread of piracy during the 'Golden Age' was by a combination of carrot – the granting of official pardons – and stick – hunting down wrongdoers, then publicly trying and executing them. The best way to discourage more sailors from turning to piracy was to demonstrate that piracy didn't pay.

If pirates were caught they faced a high-profile trial, and when found guilty they would be hanged. In Britain, trials were conducted according to Admiralty law. This meant there was no trial by jury, but instead the case was heard by a panel of officials. The onus was on the accused to prove their innocence. As most of the accused were barely literate, the whole process was less about justice than about retribution.

Once a pirate was condemned he was usually executed on the foreshore, which was within the boundaries of the authority of the Admiralty. This meant that gallows were erected on the waterfront, such as Execution Dock in London's Wapping. The pirate was allowed a last speech, a prayer would be said, and then he would be hanged. The body would be left for a day and a half, after which the corpse would be cut down and buried in an unmarked grave. Often, the dead pirate was not even granted this dignity. In keeping with the policy of deterrence, his body would be suspended in a cage overlooking the sea. These cages were positioned within sight of passing ships to serve as a warning to others. The bodies of pirates were therefore used to reinforce the argument that piracy didn't pay.

Before dawn the *Royal James* crept down the river, with her gun crews ready. Bonnet had 45 men, which meant he was outnumbered three to one. His only hope was to surprise the enemy, fire a broadside as they passed, and then escape to the open sea. As the *Royal James* approached the pirate hunters, though, she ran hard aground, right in front of her opponents. The *Henry* and the *Sea Nymph* got under way, but then they too grounded on a hidden sandbank. It was a ludicrous situation, with all three sloops stranded until the incoming tide lifted them clear.

Although their larger guns couldn't bear, both sides began shooting at their rivals with muskets. The two sides kept up the battle for five hours, by which time Rhett had lost a dozen men. However, it was the *Henry* that freed herself first, and her skipper lay his sloop across the bows of the *Royal James* at point-blank range. The game was up, and Bonnet had no option but to surrender. Rhett spent the rest of the day rounding up his prisoners, and tending to his wounded. He then set course for Charles Town, with his three prizes following him.

The squadron reached port on 3 October, and the pirates were locked up. Despite his crimes, Bonnet was still regarded as a gentleman, and so was lodged in the private house of the local marshal. A few days later he was joined by his two officers. The house was only lightly guarded, and so on 24 October Bonnet and his sailing master escaped during the middle of the night. A reward was offered for their recapture, dead or alive, and 12 days later a patrol found them hiding in a marsh. In the scuffle, Bonnet's companion was killed, but his captain was captured and put in irons. This time Bonnet was imprisoned with the rest of his crew.

The trial had actually been under way for a week by the time Bonnet returned. All except two of the pirates had pleaded not guilty, but the evidence proved irrefutable. Of the 33 men accused, 29 of them were sentenced to death. Bonnet was not among them. Being a gentleman, he warranted his own trial. At dawn on 8 November 24 pirates were marched down to the southern tip of the city and hanged in front of a large crowd. The trial reconvened on 10 November, and two days later Bonnet was found guilty. So, on 13 November, Stede Bonnet, former major and gentleman pirate, was hanged from the gallows on White Point, accompanied by the last five members of his crew.

BLACK BELLAMY

Benjamin Hornigold was very much the founding father of the Bahamian pirates, and several characters who would become pirate captains began their criminal careers sailing under his flag. Apart from Blackbeard, the most successful of these was Sam Bellamy. Bellamy was born in Devon around 1689. We know little about his early years, but he was already an experienced seaman and a candidate for a captaincy by the time he joined Hornigold's crew. Like so many others in New Providence, he once served as a privateersman based in Port Royal. Then again, according to Cape Cod legend, he was in love with Maria Hallett from Massachusetts, but as he was an impoverished sailor her parents refused to let them marry. Consequently, he set out to seek his fortune. In either case, he formed part of Henry Jennings' expedition when he raided the Spanish salvage camp in Florida in 1715, and presumably arrived in the Bahamas with Jennings and his salvors. By 1716 Bellamy was in New Providence, serving alongside Blackbeard as part of Hornigold's crew.

Bellamy sailed on Hornigold's summer cruise of 1716, and was given command of a captured sloop, the *Mary Anne*. Soon after, Hornigold and Bellamy parted company and by the late summer, Bellamy was operating with the French pirate Olivier le Vasseur, also known as 'La Buse' (The Buzzard). The two pirates cruised the waters of the Virgin Islands, capturing several small prizes before returning to New Providence in early 1717. By the summer La Buse had teamed up with the pirate Christopher Moody and was operating off the Carolinas. Moody would later accept a pardon from Woodes Rogers, but resumed his piratical career a few months later. In early 1719 Moody and La Buse would team up again, this time off the West African coast.

For his part, Sam Bellamy captured the merchant ship *Sultana* and converted her into a pirate ship of 24 guns. He handed his sloop over to his quartermaster Palgrave Williams, and the two vessels cruised in consort. Bellamy changed ships again in February 1717 when he captured the British slave ship *Whydah Galley* in the Bahamas Channel. Named after the slave port on the West African coast, the *Whydah* was a fast, well-built vessel of 300 tons, and she was reportedly laden with a cargo of rum, gold dust and money. As pirate hauls go, this was a good one.

Bellamy made the *Whydah* his flagship and fitted her with 28 guns. Her former captain was given the *Sultana* in exchange, while Bellamy and Williams resumed their cruise in the *Whydah* and the *Mary Anne*, heading northwards. During March they captured four more vessels off Virginia. The alleged conversation between Bellamy and a merchant captain of one of his prizes was recorded by Captain Johnson. Bellamy's rant against the establishment may be

The pirate ship *Whydah*, commanded by Sam Bellamy, was wrecked off Cape Cod, Massachusetts in April 1717. The wreck was discovered in 1984, and numerous artefacts have been recovered, including these guns, displayed here as part of a travelling exhibition on the ship and its pirate crew. (Photo by John Ewing/Portland Press Herald via Getty Images)

THE VOYAGES OF SAM BELLAMY

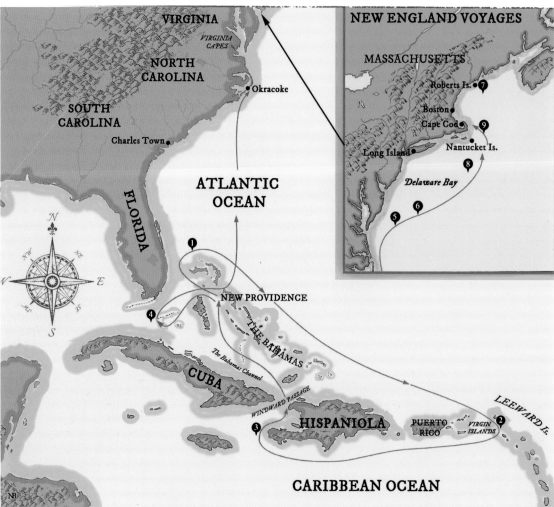

more apocryphal than a genuine speech. This said, it certainly demonstrates the views held by many pirates of the time. Bellamy railed:

> They vilify us, the scoundrels do, when there is only this difference, they rob the poor under the cover of law, forsooth, and we plunder the rich under the protection of our own courage. Had you not better make then one of us, than sneak after these villains for employment?

When the captain disagreed, Bellamy supposedly retorted:

KEY
← 1716 voyage ← 1717 voyage

1716

1. August: Benjamin Hornigold gives Sam Bellamy command of a captured sloop, the *Mary Anne*. Bellamy then parts company with his mentor and begins his own cruise.
2. September: Bellamy cruises the Leeward Islands, accompanied by the French pirate Olivier le Vasseur. Several prizes are taken.
3. November: In the Windward Passage Bellamy captures the British merchantman *Sultana*, which he takes for himself.

1717

4. February: Bellamy captures the British slave ship *Whydah* and converts her into his flagship. He releases his prisoners in the *Sultana*.
5. March: The *Whydah* and the *Mary Anne* capture several merchant ships off the Virginia Capes.
6. Early April: A storm drives Bellamy northwards towards New England, and the two pirate vessels become separated.
7. Legend has it that Bellamy planned to establish a pirate base at Roberts Island off the coast of Maine.
8. Mid April: Off Nantucket, Bellamy captures a ship carrying wine. His crew drink the cargo.
9. 26 April Off Cape Cod, the *Whydah* is overtaken by hurricane force winds and driven onto a sandbar. Only two of her crew survive the wrecking of their ship.

> You are a devilish conscience rascal, I am a free prince, and I have as much authority to make war on the whole world, as he who has a hundred sail of ships at sea, and an army of 100,000 men in the field; and this my conscience tells me: but there is no arguing with such snivelling puppies, who allow superiors to kick them about deck at pleasure.

Shortly after this encounter, the pirates were caught in a storm that drove the *Whydah* and two consorts northwards past Long Island before it abated. By 26 April 1717 they were off Cape Cod. Then a second storm hit them. Bellamy gave orders for his three ships to work their way further out to sea, but the *Whydah* was too slow, and she was driven towards the shore by hurricane force winds. The *Whydah* struck a sandbar within sight of the beach, and she rolled over. The pounding waves then broke her back, and the *Whydah* disintegrated, scattering her crew of 146 pirates into the surf. Only two men survived: a Welsh ship's carpenter who had been pressed a few months earlier, and a half-blood native of the Mosquito Coast. He was jailed, although he then disappeared from the official records, but the carpenter Thomas Davis stood trial in Boston, and was eventually acquitted.

The wreck of the *Whydah*, along with Blackbeard's *Queen Anne's Revenge*, has opened a rare window into the world of piracy in its heyday. These *grenadoes* (grenades), for instance, come from the *Whydah*, but were identical to those hurled by Blackbeard and his crew onto the deck of their assailants in the battle fought at Ocracoke Island in late 1718. (Photo By Kathryn Scott Osler/The Denver Post via Getty Images)

As for their shipmates, locals from the nearby village of Wellfleet reported that over a hundred corpses littered the shoreline. Sam Bellamy's body was never found. The prize sloop was driven ashore further up the coast, and its nine survivors were rounded up. Of these, seven were hanged in Boston. That still left Williams and the *Mary Anne*. She survived the storm, and Williams may even have visited the wreck site a few days later to see if he could recover any of the plunder. In May he captured two merchantmen off Cape Cod, but by that winter he had accepted the pardon, and so he retired from piracy.

In 1984 the wreck of the *Whydah* was discovered by wreck-hunter Barry Clifford. Over the past two decades the wreck has been excavated by Clifford and his team, and the artefacts from her are now housed in a purpose-built maritime museum in Provincetown, Massachusetts. There visitors can see the pirate ship's bronze bell, the slave shackles used by her former owners, the weaponry she carried, and even some of the plunder that for a few short months made the crew of the *Whydah* some of the richest pirates in the Americas.

THE SMALL-TIMERS

Not all the pirates mentioned in Johnson's *General History* began their careers in the Bahamas, nor did they all have spectacular successes. Many were small-time pirates, whose short careers lacked the flair of their more notorious counterparts. Richard Worley was one such pirate. In late September 1718 he and eight companions stole a ship's longboat from New York harbour and took it out to sea. They headed south, and eventually reached Delaware Bay. Off New Castle (just south of Wilmington, Delaware) they captured a small sailing ship bound for Philadelphia and then a small sloop. The pirates kept the sloop and press-ganged some of her crew, then cast their remaining victims adrift in their stolen longboat.

Their next prize was a larger sloop, outward bound for Britain, and once again the pirates upgraded their vessel. They then headed for the Bahamas. Johnson claims that Worley captured a sloop and a brig among the islands, and pressed yet more men. Worley now commanded a 6-gun sloop and 25 pirates, not all of whom were willing volunteers. They headed north again, and by late January 1719 they were off the Virginia Capes. That was when Worley's luck ran out. Colonel Rhett's veteran pirate-hunting sloops *Henry* and *Sea Nymph* were still at sea, and on 16 February they sighted Worley's sloop in the mouth of the James River.

Johnson claimed that: 'Worley and his crew determined to fight to the last gasp, and receive no quarters … so that they must either die or conquer upon the spot'. This was pure invention. With a largely pressed crew, most of the pirates would have been extremely unwilling combatants. The pirate hunters closed on each beam of the pirate sloop, fired their broadsides, and then boarded in the smoke. The one-sided battle was over in a matter of minutes, by which time all but two of the pirates lay dead. A badly wounded Worley survived the battle, and he and the other survivor were taken back to Charles Town to stand trial. They were duly hanged on the spot where Stede Bonnet had met his fate four months before.

The execution of a pirate on the gallows set up for the purpose on the foreshore at Wapping, in London. Under Admiralty law, pirates had to be executed below the high tide mark.

Another small-time pirate was John Evans, a Welsh sailing master who in September 1721 was in Port Royal, with no work. He gathered together three friends, and together they stole a large canoe. They began by robbing houses along the north shore of Jamaica, but they soon came upon a small 4-gun sloop, which they captured. They renamed her *Scowerer*. All Evans and his men needed now was a crew. They headed east, and off Puerto Rico they captured the New England merchantman *Dove*. Four of her crew joined the pirates. Then in early January 1722 they captured a merchant ship off Guadeloupe followed by two sloops. So far this had been a highly successful cruise.

Evans headed east again to Grand Cayman, where he planned to fight a duel. He and the boatswain had fallen out, and decided to settle the argument with sword and pistol. When the time came the boatswain refused to fight, prompting Evans to beat him with a stick. The man drew a pistol and shot Evans dead. He then jumped overboard and swam for the shore, but his shipmates gave chase and killed him. The pirates went ashore to bury Evans, leaving a pressed mate from the merchantman and a cabin boy on board the *Scowerer*. Between them they cut the anchor cable and sailed away to Jamaica, leaving the pirates howling for revenge on the beach.

In this Hogarth print depicting The Idle Apprentice, the young man goes to sea, while the crew of the boat taking him out to his ship taunt him about the fate awaiting him if he turns to piracy.

THE PSYCHOPATHIC EDWARD LOW

Another particularly unsavoury pirate who started his career the same way was Edward Low. He was a former London pickpocket who started afresh in the American colonies, working as a seaman. In late 1721 he joined the crew of a logwood sloop bound for the Gulf of Honduras. Once there, Low led a bungled mutiny, and was forced to flee in the ship's boat, together with 12 accomplices. As Johnson then put it, 'The next day they took a small vessel, and go in her, make a black flag, and declare war against all the world'. By December they were in the Cayman Islands, where they encountered and joined the crew of the pirate George Lowther. Low was then elected as Lowther's quartermaster. Their partnership lasted for five months, until on 28 May 1722 Lowther captured the brigantine *Rebecca* of Boston off the coast of New Jersey.

He gave command of her to Low, who converted her into a pirate ship, then set out on his own independent cruise. Low captured his first prize off Long Island, then two more off Rhode Island. The colony's governor sent out two pirate hunters, but Low avoided them, and reappeared in Marblehead in the Massachusetts colony. Johnson claims he plundered several vessels and took a schooner for himself, which he renamed *Fancy*. Although this is not supported by the historic record, Low certainly acquired a New England schooner from somewhere. He handed his brig to his quartermaster Charles Harris, and kept the 10-gun *Fancy* for himself.

Realizing the New England coast was becoming dangerous for him, he headed towards the West Indies. The *Fancy* and the brig arrived there in late August, just in time to run into a hurricane. Both vessels survived the onslaught, and, after making repairs, Low aimed to cross the Atlantic. In late September he arrived off São Miguel. In Ponta Delgada harbour Low captured several merchantmen, and destroyed all but one of them, the sloop *Rose*, which was added to the pirate squadron.

Low then captured a French merchantman, which he ransacked and left to drift. Anyone who resisted was cut down or tortured. Johnson even claims that Low and his men 'cut and mangled them in a barbarous manner'. Worse was to come. After capturing another prize a few weeks later, Low became annoyed by the quality of the meals prepared by a pressed French ship's cook. He thought that

During this period a schooner was a single or two-masted sailing vessel, although by the mid-18th century three-masted versions became more common. Their fore-and-aft sails made them popular merchant vessels, and so they were often taken by pirates as prizes.

the man, 'a greasy fellow, would fry well in the fire', so the man was bound to the mainmast, and burnt along with the ship. The pirates went on to capture several more prizes off the Cape Verde Islands, before heading back out into the Atlantic.

At the end of 1722 Low and Harris reappeared off the coast of Brazil. There Harris' brig was wrecked, but her crew were rescued by the *Fancy*. An encounter with a Portuguese sloop gave rise to another tale of cruelty. When he learned that her captain had thrown his money into the sea, Low reputedly ordered his lips to be cut out, 'which he broiled before his face, and afterwards murdered him and his crew'.

Low gave Anthony Spriggs command of the new sloop, and the cruise resumed with the two ships now heading towards the Gulf of Honduras. There they took a Spanish patrol vessel, and massacred her crew. For some reason Harris was given command of Spriggs' sloop, which he renamed the *Ranger*. The pirates then sailed north, and by late May 1723 arrived in the Carolinas where they captured two more vessels, and where Low tortured and killed one of the two captains.

On 21 June the pirates were cruising off Long Island when they spotted a sail that turned out to be the 20-gun sloop HMS *Greyhound*. Low fled in the *Fancy*, leaving Harris to fight it out. The *Ranger* was captured after a sea battle that lasted for two full hours. On 19 July, Harris and 24 of his men were hanged in Newport in the Rhode Island colony. However, Low remained at large. He fled north, capturing a small Nantucket sloop, 'the master of which ... the pirates cruelly whipped naked about the deck, making his torture their sport, after which they cut off his ears, and last of all shot him through the head, and

This 19th-century illustration shows pirates 'sweating' a prisoner – probably the captain of a newly captured merchant ship – by forcing him to run around the mainmast, encouraged by jabs from pitchforks and boarding pikes.

Another 19th-century depiction showing pirate cruelty, in this case using a captive as target practice. This actually happened to Captain Skinner of the slave ship *Cadogan* – he was pelted with empty rum bottles before being shot dead.

then sunk his vessel'. These acts of extreme violence by Low against ship captains suggested a psychopathic temperament, and a deeply held resentment against authority.

In late July he captured the large merchant ship *Merry Christmas*, which he converted into a 34-gun flagship. He also adopted the title of 'Admiral'. He crossed the Atlantic in her, capturing a sloop off the Azores and hanging half her crew. After cruising the Cape Verde Islands, he reached Sierra Leone on the West African coast, where he captured another sloop. Then, mysteriously, in January 1724, all mention of Low ceases. One suggestion was that his ship foundered in a hurricane. However, it is more likely that Low was deposed, marooned, and left to die somewhere on the African coast. In any event, Spriggs was elected as the pirates' new leader. After renaming the flagship the *Bachelor's Delight* he sailed back across the Atlantic to the Caribbean.

Johnson traced their progress to the Gulf of Honduras, then the West Indies, and finally on to the Caymans, capturing more small prizes along the way and leaving a reputation for torture in their wake. Finally though, in January 1725, Spriggs in his turn was deposed and marooned in the Gulf of Honduras; Philip Lyne then became the ship's new captain. He proved an ineffective commander,

The Dutch settlement of Curaçao lay 40 miles (64km) off the coast of the Spanish Main, but pirates avoided it, as the mercantile-oriented Dutch had little tolerance for pirates. It was here, in 1726, that the last mass hanging of pirates took place. (Westend61/Getty Images)

In 1722 Edward Low took to piracy, and went on operate from Nova Scotia down to Surinam. His fate after January 1724 is unknown. One suggestion was that his ship foundered in a hurricane, like the one depicted here.

though, and prizes were few. His cruise ended in March 1726, when the *Bachelor's Delight* was captured by two Dutch pirate hunters operating from Curaçao, where he was taken and tried. Lyne was duly hanged, along with 19 of his men, in what became the last mass pirate execution to take place in the Caribbean. The bloody path forged by Low had finally reached its end.

GEORGE LOWTHER

We know little about George Lowther, although his name suggests Scottish roots. In May 1721 he was the second mate on board the *Gambia Castle*, a 16-gun ship belonging to the Royal African Company. She arrived off Gallassee (now Banjul), on the mouth of the Gambia River, where she delivered a new garrison for the fort there. The detachment was commanded by Captain John Massey, who fell out with the traders who ran Gallassee. He and Lowther conspired to take over the ship, and duly led a successful mutiny, raised the black flag, and headed out to sea.

The pirates renamed their ship *Happy Deliverance*, and her 50-strong crew elected Lowther as her captain. He decided to head towards the West Indies, where he captured his first prize. Off Hispaniola they captured another, but there Massey made off in her with ten men. Massey threw himself on the mercy of the governor of Jamaica, but he was shipped to London, where in July 1723 he was tried, convicted and executed for piracy.

When Lowther arrived in the Cayman Islands in December 1721 he came across Edward Low. The two joined forces, and Low became Lowther's quartermaster. Then they sailed for the Gulf of Honduras, where on 10 January they captured the *Greyhound* of Boston. According to Johnson, the pirates 'not only rifled the ship, but whipped, beat and cut the men in a cruel manner'. This violence had all the hallmarks of Low rather than Lowther. They went on to capture two brigs and four sloops in the Gulf. Two sloops were added to the pirate fleet. Low was given command of one, but Lowther refused to let him operate on his own. An attempt to careen the *Happy Deliverance* ended in disaster when native tribesmen stormed the pirate camp and burned the ship. That left them with just two sloops – one commanded by Lowther (which he renamed the *Ranger*), and the other by Low.

George Lowther took to piracy after a mutiny off the African coast. His brief and not particularly successful piratical career ended with his death on a remote Caribbean island three years later.

They tried their luck in the West Indies, and captured a brig off Guadeloupe, but news of a warship patrolling in the same waters encouraged the pirates to head north towards the Virginia coast. There, in May 1722, Low sailed off on his own. On 3 June Lowther took a large New England ship, and then headed south to the Carolinas. There, they encountered the *Amy*, which fought back so effectively that the *Ranger* was deliberately run aground in an effort to avoid the *Amy*'s guns. Unable to get close enough to continue the battle, the merchant ship sailed off. A chastened Lowther refloated his ship, then took her to a secluded inlet where she was repaired. Effectively, this took all winter. By the spring of 1723 the *Ranger* was back at sea, capturing several small prizes off the Newfoundland Banks. In July they returned to the West Indies, but only captured three ships in two months.

In late September Lowther decided to careen the *Ranger*, so he sailed her down to Blanco (the Isla la Blanquilla), off the Venezuelan coast. The ship was stripped of her guns and stores, and hauled into the shallows. At that critical stage the *Eagle*, an armed merchant sloop, appeared, and her captain sailed into the bay, anchored, and pounded the defenceless *Ranger* as she lay on the beach. Lowther and a dozen other pirates escaped into the island's interior, leaving a dozen more wounded men behind to be captured. The *Eagle*'s crew managed to capture five more pirates, but Lowther remained at large. The captured pirates were all tried on St Christopher (St Kitts), and most were hanged there. The Spanish also sent a warship to Blanco, but only captured four more. Lowther and his last three men were never caught. Presumably they died of starvation on the desolate island.

In early 1725, the second-rate pirate John Gow put in to the little town of Stromness in his native Orkney and tried to pass himself off as a merchant captain. However, his identity was uncovered, and he was forced to flee to the north isles of Orkney, where he was captured. (J-P Lahall/Getty Images)

THE PIRATE GOW

One of the romantic associations we have about pirates is that they sailed among beautiful islands, fringed with palm trees, in azure seas. The career of pirate Gow reached its climax against a similar backdrop, except that there were no palm trees, and the azure waters were cold. Instead of the West Indies, this pirate is closely associated with the Orkney Islands, off the north of Scotland. In 1695 John Gow was born outside Stromness in Orkney, and like many Orcadians he took to the sea. In 1724 he signed on as a crewman on the 24-gun galley *Caroline*. Probably from the start his intention was to 'turn pirate'. He and an accomplice began by sowing the seeds for mutiny. On the night of 3 November, Gow and three accomplices set upon their captain, shooting him and throwing his body overboard. Two officers and the surgeon were also murdered. The mutineers then threatened their shipmates with a similar treatment if they objected. Gow renamed the ship *Revenge*, raised the black flag, and started hunting for prey.

The pirates captured their first prize nine days later, a sloop bound for Spain with a cargo of fish. Off Gibraltar they captured another ship carrying fish to Italy. Both ships were ransacked and sunk. Gow put in to Madeira to take provisions, but the suspicious governor refused to trade with them. Gow then sailed to the nearby Ilha de Porto Santo, where he kidnapped the governor and ransomed him for the stores he needed. The pirates then headed back out to sea. On 18 December they seized a lowly timber-carrier off the southern tip of Portugal, so Gow's luck still hadn't changed. Nine days later, though, they intercepted their first decent prize off Cape Finisterre, a French merchantman carrying Spanish wine. Gow's crew drank the cargo, then let the ship go. The *Revenge* headed south again, and on 6 January 1725 Gow captured his last prize, another fish carrier. In two months John Gow had enjoyed little success, and by now his impoverished 30-man crew were thoroughly disaffected. His solution was to head north towards his native Orkney. There he hoped to hide out amongst the islands he knew from childhood. During the voyage he changed his ship's name to the *George*, and coached his crew in their alibi: they were a stormbound merchantman on their way to Stockholm.

He arrived in Stromness harbour in late January. Inevitably, things started to go wrong. Captain Watt of the *Margaret* recognized the former *Caroline*, and knew that two of his old crew served on board her. When he met one in the street he learned the whole story, and realized that Gow was a pirate. He immediately told the authorities. Next, ten of Gow's pressed men escaped in the ship's boat, while three more hid in Stromness until Gow had sailed away. Finally, Gow threw caution aside and press-ganged eight replacements, including his own teenage

After execution the body of a pirate was often suspended in an iron cage on a prominent headland near a port, as a warning to other mariners. The body was then left there to rot away.

nephew. This caused an uproar, and so on 10 February Gow put to sea before the townspeople could storm his ship. He needed to find a safer haven where he could plan his next move.

Gow sailed the *George* around the Orkney mainland, which separates the islands into two archipelagos. Once in the North Isles they continued on to an anchorage off the northern end of the island of Eday.

The island's main landowner was James Fea of Clestrain, whose home overlooked the bay. As he approached, Gow handed the helm over to a pressed local sailor, who promptly ran the *George* hard aground on the small island off the northern part of the anchorage. The *George* could still have been pulled off if Gow had had a longboat, but his had been stolen by the deserters. His remaining boat was too small to carry the anchor and men needed to pull the ship into deeper water. Gow needed a boat. Meanwhile Fea watched the whole affair, and guessed who the mariners were. He owned the only suitable boat on the island, and he ordered his men to stave in her planks, rendering her useless. He also sent a fishing boat to ask for help.

By the time the pirates landed, Fea was ready for them. He encouraged them to drink in the hamlet of Calfsound while he invited Gow's boatswain back to his house. On the path Fea's men jumped the pirate, and the boatswain was captured. Fea then led his men back to Calfsound, where the remaining four pirates were quickly overpowered. Gow realized what had happened, but without a boat he was helpless. Instead he tried to deal his way out of trouble. During the negotiations that followed Gow and two more of his men were captured. Without a leader the remaining pirates soon surrendered.

By the time the sloop HMS *Weasel* arrived on 26 February, it was all over. The 31 pirates were all in custody, and the *George* had been refloated. By the end of March Gow and his men were safely in London's Marshalsea Prison. Gow and his men were tried on 26 May, and the trial soon reached its inevitable conclusion. On 11 June Gow and six of his shipmates were hanged at Execution Dock. An eighth pirate was hanged a week later, while the remaining pirates were released, having proved to the authorities that they had been pressed. They were lucky, as the authorities were rarely so lenient. The execution of Gow and his men represented the last substantial pirate execution to take place in London. Two more small-time pirates were hanged over the next three years, but Londoners would no longer be able to flock to see the execution of a pirate captain and his crew. The days of the 'Golden Age of Piracy' were drawing to a close.

PIRATE CODES

Once a pirate crew elected their officers they often established a set of rules that governed life on board. Several pirates used these articles, which probably had their origins in the charters set out by the buccaneers in the 17th century. Those sailors who turned to piracy from privateering would also have been used to documents of this type, which set out how prize money or plunder would be divided, or laid out compensation rates for injuries. As pirate captains, quartermasters and other officers were elected, and in most cases pirate ships were run along democratic lines, it made sense that they were unable to claim an unduly large share. Moreover, as the one-time pirate Barnaby Slush pointed out, in order to justify their extra share, captains had to prove their courage to the men who elected them: 'Pyrates and Buccaneers, are Princes to [sailors], for there, as none are exempt from General Toil and Danger; so if the Chief have a Supream Share beyond his Comrades, 'tis because he's always the Leading Man in e'ry daring Enterprize; and yet as bold as he is in all other attempts, he dares not offer to infringe the common laws of Equity; but every Associate has his due Quota.' The most detailed set of pirate articles to have survived was drawn up in 1721 by Bartholomew Roberts and his crew, and these were quoted in full by Captain Johnson:

I. Every man has a Vote in Affairs of Moment, has equal Title to the fresh Provisions, or strong Liquors, at any Time seized, & use them at pleasure, unless a Scarcity make it necessary, for the good of all, to Vote a Retrenchment.

II. Every man to be called fairly in turn, by List, on Board of Prizes, because they there on these Occasions allow'd a Shift of Cloaths: But if they defrauded the Company to the Value of a Dollar, in Plate, Jewels, or Money, MAROONING was their punishment.

III. No Person to game at Cards or Dice for Money.

IV. The Lights & Candles to be put out at eight o'Clock at Night. If any of the Crew, after that Hour, still remained inclined for Drinking, they were to do it on the open Deck.

V. To Keep their Piece, Pistols, & Cutlash clean, & fit for Service.

VI. No Boy or Woman to be allow'd amongst them. If any Man were found seducing any of the latter Sex, and carried her to Sea, disguised, he was to suffer Death.

VII. To Desert the Ship, or their Quarters in Battle, was punished with Death, or Marooning.

VIII. No striking one another on Board, but every Man's Quarrels to be ended on shore, at Sword & Pistol Thus: The Quarter-Master of the Ship, when the Parties will not come to any Reconciliation, accompanies them on Shore with what Assistance he thinks proper, & turns the Disputants Back to Back, at so many Paces, Distance. At the Word of Command, they turn and fire immediately, (or else the Piece is knocked out of their Hands). If both miss, they come to their Cutlasses, and then he is declared Victor who draws the first Blood.

IX. No Man to talk of breaking up their Way of Living, till each has shared £1000. If in order to this, any Man shall lose a Limb, or become a Cripple in their Service, he was to have 800 Dollars, out of publick Stock, and for lesser Hurts, proportionably.

X. The Captain and Quarter-Master to receive two Share of a Prize; the Master, Boatswain, & gunner, one Share and a half and other Officers, one and a Quarter.

XI. The Musicians to have Rest on the Sabbath Day, but the other six Days and Nights, none without special Favour.

HOWELL DAVIS

In September 1718 the sloops *Samuel* and *Buck* arrived off the north coast of Hispaniola. The craft had come to trade, but as most of their crew had been pirates before they accepted the pardon, Captain Brisk of the *Buck* was doubtful of their loyalty. He was right to be apprehensive. That evening the crew mutinied, and took over both vessels. The ringleaders were all former pirates: Walter Kennedy, Thomas Anstis, Christopher Moody and Howell Davis. They elected Davis as their captain.

Captain Johnson claims Davis was born in Milford Haven in Pembrokeshire, 'and was from a boy brought up to the sea'. In 1718 he was the first mate on the *Cadogan*, a Bristol slave ship, which was captured off the African coast by the pirate Edward England. England took a liking to the Welshman, so he handed the *Cadogan* over to him with orders to take her to Brazil, where he was to sell the ship and its human cargo. Instead the law-abiding crew overpowered Davis and sailed the *Cadogan* to Barbados. Davis was thrown in prison, and remained there for three months. On his release he took passage to New Providence, where he joined the crew of the *Buck*.

After the mutiny, the two captains and those men who refused to join the pirates were allowed to return to New Providence in the *Samuel*. That left Davis with 60 pirates and a 6-gun sloop. He put in to Coxon's Hole on the eastern tip of Cuba to careen the *Buck*, and then cruised the Windward Passage, where the pirates captured two French merchantmen, a ship from Philadelphia and a few sloops. Davis knew he daren't linger, as Woodes Rogers would come looking for him. So he decided to cross the Atlantic and try his luck off the West African coast.

This depiction of the Welsh pirate Howell Davis was first produced to accompany Captain Johnson's *A General History of the Robberies and Murders of the Most Notorious Pyrates* (1724). It shows Davis attacking the Royal Africa Company's fort guarding the mouth of the Gambia River.

The 'bight' of West Africa was the area where most early 18th-century slave ships picked up their human cargo, either through established trading posts or by dealing directly with the African rulers in towns such as Whydah (or Ouidah) and Calabar. Davis also knew those waters better than he knew the Caribbean. The pirates visited the Cape Verde Islands, where they spent a month pretending they were English privateers.

Then in February 1719 they captured the 26-gun ship *Loyal Merchant*, anchored off Porto Inglês. Davis renamed her *Royal James*, and, abandoning the *Buck*, he took over this new prize instead. By 23 February the pirates were off Gallassee (now Banjul) in the mouth of the Gambia River. The place was defended by a fort owned by the Royal African Company, but when Davis arrived the defences were only half-finished. Its commander lived aboard the *Royal Ann*, a company ship moored in the harbour. Davis passed himself off as a merchant, but then under cover of darkness attacked the *Royal Ann*, capturing her after a short fight. Davis then seized the fledgling fort and the town, and for the next few days Gallassee became a pirate den. Almost on cue a 14-gun pirate brig appeared, flying the Jolly Roger. The newcomer was none other than the French pirate Olivier le Vasseur, or 'La Buse' (The Buzzard), and both pirate crews celebrated for a week before heading south together. There they joined forces with yet another pirate, Thomas Cocklyn, who commanded the *Mourroon* of 24 guns. Davis was now part of a powerful pirate squadron.

In 1717 both Cocklyn and 'La Buse' had been part of the pirate crew of Christopher Moody, who operated from New Providence. Moody regarded Cocklyn as a psychopath, and so was happy to give him his own command, the galley *Rising Sun*, which Cocklyn renamed *Mourroon*. Then Moody's crew deposed him, and elected 'La Buse' as their new captain. As Moody had formed part of the original mutinous crew of the *Buck*, that meant that the three shipmates were reunited, and probably none of them trusted any of the others.

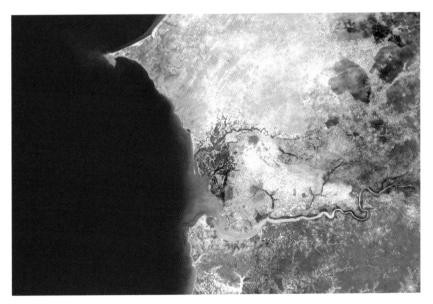

The mouth of the Gambia River on the west coast of Africa was a popular stopping place for slave ships. In late 1718 Howell Davis appeared there in search of prizes, captured a half-built fort, and turned the port of Gallassee into a temporary pirate rendezvous. (Planet Observer/ Getty Images)

THE VOYAGE OF HOWELL DAVIS

However, 'La Buse' and Cocklyn declared Davis to be their pirate 'commodore', and together they decided to attack another Royal African Company fort on Bunce Island, just down the coast at Sierra Leone (Lion Mountain). The real prize was not the fort, but the six merchantmen sheltering beneath its guns. The pirates landed and assaulted the place, which surrendered once the defenders had exhausted all their gunpowder. However, this was the only joint action taken by the three pirate crews, who fell out during the ensuing celebrations, 'the strong liquor stirring up a spirit of discord among them'.

1. January 1719: Howell Davis arrives in the Cape Verde Islands in the sloop *Buck*, and spends a month there, masquerading as a pirate hunter.

2. February: Davis raids Porto Inglês and captures the *Loyal Merchant*. He takes her for himself and renames her *Royal James*. The *Buck* is abandoned.

3. March: Davis arrives at Gallassee on the African coast and captures the Royal Africa Company fort there. He is then joined by a French pirate.

4. April: Sailing together, the pirates capture six prizes off Bunce Island. Davis keeps one, and renames her the *Royal Rover*.

5. May: The pirates avoid Cape Coast Castle, as they sail down the coast, looking for prizes.

6. June: Davis captures three more British slave ships off Anambu (now Anomabu), and some of their crews join the pirates. One of these recruits is Bartholomew Roberts.

7. Late June: The rotten *Royal James* is abandoned near Calabar, and Davis sails the *Royal Rover* south, towards Principe.

8. July: In Principe, Davis poses as a pirate hunter. However, the Portuguese learn of the deception, and ambush and kill Davis and several of his men. The survivors escape out to sea in the *Royal Rover*.

The three groups went their separate ways, and according to Johnson, Howell Davis delivered the parting lines: 'Hark ye, Cocklyn and La Bouse, I find by strengthening you, I have put a rod in your hands to whip myself, but I'm still able to deal with you both; but since we met in love, let us part in love, for I find that three of a trade can never agree'. There was probably just too much bad blood between the three captains. Worse, a group who titled themselves 'lords' set

The Welsh-born Howell Davis was the mate of a slave ship when he led a mutiny and turned to piracy. He operated on both sides of the Atlantic before his death in the summer of 1719.

themselves up as Davis' lieutenants, and considered themselves superior to the rest of the pirate crew. Leaving the others to their own devices, Davis took the *Royal James* south, capturing two British slave ships on the way. He then fought a Dutch slave ship that refused to surrender to him. She was captured after a long-running fight, and Davis kept her for himself, renaming her *Royal Rover*. Walter Kennedy was given command of the *Royal James*.

His two ships then kept clear of the powerful Cape Coast Castle, but put in to the slave trading anchorage of Anambu further down the coast. Three British slave ships lay at anchor there, and all of them were captured, yielding a small fortune in gold dust, money and trade goods. Several of the seamen joined Davis' crew, including a Welshman called Bartholomew Roberts, the second mate of one of the slavers. He would go on to become the most successful pirate of the 'Golden Age'.

The two pirate ships continued on to the east, but the *Royal James* was leaking badly, and they were forced to abandon her near Calabar. They crowded into the *Royal Rover* and turned south towards the Portuguese island of Principe. Once more, Davis pretended to be a British privateering captain. At first his deception worked. The Portuguese governor welcomed Davis, and for two weeks the crew repaired their ship and replenished her stores.

Then, in early July, the deception fell apart. A Portuguese-speaking slave escaped from the *Royal Rover* and told the governor who the visitors really were. He also revealed Davis' plan to kidnap the governor and hold him to ransom. This time it was Davis who was outsmarted. The following morning he went ashore as usual, accompanied by ten of his leading officers – the 'lords'. The pirates accepted an invitation to the governor's house and duly walked into an ambush. The island's militia cut the pirates down, and Davis was badly wounded. He tried to drag himself away, but died in the attempt. Only Walter Kennedy and one other escaped the ambush, and were picked up by the *Royal Rover*'s boats.

Before the pirates could flee they had to pass the battery guarding the harbour entrance. Kennedy opened fire on both the fort and the town. Within minutes the garrison abandoned the battery, and the pirates sailed off, leaving behind a burning town, a damaged fort and the dead body of their captain.

THE RISE OF BLACK BART

While everyone has heard of Blackbeard, Bartholomew Roberts (or 'Black Bart') is unknown to many. However, he was far more successful, and posed more of a threat before he was finally cornered off the West African coast. One of the last of the pirates of the 'Golden Age', he was known as the 'Great Pyrate' by his contemporaries, and his passing effectively marked the end of the era.

Roberts was born in the Welsh hamlet of Castell Newydd Bach (Little Newcastle), near Abergwaun (Fishguard) during the early 1680s. His original name was John Robert, but he changed his name before he became a pirate. His nickname of 'Black Bart' stemmed from his dark complexion. By all accounts he

The Welsh-born pirate Bartholomew Roberts was reputedly something of a smart dresser, and was reportedly wearing this elegant damascened coat when he was killed in battle off the coast of West Africa.

OPPOSITE This early 18th-century French slave ship is typical of the slavers that were often captured by pirates, and sometimes converted into pirate vessels themselves. They had a reputation for being fast, an important feature for ships engaged in transporting a human cargo across the Atlantic.

was good-looking by the standards of the day. In late May 1719 he was the second mate on the British slave ship *Princess* when she was captured off Anambu on the West African Coast. He promptly joined the pirate Howell Davis' crew.

Following their escape from Principe, the pirates had to elect a new captain. The surviving 'lords' were unpopular with the crew, and so, as Captain Johnson put it, 'Roberts was accordingly elected, although he had not been above six weeks among them.' On 26 July he captured his first prize off Cape Lopez, a Dutch slave ship, which he plundered on 26 July, then sent on her way. The following day they took an English slave ship, and her crew were pressed into service. Her master, Thomas Grant, recounted that the pirates took gold dust weighing 50lb (23kg), and that her crew remained involuntary pirates for another six months. Two more prizes followed. So far the cruise had been highly successful, but Roberts decided it was time to quit the African coast.

When offered a choice between Brazil or the Indian Ocean, the crew elected to head west. They spent a month crossing the Atlantic, but for two more months they cruised off the Brazilian coast without capturing a single prize. Then, in late November, they approached Bahia (now Salvador). When Bartholomew Roberts neared the harbour entrance as dusk was falling, he saw the place was filled with ships. It was the Lisbon fleet, Portugal's own small treasure *flota*. Roberts decided to attack.

Disguising the *Royal Rover* as a merchantman, Roberts entered the anchorage under cover of darkness, came alongside one of the ships, and captured her without the alarm being raised. He asked her captain which ship was the richest one in the fleet, and he pointed out the *Sagrada Familia*, a heavily armed merchantman. Roberts headed towards this new target. The Portuguese captain was no fool, and roused his men. Seeing that surprise had been lost, Roberts fired a broadside and steered his ship alongside. His men boarded the Portuguese ship, and after a short but violent fight they captured her. Dawn was now breaking, though, and the Portuguese *flota* was preparing for action. As Roberts towed his prize towards the open sea, a Portuguese man-of-war moved to cut him off. Roberts dodged round her and made it out of the harbour. The *Royal James* cast loose her prize and the two ships sailed off, leaving the Portuguese far behind.

The raid on Bahia was a triumph. The *Sagrada Familia* was carrying the Portuguese equivalent of 240,000 pieces-of-eight as well as a diamond-studded crucifix destined for the Portuguese king. Roberts presented it to the French governor when the pirates put in to the Île du Diable (Devil's Island) off what is now French Guiana, in return for a safe haven for a few weeks. On the way there Roberts had captured a brig, which he renamed the *Fortune*, and added her to his fleet. One evening his lookouts spotted a ship. Roberts used the *Fortune* to intercept her, but he lost the ship in the darkness, and a storm drove him further from the island. By the time he returned he found that the *Royal Rover* and the *Sagrada Familia* had vanished, spirited away by Robert Kennedy, together with all the plunder. Roberts and his men were furious, but there was nothing they could do. The pirates had been robbed by their own shipmates.

This depiction of Bartholomew Roberts was used to illustrate Captain Johnson's *A General History of the Robberies and Murders of the Most Notorious Pyrates*, first published in 1724. Reputedly, the jewelled crucifix around his neck was taken by him from the Portuguese treasure galleon *Sagrada Familia*.

THE ADMIRAL OF THE LEEWARD ISLES

Bartholomew Roberts resumed his piratical career with the 10-gun sloop *Fortune* and 40 men. In an attempt to avoid another desertion, he drew up a set of articles. The idea was as much to bind everyone together by an incriminating document as an attempt to enforce discipline.

In January 1720 Roberts headed north, ransacking the sloop *Philippa* off Tobago, then two sloops and a brig off Barbados. These attacks attracted attention, and so two pirate-hunting ships put to sea to hunt down Roberts.

One was the *Philippa*, now re-armed and seeking revenge, and the other was the larger *Somerset*. Together they carried 120 men, three times the crew of the *Fortune*. However, Roberts had just been reinforced, having joined forces with the French pirate Montigny de Palisse off Barbados.

When the pirates sighted two sails approaching they gave chase, and only realized they were pirate hunters at the last minute. De Palisse immediately fled, but the *Fortune* and the *Somerset* traded broadsides. The smaller *Philippa* seemed to have taken no part in the brief action that followed. Roberts kept his distance, and, realizing he was out-gunned, he turned away towards the north. The *Somerset* gave chase, but according to Johnson the pirates escaped by 'throwing over their guns, and other heavy goods, and thereby lightening the vessel'.

The fishing grounds of Newfoundland and the Grand Banks proved to be a lucrative hunting ground for Bartholomew Roberts, who captured dozens of prizes during his piratical cruise there.

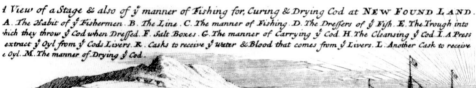

A View of a Stage & also of ye manner of Fishing for, Curing & Drying Cod at NEW FOUND LAND.
A. The Habit of ye Fishermen. B. The Line. C. The manner of Fishing. D. The Dressers of ye Fish. E. The Trough into
which they throw ye Cod when Dressed. F. Salt Boxes. G. The manner of Carrying ye Cod. H. The Cleansing ye Cod. I. A Press
extract ye Oyl from ye Cods Livers. K. Casks to receive ye Water & Blood that comes from ye Livers. L. Another Cask to receive
ye Oyl. M. The manner of Drying ye Cod.

After evading the pirate hunters, Roberts put in to Dominica to careen the *Fortune*, only to find 13 sailors who had been marooned there by the French. All of them volunteered to join his crew. The pirates spent the next few weeks dodging French naval patrols, sent out by the governor of Martinique when he learned that a pirate ship was in the area. This prompted Roberts to design a new flag, featuring an image of him, sword and hourglass in hand, standing astride two skulls. One was marked ABH ('A Barbadian's Head'), the other AMH ('A Martiniquan's Head').

It was now clear that the West Indies was a dangerous place, so Roberts headed north to attack the Newfoundland fishing and whaling fleets. Both fishing and whaling were lucrative businesses in 1720, and the pirates expected rich pickings. The *Fortune* arrived off the Newfoundland coast in June, and Roberts began by attacking the large fishing station of Trepassey, in north-eastern Newfoundland. On 21 June the pirates sailed into the harbour 'with their black colours flying, drums beating, and trumpets sounding'. Rather than fight, the crew of the guardship *Bideford* fled ashore, leaving the harbour defenceless. As Johnson recalled, 'It is impossible particularly to recount the

Pirates had no access to shipyards or repair facilities. When underwater growth on their hulls began to slow ships down, the pirates took them to a remote beach and careened them – beaching the ships to scrape their hulls. This beach in Tortola was considered a suitable careening place. (Walter Bibikow/Getty Images)

THE VOYAGES OF BARTHOLOMEW ROBERTS

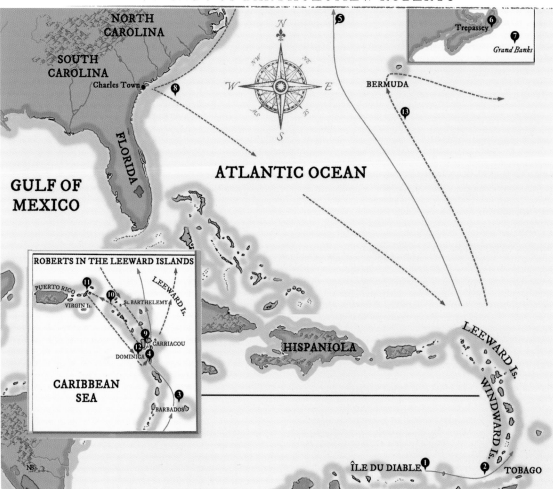

destruction and havoc they made here, burning and sinking all the shipping, except a Bristol galley, and destroying the fisheries, and [landing] stages of the poor planters, without remorse or compunction'. Some 22 ships were captured that day, along with 250 small fishing boats.

Roberts abandoned his worn-out sloop for the 16-gun Bristol galley, and the pirates then cruised off the Newfoundland Banks, capturing another ten ships, most of them French. One was a powerful 26-gun merchantman, which Roberts took for himself, giving her crew the Bristol ship instead. He renamed her the *Good Fortune*. At this point de Palisse arrived in his sloop *Sea King*, apologizing for fleeing the fight off Barbados, and the two ships continued the

KEY

◀—— Outward voyage to the Caribbean   ◀ - - -Return voyage from Newfoundland

1. November 1719: Having captured a Portuguese treasure galleon, Bartholomew Roberts puts in to the Île du Diable to divide her cargo. When a sail is sighted, Roberts gives chase. His deputy Charles Kennedy seizes his moment and makes off in the Portuguese galleon.

2. January 1720: Having lost his treasure, Roberts sails to Tobago in his remaining sloop, where he captures a prize.

3. February: Three more prizes are captured off Barbados. He joins up with the French pirate Montigny de Palisse, but the pair are soon driven off by Barbadian pirate hunters.

4. March: Roberts careens his sloop in Dominica, but again he is driven away from the Windward Islands by pirate hunters.

5. May: He sails north towards Newfoundland in search of easier prey.

6. 21 June: He attacks the fishing station of Trepassey in Newfoundland, capturing one ship and destroying 22 others.

7. July: After de Palisse rejoins him, Roberts captures several more prizes off the Grand Banks. He then heads south again.

8. August: Roberts captures a prize off Charles Town, and then sets a course towards the West Indies.

9. Early September: On reaching the West Indies, Roberts careens his ship at Carriacou.

10. Late September: Roberts and de Palisse join forces again and attack Basseterre and St Barthelemy. They also capture two ships.

11. Early October: Roberts renames one of the ships the *Royal Fortune,* which now becomes his flagship. He cruises the Virgin Islands, where he captures a brig, which becomes his latest *Royal Fortune,* the previous one being abandoned.

12. Late October: Off Dominica Roberts captures a large Dutch merchant ship, which becomes the third *Royal Fortune.* He and de Palisse then destroy 15 more ships lying off the island.

13. November: Roberts leaves the Caribbean, to avoid pursuit, and abandoning de Palisse sails northwards to Bermuda. He then heads across the Atlantic to the west coast of Africa.

cruise together. Several more prizes followed in quick succession. In all, Roberts' Newfoundland cruise resulted in the pillaging or destruction of more than 40 ships, and hundreds of smaller craft. However, Roberts knew that warships would be sent to the area, so he moved south again.

By late August he was off South Carolina, where he captured a small vessel and stripped her of her water casks. By September Roberts and de Palisse had returned to the West Indies and put in to Carriacou (now La Désirade), between St Vincent and Grenada, to repair their ships. In October, Roberts sailed the *Good Fortune* into the harbour of Basseterre on St Christopher (St Kitts) 'where being denied all succour and assistance from the government, they fired in revenge on the town, and burnt two ships in the road'. These ships also provided Roberts with a handful of new recruits.

Then Roberts sailed north to the tiny French island of St Barthelemy, between St Christopher and Anguilla. The French governor lacked the power to resist, so as well as indulging in rum and the company of the local women, as Johnson claims, they were also able to trade their plundered goods with impunity. Roberts also renamed his ship again, this time calling her the *Royal Fortune*. In turn, de Palisse adopted Roberts' old name of *Good Fortune* for his sloop. Roberts also adopted an even fancier title, as a newspaper reported that 'They write from St Christopher that Captain Roberts, who is the most desperate pirate of all who range these seas, now calls himself Admiral of the Leewards Isles'. However, by the time the newspaper came out the admiral was thousands of miles from the area, terrorizing his way along the African coast.

THE 'GREAT PYRATE'

After quitting St Barthelemy, the pirates captured a 22-gun brig off Tortola. As she was in much better condition than his own ship, Roberts transferred into her, and she became the new *Royal Fortune*. By late October he was off St Lucia, where he captured a brig and a sloop. He kept the sloop as a store ship, then moved back north to Dominica. There, off the main harbour, the *Royal Fortune* fought a well-armed Dutch merchantman of 42 guns. The two sides battled it out, and this time de Palisse stayed to lend a hand. The pirates eventually captured the Dutch ship and massacred her crew. She duly became the third *Royal Fortune*. After watching the massacre, the 15 small vessels in the harbour all meekly capitulated.

While in Dominica, Roberts announced his decision to sail to West Africa. He pointed out that every warship in the Americas would now be looking for them, and so Africa represented a safer option. So in early November they sailed to Bermuda, where they picked up the trade winds that would carry them eastwards. In early December they came upon a Portuguese convoy off the Cape Verde Islands. Roberts gave chase, but not only did the convoy escape, contrary winds also made it impossible to reach the African coast. So Roberts returned to the West Indies, capturing several vessels before putting into Samana Bay on Hispaniola for repairs. There, Roberts shot a group of deserters, so clearly morale was a problem. Roberts needed a few dramatic successes to bolster his men.

On 18 February 1721 the *Royal Fortune* and the *Good Fortune* appeared off St Lucia, where Roberts cut out a Dutch merchantman. He then used her as a decoy, pretending to be a slaver. Several local sloops were captured, and Roberts had his morale-boosting success. He lingered in the West Indies until late March, then sailed north towards Virginia. At that point de Palisse decided to go his own way. Left with only two ships, Roberts decided it was time to make another attempt to reach Africa. However, in late April, somewhere near

Bermuda, the *Good Fortune* parted company with the pirate flagship, as her captain Thomas Anstis went off on his own cruise. This desertion left Roberts with only the *Royal Fortune*, his plunder and some 228 men.

Roberts arrived off the Cape Verde Islands in late May, and after taking on stores he finally made his African landfall off the mouth of the Senegal River. There he captured two French sloops. Roberts kept them as scouting ships, renaming one of them the *Ranger*. By the time he reached Sierra Leone it was the end of June, and the anchorage was empty. His men spent six weeks there, repairing their ships, and what Johnson described as 'whoring and drinking'. Eventually they continued on down the coast, and off the mouth of the Cestos River (now in Liberia) they came upon the Royal African Company ship *Onslow*, commanded by Captain Gee. When the pirates arrived most of the crew were ashore, and the ship was captured with ease. Many of her crew even volunteered to join Roberts' band. Roberts gave Gee his own ship and commandeered the 40-gun *Onslow*, which became the fourth and last *Royal Fortune*.

Bartholomew Roberts, shown off the west coast of Africa. Behind him is his flagship *Royal Fortune*, the fourth ship he gave that name to, accompanied by the smaller pirate ship *Great Ranger*, about to capture a fleet of slave ships anchored off Whydah.

BARTHOLOMEW ROBERTS IN AFRICA

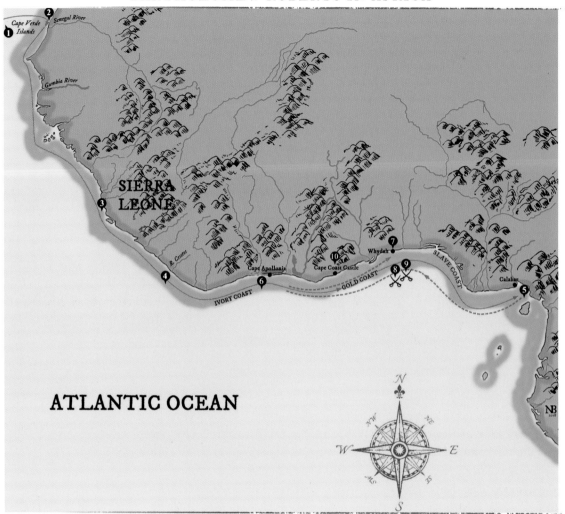

The cruise continued, with the new *Royal Fortune* and the *Ranger* following the coast as far as Old Calabar (now in Nigeria), which they reached in October. They captured three slave ships there, but the hostility of the locals prompted an early departure, so they continued down to Cape Lopez. After watering, Roberts headed back to Cape Apollonia, where the pirates captured two more slave ships. From there they headed to Whydah (now Ouidah), arriving there in early January 1722. The anchorage was crowded with 11 slave ships, all of which surrendered as soon as the pirates appeared. One of them was added to the fleet, becoming the 32-gun *Great Ranger*, while the original sloop *Ranger* was renamed the *Little Ranger*.

KEY

———1721 voyage   ◄ ─ ─1722 voyage   ✕ Battle

1721

1. Late May: Bartholomew Roberts arrives at the Cape Verde Islands in the *Royal Fortune*, and takes on provisions there.
2. June: He makes his African landfall off the Senegal River. He captures two French sloops there and renames one the *Ranger*.
3. Late June: Roberts spends six weeks careening his ships on the coast of Sierra Leone.
4. August: Off the Cestos River he captures the Royal African Company's slave ship *Onslow*. She becomes the fourth and last *Royal Fortune*.
5. October: On reaching Calabar, the pirates capture three British slave ships. Attempts to careen the *Royal Fortune* are foiled by the hostility of the locals.

1722

6. Early January: Off Cape Apollonia Roberts captures two more slave ships.
7. 11 January: Roberts arrives off Whydah and captures 11 slave ships. One of them is renamed the *Great Ranger,* while the *Ranger* is renamed *Little Ranger*. One slave ship is burned when its captain refuses to pay the pirates any protection money.
8. 5 February: The British frigate HMS *Swallow* arrives off Whydah, and not knowing her identity Roberts sends the *Great Ranger* off in pursuit. Captain Ogle of the *Swallow* leads the *Great Ranger* over the horizon, then turns, attacks and captures her.
9. 10 February: When the *Swallow* reappears off Whydah, Roberts sails the *Royal Fortune* out to give battle. In the fight that follows he is killed by the *Swallow's* first broadside. His crew fight on, but eventually the pirate flagship is captured.
10. April: The surviving pirates are tried at Cape Coast Castle, and 52 of them are hanged.

The pirates were still at anchor off Whydah as dawn rose on 5 February. Lookouts spotted a ship approaching. Roberts and his men had spent the night drinking, so the pirates were caught napping. The newcomer was HMS *Swallow* of 50 guns, commanded by Captain Chaloner Ogle. Roberts sent the *Great Ranger* after her, the *Swallow* pretended to evade, and the chase continued over the horizon. Ogle then slowed down. When the *Great Ranger* was too close to escape, Ogle sprang his trap and fired a broadside. A two-hour sea battle followed, by the end of which the *Ranger* was a bloody shambles. The pirates finally struck their colours. On 10 February the *Swallow* reappeared off Whydah, and this time Roberts sailed out to give battle. Roberts put on his finest clothes: 'a rich crimson damask waistcoat and breeches, a red feather in his hat, a gold chain around his neck, with a diamond cross hanging to it'. As he got under way, Roberts also ordered the black flag to be hoisted.

Ogle recalled, 'The pirate sailing better than us, shot ahead about half a gunshot'. He fired a broadside, and then, 'We continued firing (without intermission) such guns as we could bring to bear'. Bartholomew Roberts was killed in the first salvo. The death of the pirate captain took the fight out of his crew: 'many deserted their quarters.' The *Swallow* continued firing, 'till by favour of the wind we came alongside again, and after exchanging a few more shot, about half past one, his main-mast came down, being shot away … at two she struck, and called for quarters.'

The 'Great Pyrate' Bartholomew Roberts was dead, and those who survived of his crew were taken in chains to Cape Coast Castle, just along the coast from Whydah. The 77 African pirates were sold to slave traders, while their remaining shipmates were tried for their crimes. Their trial began on 28 March, and lasted for three weeks. Finally, on 20 April 1722, 52 of the pirates were sentenced to

On 5 February 1722 Captain Chaloner Ogle (1681–1750) commanding the 50-gun frigate HMS *Swallow* caught up with Bartholomew Roberts off the West African coast. His frigate and Roberts' *Good Fortune* exchanged fire, and Roberts was killed by Ogle's second broadside.

death, while another 37 received lengthy sentences in the Cape Coast mines, or were incarcerated in a London prison. A further 79 were acquitted or respited, having proved they had been forced to join Roberts against their will. The remainder died of the wounds or of disease while in prison. For some historians, this mass hanging marked the end of the 'Golden Age of Piracy', although, as always, there were still a few piratical loose ends to tidy up. So, the pirate scourge would continue.

The end of the line for Bartholomew Roberts' crew was Cape Coast Castle on West Africa's Gold Coast (now Ghana). It was here, on 28 March 1722, that 52 pirates were hanged. Another 37 were imprisoned in England or sentenced to work in the Cape Coast mines. (MyLoupe/UIG/Getty Images)

BLACK BART'S LORDS: KENNEDY AND ANSTIS

Two pirates who once sailed with Bartholomew Roberts went on to forge their own piratical careers. The first of these was Walter Kennedy, born to Irish parents in London in 1695. He began his criminal career as a pickpocket before gravitating to burglary. Later he became a sailor, and in 1718 he took part in Woodes Rogers' expedition to the Bahamas. Later that year he was one of the crew members of the sloop *Buck* who mutinied off Hispaniola. He subsequently sailed with Howell Davis, and then Bartholomew Roberts. In late November 1719, at the Île du Diable, Roberts left Kennedy in charge of his flagship the *Royal Rover* when he went chasing after a prize. Kennedy might have been left in charge, but he was unpopular, and, being illiterate, he lacked the navigational skills required by any captain. All that held his crew together was his ferocity.

WALTER KENNEDY, THE PIRATE LORD

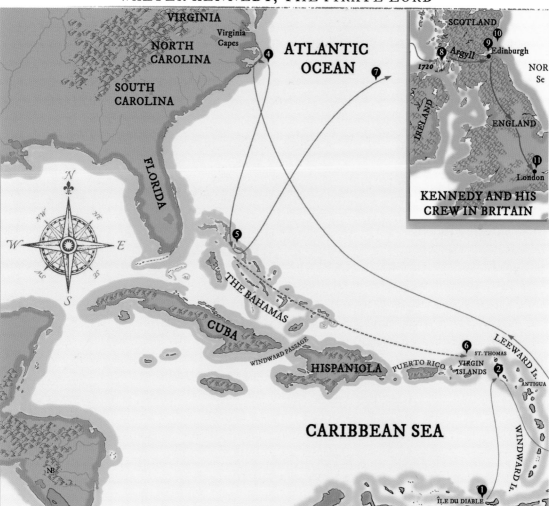

Imposing his will on the reluctant crew, Kennedy moved the treasure from the *Sagrada Familia* into the *Royal Rover*, and gave the treasure ship to his prisoners, who sailed her to Antigua. Kennedy then abandoned Roberts, and sailed off in the pirate flagship. On 15 December he captured a small merchantman off Barbados, then headed to Virginia, where he spent a fruitless month cruising off the Chesapeake. Eventually giving up, he headed south towards warmer waters. His one encounter resulted in little plunder and the defection of eight more pirates, who chose to risk sailing with the merchant captain rather than with Kennedy. Six of them were eventually tried and hanged.

1. November 1719: The pirate Bartholomew Roberts puts in to the Île du Diable with two vessels, plus a captured Portuguese treasure ship, the *Sagrada Familia*. A sail is sighted, and when Roberts sets off to investigate, Walter Kennedy, commanding the other vessel, the *Royal Rover*, seizes the *Sagrada Familia* and makes off with the plunder.

2. Early December: Somewhere in the Leeward Islands Kennedy transfers the plunder to the *Royal Rover* and divides up the treasure. He then frees his Portuguese prisoners, who sail the empty treasure ship into Antigua.

3. 15 December: Kennedy is cruising off Barbados when he captures the brig *Sea Nymph*. Some of his crew wish to leave with their share of the plunder, so he hands the prize over to them and heads north.

4. January 1720: Kennedy appears off the Virginia Capes, where he captures a small prize. Once again some of his crew abscond in her, leaving the *Royal Rover* short-handed.

5. Mid-February: Having sailed south again, Kennedy captures the merchantman *Eagle* of New York while cruising off the Bahamas. While most of the pirates drink her cargo of rum, Kennedy transfers his share of the plunder into the *Eagle* and sails off in her with 48 men.

6. Early March: The remaining pirates sail the *Royal Rover* down to the Leeward Islands, and anchor off St Thomas. While most of them are ashore, their pirate ship is captured by pirate-hunters. However, the *Royal Rover* founders in a storm while being escorted to the island of Nevis.

7. March–April: Meanwhile, Kennedy embarks on a transatlantic voyage in the *Eagle*, in an attempt to make a landfall in his native Ireland.

8. May: Instead, the *Eagle* is caught in a storm as she approaches the Irish coast, and the damaged ship makes landfall of the west coast of Argyll in Scotland. Kennedy and his crew abandon the *Eagle*, and go ashore with their plunder.

9. June: The pirates split up. While Kennedy and a few others set off to the south, the bulk of his crew heads to Edinburgh. However, their wealth arouses suspicion, and they are arrested.

10. December: The pirates are tried in Edinburgh, and nine of them are sentenced and hanged.

11. July 1721: In London, a now penniless Kennedy is arrested for theft. He is identified as a pirate, and is tried and sentenced. On 21 July he is hung in Wapping's Execution Dock.

In February 1720 Kennedy in the *Royal Rover* captured the merchantman *Eagle*, which he claimed for himself. He abandoned his old pirate ship and sailed away with the Bahia plunder, abandoning the *Royal Rover* and her skeleton crew. She was eventually captured off St Thomas by British pirate hunters from Nevis, but she foundered in a storm off St Croix before she could be brought into port. Meanwhile, Kennedy crossed the Atlantic in the *Eagle*, but his ship was damaged in a storm, and the pirates abandoned her on the coast of Argyll, in western Scotland. They split into two groups, as Kennedy and one party walked south to England, while the remainder headed towards Edinburgh. This second group aroused suspicion when they spent Portuguese coins on drink, and they were arrested and tried when they reached Edinburgh in December. Nine of them were hanged. As for Kennedy, he reached London, but was arrested for theft, and in prison he was identified as a pirate. On 21 July 1721 he was hanged at Execution Dock.

The next defector from Bartholomew Roberts' crew was Thomas Anstis. He was another of the men who mutinied on the *Buck* in 1718. Like Kennedy he was one of the 'lords', or inner cabal of Howell Davis' crew, and he continued to serve as Roberts' trusted deputy, eventually being given command of the 18-gun pirate brig *Good Fortune*. However, in April 1721 he deserted Roberts during a transatlantic crossing, and thereafter he forged his own career. In the West Indies he captured several small merchantmen, but ran into two French warships off Martinique, forcing him to flee to the Gulf of Campeche. There he was joined for a time by Montigny de Palisse. In late October he captured two large merchantmen, keeping one of them called the *Morning Star* as his consort, and giving command of her to John Finn, one of his lieutenants.

Their next attack took place off Tobago in December, and then, after a second unsuccessful cruise through the West Indies, the pirates were reported off the Venezuelan coast. However, by early 1722 most of the pirates were thoroughly demoralized. They deposed Anstis as captain, and then tried to appeal to the authorities in Jamaica for clemency and a pardon. They spent four months hiding out in Cuba, waiting for a reply that never came. Johnson suggests they spent their time holding mock pirate trials. These involved the pirates appointing a judge and jury, and then trying one of their own. Finally, by the end of August, they gave up the wait and resumed their piratical voyage.

They cruised off the southern coast of Cuba, but no worthwhile ships appeared for them to attack. Then in late September, Finn ran the *Morning Star* aground off Little Cayman. Hours later two British warships arrived, and, while the *Good Fortune* escaped, some 40 pirates were left behind to be captured. Finn took the *Good Fortune* through the Leeward Islands that winter, and reached Tobago in the spring of 1723. They put in to careen the ship, but on 17 May HMS *Winchelsea* appeared, and this time, while the *Good Fortune* escaped, Finn and five pirates were left behind to be captured. They were all eventually tried and executed on Antigua.

Anstis tried to regain his old command, but instead some of the crew mutinied, shot Anstis in his hammock as he slept, and sailed the pirate ship to Curaçao. There the Dutch authorities pardoned the mutineers and imprisoned the rest. Their trial was delayed for several months as the Dutch prosecutors gathered evidence, but eventually in early 1726 it was held, and 18 pirates were condemned and hanged. That was effectively the end of the chain of events that had begun eight years before with the mutiny on the *Buck* piracy.

The execution of Anstis' crew was the last mass hanging of the period. By then it was clear that piracy didn't pay. A string of recent high-profile trials and hangings in London, Boston, West Africa and the West Indies underlined the point. So those pirates became the last of their breed. By then the mythology of piracy had already begun to overshadow its grim reality. On 24 May 1724, Captain Johnson published his first edition of *A General History of the Robberies and Murders of the Most Notorious Pyrates*. From that point on, piracy became a subject of vicarious titillation rather than first-hand terror.

When the pirate Thomas Anstis and his crew applied for a pardon in 1722, they spent several months in Cuba waiting for a reply. Johnson suggests that they passed the time by holding mock pirate trials, acting as judge and jury to their shipmates.

Chapter Seven

THE PIRATE ROUND

THE LURE OF THE INDIAN OCEAN

Piracy was not just limited to the waters of the Caribbean and West Africa. During the last decades of the 17th century, pirates began to venture as far as the Indian Ocean. The big advantage of operating there was the wealth being shipped between India or the Far East and Europe. Ever since Vasco da Gama opened up a new sea route to the Indies in the late 15th century, European seafarers had been shipping the spices of the East to an appreciative market back home.

At first it was the Portuguese who held this trade monopoly, and their ships severed Arabian control of the spice trade by transporting these exotic cargoes by sea rather than across the desert. Consequently, huge fortunes could be made in trade with the Spice Islands of Indonesia, or with the great coastal cities of the Indian sub-continent. By the start of the 17th century other European maritime nations had ventured into the Indian Ocean.

The Comoros Islands lie astride the northern entrance to the Mozambique Channel, between East Africa and Madagascar. They were often used as a watering place for passing merchant ships – and for pirate ones. Johanna Island (now Anjouan) shown here was the most popular watering place in the Comoros archipelago. (John Seaton Callahan/Getty Images)

The first of these was the Dutch East India Company, known as Vereenigde Oostindische Compagnie (or VOC), which was founded in 1602. The following year it opened up its first trading post in Indonesia, and by 1640 the Dutch rather than the Portuguese dominated trade between Europe and the East Indies.

It was generally considered to be the largest and richest private company in the world, maintaining a fleet of more than 150 merchantmen and almost 50 warships. However, it also had a rival. In 1600 Queen Elizabeth I of England signed a charter granting a monopoly of trading rights in India to a new organization – the Honourable East India Company (HEIC). In 1617 the Mughal emperor of India signed a trade deal with them, and over the next few decades the HEIC consolidated its hold on India. At first it limited its main interests to cotton, silk, indigo and tea, but it soon began making inroads into the spice trade.

This huge increase in trade meant that by the end of the 17th century the Indian Ocean had become the perfect hunting ground for pirates. Of course the European or colonial American pirates were not the first sailors to attack shipping in the Indian Ocean. Small communities of pirates fringed the coast of India,

For a few decades from the 1690s onwards, St Mary's Island (or the Île Sainte-Marie) off the north-eastern coast of Madagascar in the Indian Ocean became a popular pirate haven, even though it lacked a marketplace for stolen goods. (Olivier Cirendini/Getty Images)

Persia and Arabia. The Turks maintained regular naval patrols in the region, as too did the Mughal emperors of India, but by the late 17th century these anti-piracy operations had largely been abandoned, and only important convoys were escorted. Consequently, it was left to the Europeans to protect their own trading bases and ships.

The Dutch and the English were already stretched by the need to protect their interests from rival European powers. The need to protect themselves against pirates merely added to the problem. Consequently, by the time the European pirates first made an appearance, the resources of the two great trading companies were fully stretched. So, pirates enjoyed a degree of freedom that they were unable to find elsewhere.

The end of the 17th century also marked a burgeoning of the African slave trade. The Portuguese monopoly of slave trading on the west coast of Africa had been broken a century before, allowing English and French slave traders to establish their own links in the region. The English organized the trade by means of another trading organization, the Royal African Company, which, like its larger counterpart in India, maintained its own forts, trading stations and ships. Despite this, it was inevitable that pirates would find West Africa a lucrative hunting ground. Soon some of these pirates would continue their voyages further down the coast to reach the Cape of Good Hope and the Indian Ocean that lay beyond it. What they found was a pirate's dream – rich and poorly protected prizes, a range of suitable hideaways to evade any pursuers, and a collection of European trading companies too busy fighting each other to worry about the pirate threat. The result was that from around 1690 until the 1720s, the Indian Ocean became the most lucrative pirate destination in the world, and the men who sailed its waters were presented with opportunities that were simply not available anywhere else.

The popular myth that pirates were capable of capturing huge caches of gold coins and other specie began with the successes of the Red Sea Roundsmen, but rather than bury them, these hauls were always shared out among the crew.

Howard Pyle's Captain Scarface, although used to illustrate a fictitious pirate character in a children's book, was actually based on an amalgam of Thomas Tew, Henry Every and William Kidd.

THE ROUNDSMEN

The pirate threat that enveloped the Indian Ocean in the 1690s had its roots in Bermuda. That was where Thomas Tew from Newport, Rhode Island found himself in 1692. Tew was wealthy enough to buy a share in a local sloop called the *Amity*. Nobody really knew where his money came from, but an official later reported that 'it was a thing notoriously known to everyone that he had before then been a pirate'. In late 1691 a 'Captain Tew' raided an island off Cape Cod, and while we can't prove it was the same man, the coincidence of name is suspicious. However, in 1692 the War of the Grand Alliance (1688–97) was at its height, and so Tew persuaded Governor Ritchier of Bermuda to grant him a letter-of-marque that permitted him to attack the French. He decided to cruise off the West African coast, and so he headed out across the Atlantic in consort with another small Bermudan privateer commanded by a Captain Drew. However, Tew had no intention of limiting his attacks to the French.

His crew seemed to be in full agreement. When the two sloops were parted in a storm off the West African coast the *Amity* headed for the Cape of Good Hope. Once in the Indian Ocean they sailed north towards the Red Sea. The Bab-el-Mandeb ('Gate of Tears') was the Arab name for the 17-mile-(27km-) wide passage between East Africa and the Arabian Peninsula that marked the boundary between the sea and the ocean. It was there that Tew and his men captured their first prize.

In July 1693 they sighted a 'tall vessel' heading north into the Red Sea. According to Johnson the larger ship carried 300 soldiers, 'yet Tew had the hardiness to board her, and soon carried her, and, 'tis said, by this prize, his men shared near three thousand pounds apiece'. It was a stupendous achievement. The prize turned out to be a warship belonging to the great Indian Mughal emperor Alamgir I (1618–1707), and she yielded up a fortune in specie, gems, ivory, spices and silks. The pirates learned that the ship was part of a convoy, and five more vessels were nearby. Tew wanted to give chase, but he was overruled by his crew, who wanted to safeguard their plunder. As Johnson put it, 'This differing of opinion created some ill blood amongst them, so that they resolved to break up pyrating, and no place was so fit to receive them as Madagascar.'

There, Tew allegedly met up with another pirate. Captain James Misson and his ship *Victoire* had recently arrived there, and the French pirate had apparently established a piratical settlement he called 'Libertaria' on St Mary's Island (or the Île Sainte-Marie, now Nosy Boraha), off north-western Madagascar. Tew and his men certainly spent a few months on the island. However, the likelihood is that this mysterious Captain Misson was little more than a literary fiction dreamed up by Johnson.

When Tew decided to return to America, half his crew remained behind in Madagascar. In April 1694 he arrived in Newport, Rhode Island. As his prize had been captured from a non-European power, the governor of the colony treated Tew more as successful privateer than as the pirate he really was. Tew found himself fêted, and after selling his share of the plunder he was invited to pay a visit to Governor Fletcher of New York, as the governor wanted to back Tew in further ventures. When he was criticized for consorting with a known pirate, Fletcher wrote that he found Tew an interesting character, and that 'at

Howard Pyle's depiction of Thomas Tew, entertaining Governor Benjamin Fletcher of the New York colony with tales of his exploits as a 'Red Sea Roundsman'. This kind of fraternization led directly to the arrangement between William Kidd and another New York governor, the Earl of Bellomont.

THE VOYAGES OF THOMAS TEW

some times when the labours of my day were over it was some divertissement as well as information to me, to hear him talk'.

As a contemporary New Yorker wrote, 'We have a parcel of pyrates called the Red Sea Men in these parts who got a great booty of Arabian gold'. Fletcher was not alone, as other colonial businessmen were eager to finance further ventures into the Red Sea, a lucrative 'privateering' voyage that was soon dubbed the 'Red Sea Round'. Tew returned to sea in November 1694, armed with a letter-of-marque signed by Fletcher. This time he sailed with four other New England 'privateers', their crews eager for their share in the riches of the East.

KEY

← 1693 voyage   ← 1695 voyage

1693

1. May: Thomas Tew and his sloop *Amity* enter the Indian Ocean.
2. June: After taking on supplies in Madagascar, Tew heads north towards the Red Sea.
3. July: Tew captures an Indian warship belonging to the Mughal emperor, which yields a fortune in plunder.
4. Tew wants to continue the cruise, but his men opt to return home with their loot.
5. Tew probably put in to St Mary's Island, marking the start of its use as a pirate base.

1695

6. May: Tew returns to the Indian Ocean and sails north again.
7. It has been claimed that Tew used St Mary's Island as a base, and as a rendezvous with other pirates, but this has never been proven.
8. Late May: Off the Comoros Islands Tew encounters Henry Every, and the two pirates join forces.
9. June: The pirates enter the Bab-el-Mandeb, where the Red Sea narrows. They see this as the ideal hunting ground.
10. July: Tew spots Indian ships and gives chase. The merchantman *Ganj-i-Sawai* slips away, so Tew decides to attack the warship *Fateh Mohammed*, in the belief that it is filled with treasure.
11. Tew is killed in the ensuing battle, and the remaining pirates are captured.
12. Henry Every attacks and captures the *Fateh Mohammed* and rescues Tew's men. He goes on to capture the *Ganj-i-Sawai*, which is laden with plunder.

Tew became the commodore of this pirate squadron, and Johnson dubbed him 'Admiral of the Fleet'. Once in the Indian Ocean, they were joined by another ship, the *Fancy*, commanded by Henry Every.

By June 1695 the pirates were back in the Bab-el-Mandeb. There, Tew decided to attack a large Indian south-bound merchantman, part of a convoy bound for Surat. His target was the Mughal treasure ship *Ganj-i-Sawai*, which was escorted by the well-armed Indian warship *Fateh Mohammed*. The *Amity* approached the escort, but was met by a devastating broadside. Johnson claimed that 'in the engagement, a shot carried away the rim of Tew's belly, who held his bowels with his hands some small space; where he dropped'. The original 'Red Sea Roundsman' was dead. This 'struck such a terror in his men that they suffered themselves to be taken, without making resistance'. At that point the story of the 'Red Sea Roundsmen' is taken up by Henry Every.

For a man who has been touted as the most successful pirate of them all, we know very little about Every before he joined Tew's pirates. Johnson claimed he was born at Plymouth in Devon, and was 'bred to the sea'. Other accounts describe him as the son of a Plymouth innkeeper, born in the early 1650s. Another intriguing fact

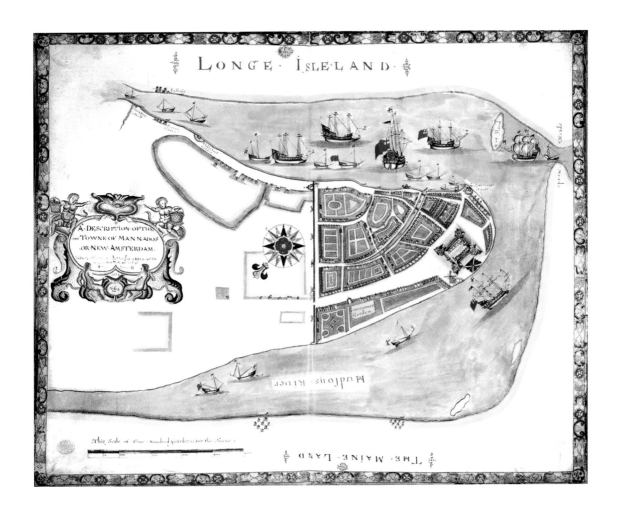

New York as it looked in 1664, the year it was captured from the Dutch and became an English colony. While the city was not considerably bigger by the time of Tew and Kidd, it had become a thriving port. The city expanded much more rapidly from 1694.

is that he was raised as John Every, but the name Henry appears in all surviving documents, including those written by the man himself. During the late 1680s he appeared in the Caribbean as the captain of a logwood sloop. In 1693 'Long Ben, alias Every' is mentioned in the papers of the Royal African Company, where he was described as an unlicensed slave trader. Until the end of the century the company held a monopoly of slave trading on the West African coast, but the trade suffered from the activities of 'interlopers' such as 'Long Ben'. Finally in 1698 it bowed to the inevitable and granted non-company ships permission to operate from its ports, in return for a share of the profits. In 1694 Every reappeared as the first mate of the fast 46-gun privateer *Charles II*. That June she set sail from Bristol, bound for Martinique, and her captain held a letter-of-marque authorizing him to prey on French shipping.

The *Charles II* put in to La Coruña in north-east Spain, but the crew were discontented enough for Every to stage a mutiny when the captain was ashore. The mutinous crew elected Every as their captain, who renamed the privateer the *Fancy*, then headed to the Indian Ocean in search of plunder. On the way south they ransacked three English and two Danish ships in the Cape Verde Islands. After rounding the Cape of Good Hope the *Fancy* put in to Johanna Island (now Anjouan) in the Comoros archipelago for water. It was there that Every captured another ship, a French privateer.

Every then penned a letter to be passed to the captains of all English ships operating in the Indian Ocean. In it he claimed, 'I had not wronged any English or Dutch, nor ever intend whilst I am commander'. It seems that he was still trying to pretend he was a law-abiding privateer captain rather than the pirate leader of a mutinous crew. Nobody was fooled.

It was at this point that he encountered Thomas Tew, and joined forces with him. Every took part in the attack on the Mughal convoy in which Tew was killed, and while the other ships in the squadron held back, he shadowed the convoy until the evening. When the *Fateh Mohammed* dropped astern of the convoy, he made his move. Every closed in, raked her, then led his men aboard the Mughal warship. The battle was over in minutes. Every's men massacred the Indian crew, released the prisoners from Tew's *Amity*, and helped themselves to the plunder on board, valued at around £50,000. This was a substantial achievement, but for Every it was only the start. He continued to shadow the convoy, and this time his goal was the treasure ship *Ganj-i-Sawai*.

She was a tough opponent, mounting 62 guns, and carrying 500 Mughal soldiers. However, the *Fancy* was more manoeuvrable, she had 46 guns, and her 190-man crew were fuelled by avarice. Judging his moment, Every steered towards the *Ganj-i-Sawai*, and both sides began exchanging broadsides. Then a lucky shot from the *Fancy* brought down the treasure ship's mainmast, making her almost impossible to steer. Every was able to rake his opponent, causing devastation aboard the Indian ship. He then brought the *Fancy* alongside and boarded her.

It was a rash move, as he was still heavily outnumbered. However, in the hard-fought mêlée that followed the pirates gradually got the upper hand. After two hours the remaining Indians finally surrendered. The *Ganj-i-Sawai* now belonged to Every, and even the most rapacious members of his crew would have been stunned by their plunder. The specie, precious stones and silks and

The pirate Henry Every was often regarded as one of the most successful of all pirates, as, after capturing a fortune in Indian treasure, he divided the loot amongst his crew and then slipped from the pages of history. While some claim he died in poverty, others claimed he ended his days as a rich and pampered landowner.

THE VOYAGE OF HENRY EVERY

more was valued at around £600,000, and included half a million gold and silver coins. The pirates then went on a two-day spree, torturing or raping the rich Indian passengers to find hidden caches of money or jewels. Then they sailed away, leaving the survivors reeling from the violence of the assault they had endured.

Every sailed to the French island of La Réunion, where he shared out most of the loot, giving each man a handful of gems as a bonus. He then quit the Indian Ocean and set sail for the West Indies, putting in to St Thomas in the Virgin Islands, where they sold some of their plunder. There Every discovered that news

1. Spring 1695: Henry Every enters the Indian Ocean in the former privat[...]
2. Early June: He makes a landfall at Johanna Island.
3. At Johanna Island he captures a French ship, but releases it and its crew, claimin[...]
4. Late May: He encounters Thomas Tew, and together the pirates head towards the Re[...]
5. July: In the Bab-el-Mandeb they attack a two-ship convoy, but Tew is killed while attacki[...]
6. Every gives chase, and captures the *Fateh Mohammed* after a sharp fight. He then sets off i[...]
    been escorting.
7. Every attacks the treasure ship *Ganj-i-Sawai*, and captures it after a particularly bloody boarding actio[...]
8. Every sails to La Réunion, where he divides the plunder.
9. He then leaves the Indian Ocean, and on reaching the West Indies his crew disperses. Every's fate remains a[...]

In this depiction of Henry Every, from Captain Johnson's *A General History of the Robberies and Murders of the Most Notorious Pyrates* (1724), the background shows his fight with the Mughal treasure ship *Ganj-i-Sawai*.

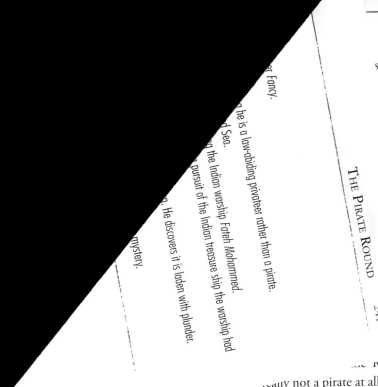

s, and that he was a wanted man. He
everyone went their own way.
Ireland on the sloop *Isaac*, landing
il went cold. There were several
about his fate. Captain Johnson
nd died in poverty. The truth is
m. History has labelled Henry
th it. He probably did. Unlike
nry Every knew to quit while
successful pirate of them all.

TEER

Kidd, who is probably the
owever, stems more from
om anything he actually
Red Sea Roundsmen'. In fact, it can
really not a pirate at all, only a privateer who made errors
judgement that ended up costing him his life.

Born in Dundee in Scotland in January 1654, he had a
tough childhood, his father dying when he was five, and his
mother reduced to receiving handouts from a seafarers'
benevolent society. He went to sea as a youth, and spent the
next few decades perfecting his trade. In February 1689 he
joined the crew of the French privateer *Sainte Rose*, based in
Petit Goâve. Then France declared war on the two kingdoms
of England and Scotland, and Kidd found himself taking
part in a French attack on the English island of
St Christopher. When most of the French were busy
attacking Fort Charles, Kidd, his accomplice Robert
Culliford and six other Britons managed to overpower the
men guarding a 16-gun brig, and sail her to the English-
owned island of Nevis.

A grateful governor let Kidd keep the brig, which he
renamed the *Blessed William* in honour of the king. He was
also given a letter-of-marque. However, on 2 February 1690
Culliford stole the brig while Kidd was ashore on Antigua,
leaving her captain stranded. It was several months before

Kidd was able to capture another French ship, which he called the *Antigua*. He sailed her to New York in a forlorn attempt to catch up with Culliford.

It was there that he met Sarah Oort, a wealthy widow, and in 1691 they were married. Kidd's fortunes were transformed, and he was now regarded as a sea captain of repute and a member of New York society. He became a merchant captain, sailing to the West Indies and back, and he even made a few privateering voyages on the side. Then in 1695 he sailed to England in the *Antigua*, hoping to win a more wide-ranging letter-of-marque. That was when it all started to unravel.

In London, he ran into an old New York acquaintance, Richard Livingston, who in turn introduced him to Richard Coote, the Earl of Bellomont. Livingston convinced the earl that his fellow Scot would make an ideal commander of the 34-gun privateering vessel he was building, called the *Adventure Galley*. Bellomont agreed and offered to

Richard Coote, 1st Earl of Bellomont (1635–1701), was William Kidd's main backer, and promised the privateer his political and legal protection. Instead, when Kidd was accused of piracy, Bellomont and his friends abandoned him to his fate.

fund the venture, along with a group of his political friends, Lord Romney, the Earl of Salisbury, Lord John Somers and Admiral Edward Russell, all members of the ruling Whig government. As a result, Kidd was drawn into a web from which he would be unable to escape. He sold the *Antigua* to raise money for his stake in the enterprise. However, the terms of the agreement left little scope for Kidd and his crew to reap a decent profit from the venture.

Kidd was given letters-of-marque authorizing him to attack both the French and pirates. Finally, in early April 1696 he headed down the river Thames and put to sea. In New York, he recruited more crew. The governor described them as 'men of desperate fortunes', adding, 'twill not be in Kidd's power to govern such a horde of men under no pay'. Privateers operated on a strict 'no prey, no pay policy', and without prizes the crew could become disaffected. Kidd finally set sail in September, bound for the Indian Ocean. This in itself was a curious decision – he had clearly set his heart on the tracking down of the 'Red Sea Roundsmen' rather than French merchant ships, which could more readily be found in the West Indies.

On 28 January 1697 the *Adventure Galley* arrived off Madagascar. He had considered attacking the pirate base on St Mary's Island, but thanks to an outbreak of the 'bloody flux' during his passage he lacked sufficient men for the task. So he

THE VOYAGE OF CAPTAIN KIDD

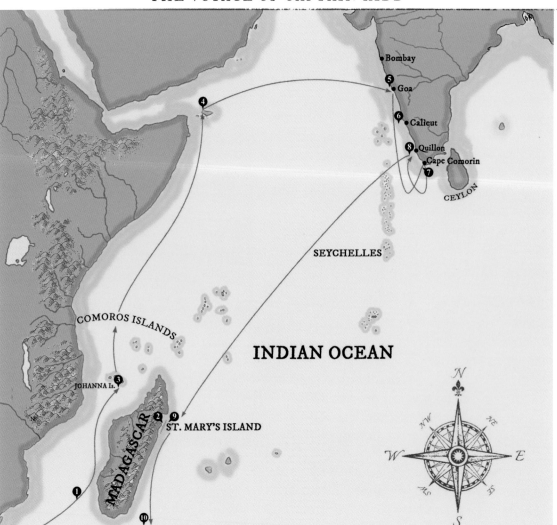

lingered off Madagascar, hoping that a pirate ship would appear. Eventually he grew tired of waiting, and headed north to Johanna Island, where he came across the *Scarborough*, an English merchantman. Kidd sailed towards her, but found his way blocked by a new arrival, the East India Company warship *Shirley*. Kidd backed off, but the East India Company captain would later report that he was certain Kidd was a pirate, or at least planned to become one. By then the *Adventure*'s crew were ravaged by disease, and so Kidd remained in the Comoros Islands for two months as the illness ran its deadly course. It was July before he

1. January 1697: Kidd makes a landfall in Madagascar in the *Adventure Galley*.
2. He plans to attack the pirates on St Mary's Island, but lacks the manpower to carry out the assault.
3. March: Kidd takes on water at Johanna Island, and remains there while he and his crew fight off the illness that has ravaged them.
4. August: Kidd attempts to attack an Indian convoy at the entrance to the Red Sea, but cancels the attack when he finds it is escorted by an East India Company warship. The captain of the warship reports that Kidd has turned to piracy.
5. October: Kidd sails to the coast of Malabar and captures a Dutch trading ship, the *Rupparell*.
6. November: He evades two Portuguese warships, which had tried attack him, having taken him for a pirate.
7. 30 January 1698: Off Cape Comorin he captures the Indian ship *Quedah Merchant*, which carries French papers. He uses plunder from her to pay off his mutinous crew.
8. February: Kidd puts in to Quillon (now Kollam) to sell some of his cargo. He remains there for several weeks.
9. April: Kidd puts in to St Mary's Island, where he abandons the rotten *Adventure Galley* and the *Rupparell*. Many of his crew desert and join the pirates based there.
10. Kidd sails for home in the *Quedah Merchant*.

St Mary's Island lies less than 5 miles (8km) off the north-eastern coast of Madagascar. It became a pirate haven, although claims that it was also a libertarian commune were much exaggerated.

was able to set sail again, and he headed towards the Red Sea, where he hoped to intercept pirates lurking in the Bab-el-Mandeb. By now, though, his much reduced crew were becoming restless. He needed a prize.

On 15 August the *Adventure Galley* encountered a Mughal convoy in the Bab-el-Mandeb. Kidd ran up a French flag and attacked, a clear act of piracy. However, the convoy was being escorted by the East India Company warship *Sceptre*. Unknown to Kidd the Mughal emperor had hired the Company to protect his shipping. As soon as he spotted her Kidd turned away, but the damage had already been done. In the eyes of the East India Company, Kidd had become a pirate.

KIDD THE PIRATE

Kidd was now desperate, as his crew were on the verge of mutiny. He headed to the Malabar coast and loitered off Goa, hoping to meet an unescorted Indian merchantman. He captured a small Arab merchantman, and escaped from two Portuguese warships, but there was still no sign of any lucrative merchantman. Kidd knew his crew were about to mutiny, and so when he overheard his gunner William Moore plotting, Kidd decided to act. There was a brief exchange of curses, which ended when Kidd grabbed a wooden bucket and smashed Moore over the head with it. The gunner died the next day. This, and the capture of the small Dutch merchantman *Rupparell* in November, helped stave off the mutiny.

His big chance came on 30 January 1698, while the *Adventure Galley* cruised off the southern tip of India. The *Quedah Merchant* appeared, an Indian vessel homeward bound from the Far East. Kidd ran up the French flag and ordered her to heave to. Her English captain complied, and Kidd and his men ransacked the ship, then took her into the nearby Portuguese-run port of Quillon (now Kollam). Kidd sold some of the cargo and used the money to pay his crew. It wasn't much, but it was sufficient to buy their loyalty until Kidd made it home. He kept the rest of the plunder to pay off his backers, although he also promised his men their share when the ship returned to New York. Best of all, the *Quedah Merchant* had passes proving she was under French protection, which technically meant she was a legitimate prize.

He now had three ships: the *Adventure*, the *Rupparell*, and the *Quedah Merchant*. It was just as well, as his flagship was rotten after a year in the Indian Ocean. On 1 April Kidd put in to St Mary's Island. It says much about Kidd's changed circumstances that he now sailed into the pirate den without fear of attack. However, one of the pirate ships in the port was the *Revenge*, commanded

OPPOSITE Captain William Kidd was a successful privateer, but while operating in the Indian Ocean in 1697–98 he may well have stepped over the line between privateering and piracy. In any case, he was accused of being a pirate and executed for it in 1701, after what amounted to a sham trial.

by Robert Culliford, the man who had stolen Kidd's first ship. Most of Kidd's crew now defected, leaving him with barely enough to make the voyage home. Feelings must have been running high, but Kidd was outnumbered, and he was out of options. The *Adventure Galley* was beyond repair, so he abandoned her and the *Rupparell*, and in November he sailed for home in the *Quedah Merchant*.

Kidd must have known that he would face a hostile reception. His big hope was that his influential backers would support him and understand that his

Before returning to New York, Kidd realized he faced charges of piracy, so he buried the bulk of his plunder on Gardiners Island, off Long Island. After his arrest it was recovered by Lord Bellomont and the colonial authorities.

mutinous crew had forced his hand. On reaching Hispaniola, he discovered that he was branded a pirate, but that his backer Lord Bellomont was now the governor of New York. So he decided to leave the *Quedah Merchant* in Antigua, and then take passage north with the bulk of her remaining cargo. He put in to Gardiner's Island off the southern tip of Long Island, where he buried the bulk of his plunder – an insurance policy in case Bellomont didn't support him. He then wrote to the governor, asking for help. Bellomont was in Boston at the time, so after visiting his family Kidd made his way there, arriving on 1 July 1699. If he expected a friendly reception, he was disappointed. The earl refused to see him, and five days later Kidd was arrested.

He confessed where he had hidden the stolen goods, and within weeks Bellomont had recovered plunder valued at around £14,000. The trouble was that while Kidd had been away the political climate had changed. England and France were no longer at war, and the privateers had been recalled. This inevitably led to an increase in piracy, so the government had adopted a tougher stance. Consequently any association with a known pirate would harm Bellomont's career and those of his fellow backers. In other words, Kidd was being thrown to the wolves. The story of Captain Kidd's trial is probably better known than his piratical exploits. In March 1700 he arrived in England, and immediately became the epicentre of a political storm.

During the two months he was held in Newgate Prison, the Tory opposition demanded that Kidd name his Whig backers, while Bellomont's colleagues avoided a political scandal by destroying all the evidence they could that linked them to the prisoner. Kidd still believed he would be exonerated, so he kept silent during two parliamentary hearings. The trial began on 8 May, and Kidd was charged with five acts of piracy and one of murder, the killing of William Moore. As the proceedings were governed by Admiralty law, Kidd was forced to maintain

his own defence. Proof that the *Quedah Merchant* was a legitimate prize was conveniently lost. Denied access to the evidence he needed to support his story, and condemned in advance by the East India Company and the government, the outcome was never in doubt. Kidd was duly found guilty of piracy and murder.

The whole trial had lasted just three days. Its real aim was to avoid further political scandal rather than to achieve justice. The judge set the date of the execution for two weeks' time. Kidd probably still hoped for a reprieve, but his backers kept their distance. So, on Friday 23 May 1701, a cart brought William Kidd to Execution Dock in Wapping, the procession headed by an official carrying a ceremonial oar – the symbol of the authority of the Admiralty. By all accounts Kidd was drunk, having been allowed to drown his sorrows in rum the night before. A gallows had been set up on the foreshore of the river, and a crowd of jeering onlookers watched as Kidd was led to the scaffold and a minister prayed for his soul. His last slurred words were uttered, protesting his innocence, and then, as a psalm was sung, the block he stood on was kicked away, and he began his final dance.

A fanciful depiction of the pirate haven on St Mary's Island, off Madagascar, as it might have looked in the early 18th century. The site of the settlement has been investigated, as have the remains of abandoned pirate ships in the harbour, one of which was Kidd's *Adventure Galley*.

The fact that Kidd buried plunder prompted four centuries of treasure hunting, spurred on by the discovery in 1929 of treasure maps that supposedly belonged to Kidd. The fact that these were almost certainly fake did little to deter people searching for Kidd's hidden plunder.

That, though, wasn't the end of the affair. His body was hung in a cage on the banks of the river Thames as a warning to other would-be pirates. Then came the claims, demands and recriminations over the plunder – a long-running legal tussle that involved Bellomont, the government and the Admiralty. It was never satisfactorily resolved.

Then there was the business of Robert Culliford. In September 1698 he captured the Mughal treasure ship the *Great Mohammed*. He was back in St Mary's Island when a squadron of English warships appeared, and he was arrested. Culliford stood trial, but for some reason he was reprieved and set free. It has been argued that he gave false evidence against Kidd in return for his freedom. William Kidd and his nemesis Robert Culliford were probably the last of the 'Red Sea Roundsmen'. After their passing, the East India Company vigorously patrolled the Indian Ocean, so preventing any fresh wave of attacks from occurring. While St Mary's Island would remain a pirate haven, none of these small-time pirates would ever have the opportunities enjoyed by the likes of Tew, Every or even Kidd.

THE MADAGASCAR PIRATES

The story Captain Johnson tells of the founding of an idyllic pirate community called 'Libertaria' was a myth. He claimed that around 1695 the colony of 'Libertaria' was founded by the French pirate Captain Misson, and was located on the island of St Mary. The island's main anchorage of the Baie des Forbans provided good protection from storms, while the island itself was well provided with food and water, and the local population was tolerant of visiting mariners. Above all, Madagascar itself was ideally located astride the main sea route between Europe and the Orient. In other words, St Mary's Island was piratical paradise. It is little wonder it came to be associated with a pirate utopia.

The legend of Captain Misson is really a tale of idealism. A supposed native of Provence, James Misson is said to have served in the French Navy Royal, where he met Father Caraccioli. This unorthodox priest called for the establishment of an egalitarian commune, in which everyone was equal, without distinctions of race, class or creed. The notion that these admirable virtues were made reality by a radical priest and pirate captain has never been documented outside the pages of Johnson. It is far more likely that this was a literary invention.

That said, the social structures adopted by pirates were already extremely liberal for their day, and what might be construed as a social experiment was merely a pirate settlement run on democratic lines, following a generally held code of piratical conduct. Johnson's account simply pandered to widespread tales of pirate kingdoms, fuelled by the wealth and abundance that many Europeans imagined was there for the taking in the Indian Ocean. On St Mary's Island, as in other known pirate haunts in the area such as Ranter Bay (now the Baie d'Antongil) and Saint Augustine's Bay, both on Madagascar's east coast, the remoter islands of La Réunion and Mauritius to the east, and Johanna Island to the north-west, visiting pirate crews seem to have been welcomed by those who were already there. In effect this pirate utopia was little more than interaction governed by the principles laid down in pirate codes.

Far from being an example of a social utopia, this was merely a pragmatic way of controlling life beyond the reach of the law. It has been argued that

Johanna Island in the Comoros Islands, between Madagascar and the East African mainland, was a popular watering place for both pirates and law-abiding mariners alike. This sketch of the island was drawn in the 1670s.

Johnson's chapter was merely a political essay, disguised as pirate history. He proposes that this vision was based on the ideas espoused by the English Levellers during the late 1640s: 'all land in common, all people one'. It hardly sounds as if this creed was designed to govern life amongst a disparate collection of maritime renegades and criminals. In fact, there are clear indications that, just as in any criminal society, some men rose to the top. In the late 1690s the pirate Abraham Samuel styled himself 'King of Port Dolphin' (Fort Dauphin, now Taolanaro in southern Madagascar), while another pirate, James Plantain, called himself the 'King of Ranter's Bay'. So much for an egalitarian pirate utopia.

What is clear is that for a while, St Mary's Island and these other anchorages provided a fairly safe refuge for pirates. A recent exploration of the Baie des Forbans on St Mary's Island has not only produced what is probably the wreck of the *Adventure Galley*, but also the remains of several other suspected pirate ships, which were probably abandoned for the same reason as Kidd's flagship.

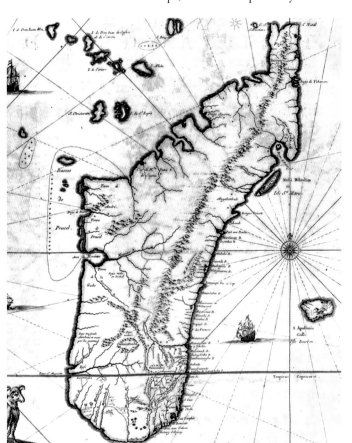

In this Dutch map of Madagascar dated 1665, St Mary's Island can be seen lying off the eastern side of the island, almost directly above the compass rose. Other smaller and less permanent pirate lairs have also been recorded, in secluded bays on the main island.

The visit to the Baie des Forbans by a Royal Navy squadron in 1699 may well have marked the end of Madagascar's heyday as a pirate sanctuary. Many of the pirates there accepted the offer of a pardon, while others gave up piracy to live as settlers. When Woodes Rogers visited the Cape of Good Hope in 1711 he spoke to two former pirates from St Mary's Island, who told him that fewer than 60 or 70 pirates now remained in Madagascar, 'most of them very poor and despicable, even to the natives'.

It seemed that by the start of the 18th century the Indian Ocean had seen the last of the pirates. However, they would return for one last hurrah. This all began with John Halsey, an American privateer-turned-pirate. He arrived in St Mary's Island in 1706, then for more than two years he used the decaying pirate haven as a base. His greatest success came in August 1707, when he captured two British ships off Mocha (now in the Yemen), but soon after his return his ship and her prizes were destroyed in a typhoon. Halsey died on St Mary's Island soon afterwards, and his crew joined the other 'poor and despicable' inhabitants of the island.

The next to appear was the Englishman Christopher Condent, who was one of the 'die-hards' who fled New Providence with Charles Vane in 1718. He soon went his own way, and off the Cape Verde Islands he captured a small Dutch sloop-of-war, which he renamed the *Flying Dragon*. He arrived on St Mary's Island in the summer of 1719. There he came across the survivors of Halsey's crew, and he used their local knowledge to good effect, spending the next year cruising the Indian Ocean in search of prey. In October 1720 he captured an Arabian merchantman off Bombay, which yielded a substantial fortune in plunder, possibly as much as £150,000.

In this Howard Pyle painting, pirates have come to blows during the burying of their treasure. In fact, with the exception of Captain Kidd, no pirates were ever known to have buried their plunder.

Condent was another pirate who knew when to quit. He sailed to St Mary's Island and dispersed the crew of the *Flying Dragon*. In fact, archaeologists think they have now identified her remains lying at the bottom of the Baie des Forbans, not far from the wreck of the *Adventure Galley*. Condent and 40 of his men then headed east to the French island of La Réunion, where he negotiated a pardon from the French governor. The story goes he married the governor's sister-in-law, then retired to St Malo in Brittany, where he set himself up as a merchant.

The next one to try his luck was Edward England, who despite his name was an Irishman who had changed his name from Edward Seegar. During the War of the Spanish Succession (1701–14) he served as a privateer in Jamaica, before gravitating towards New Providence in 1716. England accepted Woodes Rogers' pardon, then returned to his old ways. He was operating off the West African coast in early 1719, and he may well have encountered Howell Davis during his cruise, as the two pirates were both identified as operating together off the coast of Guinea. By this time he had replaced his sloop with a larger vessel called the *Pearl*.

He kept another of his prizes, renaming her the *Victory*, and gave command of her to his quartermaster, John Taylor, another New Providence renegade.

The Irish pirate Edward England, pictured in an early version of Captain Johnson's *A General History of the Robberies and Murders of the Most Notorious Pyrates*. He was one of the New Providence 'die-hards', but he eventually ended up operating in the Indian Ocean.

They decided to try their luck in the Indian Ocean. Captain Johnson claims that they made landfall in Madagascar, where they 'Liv'd there very wantonly for several weeks, making free with the Negroe women'. From the description it sounds like St Mary's Island. Eventually England and Taylor grew tired of these diversions and returned to sea, cruising in consort off the north-west coast of India. Again, England moved into one of his prizes, a 34-gun three-masted ship he called the *Fancy*.

A little after noon on 27 August 1720 the pirates made a landfall at Johanna Island, where they put in for water. However, they were not alone. The pirates found three ships already at anchor, a small Dutch Indiaman, and two larger vessels, both British East Indiamen. The *Greenwich*, the smaller of the two British ships, and the Dutch vessel both cut their anchor cables and fled, but Captain James Macrae of the Indiaman *Cassandra* elected to stay and fight. While Taylor chased the two fleeing ships in the *Victory*, England steered the *Fancy* towards the Indiaman. As the Scottish captain wrote in his report, the two other ships 'left us engaged with barbarous and inhuman Enemies, with their black and bloody Flags hanging over us'.

The lack of wind made it difficult to manoeuvre, so the two simply blazed away at each other. The fight lasted for three hours, and both sides fired broadsides into the other at close range until both vessels were holed and damaged. At one point England tried to use long oars ('sweeps') to bring the *Fancy* alongside the *Cassandra*, but, as Macrae put it, 'by good Fortune we shot all her Oars to Pieces, which prevented them, & by consequence saved our lives'. However, it was clear that the better-armed pirate ship was winning the fight, and so Captain Macrae decided to run his battered ship onto the beach. His crew scrambled ashore and hid out on the island for several days before surrendering to the pirates.

This involved throwing themselves on the mercy of the cutthroats. To Macrae's surprise England turned out to be a gracious victor, and he granted the British sailors their freedom. Taylor was furious, and accused England of being far too lenient. The pirate ignored him, and allowed Macrae and his men to limp away in the shattered and leaking *Fancy*, which somehow made it to the safety of Bombay. The doughty Scotsman was fêted as a hero, and went on to become the governor of Madras.

Meanwhile England had Taylor in the *Victory* pull the *Cassandra* off the beach, and then set about turning her into his new flagship. However, the rift between the soft-hearted England and the callous Taylor reached a head six months later in early 1721. As Johnson put it, 'he [England] was soon abdicated and pulled from his government, and marooned with three more on the island of Mauritius'. Marooned and abandoned by his own men, England and his companions managed to sail across the Indian Ocean in 'a little boat of staves, and odd pieces of deal', and he reached St Mary's Island. There he 'subsists at present [1724] on the charity of some of their brethren'. England reportedly died shortly afterwards.

In this depiction of Edward England, he is shown in front of a sea battle, representing the fight in 1720 between his pirate ship *Fancy* and the East Indiaman *Cassandra*. The battle was essentially a draw, with both ships badly damaged and driven aground during the fighting.

THE VOYAGES OF ENGLAND AND TAYLOR

As for John Taylor, he continued his cruise in the *Victory* and the *Cassandra* after marooning his former captain, capturing a string of prizes off the Indian coast. He returned to St Mary's Island, where he met Olivier le Vasseur, or 'La Buse' (The Buzzard), the Frenchman who had once sailed with Howell Davis and Sam Bellamy. Taylor gave the veteran French pirate command of the *Victory*. The two pirates then sailed to La Réunion, where they came across a Portuguese merchantman which had lost her mast in a storm. She was captured after a brief action, and the pirates found she was laden with plunder, including a hoard of diamonds destined for King João V of Portugal. Instead, the jewels were divided between the pirate crew.

KEY

◄─── England's voyage   ◄─ ─· Journey of makeshift boat   ◄───Taylor's voyage

1. Spring 1720: Edward England in the sloop *Pearl* and John Taylor in the *Victory* enter the Indian Ocean in search of plunder.

2. The pirates loiter on St Mary's Island for several months.

3. July: The pirates cruise between Africa and Madagascar, capturing several ships. England keeps one of the prizes, which he renames the *Fancy*.

4. August: They head north, and on 27 August they put in to Johanna Island, to take on water.

5. There they encounter three ships – a Dutchman and two East Indiamen. Taylor chases two of them, while England takes on the Indiaman *Cassandra*, which stayed to fight. After a hard-fought battle the *Cassandra* is captured.

6. England frees his prisoners, giving them the *Fancy*, but takes the *Cassandra* for himself.

7. March 1721: England and Taylor fall out over the former's leniency to his prisoners. England's crew side with Taylor, and England and three supporters are marooned on Mauritius.

8. May: England builds a boat and sails it to St Mary's Island. He dies there several months later.

9. June: Taylor cruises off the Malabar coast, capturing several prizes, then returns to St Mary's Island.

10. Taylor allies himself with Olivier le Vasseur, and together they capture a Portuguese merchantman off La Réunion.

11. Taylor decides to return home to Britain by crossing the Pacific. After making landfall near Panama his crew disperse, taking their plunder with them.

Le Vasseur replaced the rotten *Victory* with the prize, which was renamed *Victoire*, and the pirates sailed to the East African coast, where they lay low, while a squadron of British warships scoured the Indian Ocean for them. The two men then split up. Le Vasseur destroyed the *Victoire* and disappeared, probably having taken passage home to France. Taylor decided it was clearly no longer safe to return to St Mary's Island, so he headed east across the Pacific, reaching Panama in May 1723. Although Spain and Britain were at peace, the governor accepted Taylor's present of the *Cassandra* in return for a pardon and a safe passage. What eventually happened to Taylor after that is still a mystery.

England, Taylor and le Vasseur were the last of the Madagascar pirates. In 1721 the same squadron from which Taylor and le Vasseur had hidden destroyed any remnants of pirate havens in Madagascar, while the French did the same in Mauritius and La Réunion. For the first time in decades the British, French and Portuguese were at peace with each other, and their governments co-operated in an effort to end all piracy in the Indian Ocean. It was the end of the 'Pirate Round', and, just as in the waters of the Caribbean or on the coast of West Africa, organized piracy in the Indian Ocean became a thing of the past. In fact, it was also the beginning of the end of that whole great pirate era known as piracy's 'Golden Age'.

Chapter Eight

THE LAST OF
THE PIRATES

THE LATIN AMERICAN PROBLEM

The end of the 'Golden Age of Piracy' didn't mean the end of
pirate attacks. However, these became isolated incidents, and any
larger outbreaks were soon dealt with by the navies of the leading
maritime powers, which for the most part meant Great Britain.
The government campaign against the pirates had clearly been
successful, and ship owners could now sit back and watch the
profits roll in. Unfortunately, life was rarely that simple. A near-
constant string of wars between Britain and France meant that
privateers remained in demand for much of the 18th century.

The War of the Austrian Succession, also known as the War of
Jenkins' Ear (1740–48), saw the widespread use of privateers in the
Mediterranean, the Caribbean and the English Channel. Then came
the Seven Years' War (1756–63), when British naval supremacy was
established on both sides of the Atlantic. The French were out for
revenge, and so during the American War of Independence (1775–83)

Small boats from Commodore Porter's anti-piracy squadron attack a schooner
belonging to Cuban-based pirate nicknamed Diabolito ('Little Devil'). In this
action fought in 1823, over 70 pirates were killed by the American sailors and
marines.

their privateers joined those of the Americans. The great Anglo-French struggle resumed following the overthrow of Louis XVI in the French Revolutionary Wars (1792–1802), and came to a head in the Napoleonic Wars (1805–15). In between came a host of other smaller conflicts, the most important of which was a series of wars of independence in Latin America and the Anglo-American War of 1812 (1812–15). What all these wars meant for sailors was that privateering became extremely lucrative, and by the end of the string of conflicts this form of state-sponsored piracy had become big business.

When these wars ended in 1815, thousands of privateers found themselves out of work. While most found regular employment, others turned to piracy, or operated under dubious letters-of-marque issued by rebel governments whose authority wasn't recognized by the rest of the world. The emerging countries of Latin America were a major source for these privateering licences. When the French launched their devastating invasion of Spain in 1808, many Spanish colonies in the Americas seized the opportunity to rebel against their colonial overlords. The Latin American Wars of Liberation that followed soon engulfed most of South America, and the rebel juntas in Venezuela, Colombia and Ecuador all embraced privateering as a means of striking out against their Spanish masters.

By 1826, Peru and Chile had become independent states, while Ecuador, Colombia and Venezuela had also effectively freed themselves from the Spanish.

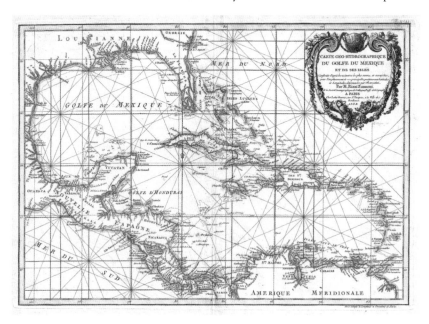

The end of the Napoleonic Wars in 1815 ushered in a new era of piracy in the Caribbean, as the Spanish Empire tore itself apart and pirates took advantage of the political chaos that ensued.

A small pirate vessel is driven off by a well-armed merchant ship. The rapid growth in merchant shipping after 1815 led to a corresponding boom in crime, as many former privateers turned to piracy.

While Mexico gained its independence in 1821, the rest of Central America was still in turmoil. Only Cuba remained under Spanish control, although it too was ravaged by guerrilla fighting. The problem caused by these privateers did not go away after independence, as many kept on attacking Spanish shipping, claiming that they held their letters-of-marque from juntas who were still fighting for their independence. Others simply crossed the line from privateering into piracy, and attacked anyone they wanted. Not all of these pirates were capable of operating on the high seas – some were little more than local fishermen and bandits, who attacked passing ships to supplement their income. In effect, the Caribbean had become a dangerous and semi-anarchic place where a once powerful central authority had been replaced by a patchwork of warlords, revolutionary juntas and petty rulers.

This coincided with a post-war boom in shipping. As the war economies of Europe and the United States turned to manufacturing, the growing demand for materials created by the Industrial Revolution meant that the volume of shipping on the world's sea lanes increased dramatically. For the most part, these ships operated without hindrance. However, those who sailed through pirate 'hot-spots' such as the Caribbean placed themselves in danger. An example of one such attack was the plunder of the American brig *Washington*, which was seized by pirates off the coast of Cuba in 1822. Captain Lander reported that the Hispanic pirates who swarmed aboard his vessel stole food, cooking equipment, clothing and a compass, as well as $16 in cash. This was typical of the opportunist attacks carried out on Caribbean shipping during this

This depiction of a pirate attack on a ship anchored off a Spanish port in the Caribbean might be over-dramatic, but it reflected a growing threat in the region during the second decade of the 19th century.

period. The American captain was fortunate to have escaped with his life – in several instances the pirates massacred the crew, following the old pirate adage that 'dead men tell no tales'.

In a few cases the pirates ranged further afield, attacking ships on the high seas. Still, unlike the great upsurge of piracy a century earlier, these ocean-going pirates were exceptions to the rule, and this time the maritime powers were better prepared and willing to co-operate to bring the pirates to justice. For the most part, the main anti-piracy force at this time was the Royal Navy. However, since attaining its independence in 1783 the United States of America had also become a major mercantile power. By 1820 American ships had come to dominate the maritime trade of the Caribbean. This meant that American shipping was particularly badly hit by the increase in piratical attacks.

As the number of pirate incidents increased, maritime insurance premiums soared, and consequently American ship owners demanded that their government do something. From 1820 on, major efforts were made by both the US Navy and the Royal Navy to stamp out piracy in the Caribbean. This response involved three main phases. The first was the patrolling of major shipping lanes such as the Florida Straits and the Bahamas Channel. That was followed by a series of aggressive naval patrols in pirate waters, in which pirate ships of all sizes were hunted down and destroyed. Finally, attacks were launched against known pirate bases, particularly those on the coast of the Gulf of Mexico and along the northern coast of Cuba. This was supported by a diplomatic mission in which the Spanish authorities in Cuba and the fledgling nations of Central and South America were encouraged to deal with the pirate problem within their own territorial boundaries. The result was that by the late 1820s the pirate problem had been almost completely eradicated, and the waters of the Caribbean were once again deemed safe for maritime trade. This success was reflected by the great maritime insurers Lloyds of London, when in 1829 they removed their special insurance tariff for voyages to or from the Caribbean.

Although painted more for entertainment than anything else, this early 19th-century scene typifies the ruse pulled by many pirates of all eras, attempting to lure their prey closer by giving the appearance of being an innocent merchant ship.

THE LAST PIRATES OF THE CARIBBEAN

Piracy was becoming a real problem. In 1823 the American newspaper *Niles Weekly Register* reported that between 1815 and 1823 over 3,000 acts of piracy had taken place in the Gulf of Mexico and the Caribbean. In 1820 there were 52 piratical attacks in the Florida Straits alone, of which 27 were against ships flying the American flag. That year, insurance premiums were raised to a higher level than during the recent War of 1812, when British and American ships were regularly attacked by each other's privateers.

The newspapers of the period were filled with horror stories. For instance, in February 1819 the *Boston Daily Advertiser* carried a report from the American brig *Emma Sophia*:

> On Saturday 19th [December 1818] between the Bahama Bank and Key Sal we were boarded and taken possession of by a small schooner of about 30 tons, having one gun mounted on a pivot and 30 men. She manned us with twelve men, Spaniards, French, Germans and Americans, and carried us towards the Florida coast … every man had a knife about a foot long, which they brandished, swearing they would have money or something more valuable, or they would kill every soul of us.

One such small-time pirate was the Frenchman Louis-Michel Aury, a privateer based in Cartagena during the Latin American Wars of Liberation. When the Spanish reconquered the city in 1815 he turned to piracy, attacking shipping of any nationality he could find. Then in 1817 he arrived off Amelia Island in north-eastern Florida, where a revolt was taking place against Spanish rule. He turned the place into a pirate haven, where slaves were illegally sold to buyers on the Florida mainland. Two months later a force of US Marines landed, rounded up the pirates, and put an end to Aury's island state. This move was followed a year later by the American annexation of Florida.

Another area troubled by pirates was the Gulf of Mexico. By far the most notorious of these was Jean Lafitte, a smuggler who turned to piracy, and whose close association with New Orleans has become part of the city's folklore. Today he is viewed as something of a romantic hero, a man who helped save the city from the British. Of course the truth is somewhat different. His birthplace is usually given as Bayonne in southern France, sometime around 1780. He left the country at the time of the French Revolution, and by 1809 he and his brother Pierre were in New Orleans, where they reputedly ran a blacksmith's shop. It appears that if this ever existed it was just a front, as their real business was smuggling.

In 1810 Jean Lafitte was named as the leader of a group of smugglers who operated from 'the Kingdom of Barataria', a bay on the western side of the Mississippi Delta, just south of New Orleans. Then in 1812 the brothers were arrested and charged with smuggling – charges of piracy were dropped through lack of evidence. The pair were released on bail, then fled to Barataria, where they resumed their activities. According to a well-known New Orleans legend, when the newly elected Louisiana governor, William Claiborne, put a price of $500 on the head of Jean Lafitte, the smuggler responded by offering ten times that for the head of the governor! Unfortunately, there is no evidence that this exchange ever took place.

Barataria Bay was linked to the Mississippi River by a network of small rivers and bayous, and Lafitte and his colleagues used these waterways to transport goods between the Gulf of Mexico and the city, and stood ready to use them as a means of escape if the authorities came looking for them. Lafitte's main base was a barrier island called Grand Terre, to which slave owners and merchants came from the city to trade directly with Lafitte and his men. The authorities raided the island in September 1814, and although Jean escaped, his brother was captured and the base destroyed. Then three months later the British arrived and landed a small army, which attempted to assault New Orleans. This time Lafitte and his men sided with the American authorities and played a part in repulsing the British assault in an engagement known as the battle of New Orleans (1815).

In retrospect, Lafitte probably backed the wrong side. In the aftermath of the American victory, General Andrew Jackson and Governor Claiborne refused to deal with the Baratarians, and within two years Jean Lafitte was forced to flee from Louisiana. He moved to Galveston (then known as Campeche) in what is now Texas, a port on the fringes of the authority of the Spanish government in Mexico. It served as a marketplace for frontiersmen, slave traders, pirates and Mexican traders. One of these slave traders was Jim Bowie, who later achieved fame because of his knife and his participation in the defence of the Alamo. By 1818 it was claimed that 20 pirate schooners operated out of the port, including those owned by Lafitte. However, a hurricane flattened the port later that year, and Lafitte's operation suffered a major setback.

At this stage there was no anti-piracy squadron, but attacks on American ships operating out of New Orleans resulted in the US Navy sending a Lieutenant Kearney, captain of the USS *Enterprise*, to deal with the problem. The *Enterprise* was a 14-gun brig, and in May 1821 Kearney threatened to bombard the port unless the pirates dispersed. Instead they responded with a dramatic gesture of defiance. As Kearney put it, 'Laffite set fire to Campeche. Men aboard the USS *Enterprise* saw it burst into flames … When they went to shore at dawn they found only ashes and rubble. The ships of Lafitte were gone …' What happened to Jean Lafitte afterwards remains a mystery.

In October 1821 the USS *Enterprise* caught the fleet of the Rhode Island native Charles Gibbs, a former privateer and now one of the most notorious

This dramatic scene depicts an incident that supposedly happened during Jean Lafitte's piratical career, when he turned a gun on the crew of a British East Indiaman that continued to resist him. The defenders promptly surrendered. Unfortunately, there is no evidence to suggest this ever happened.

THE ROUTES OF JEAN LAFITTE

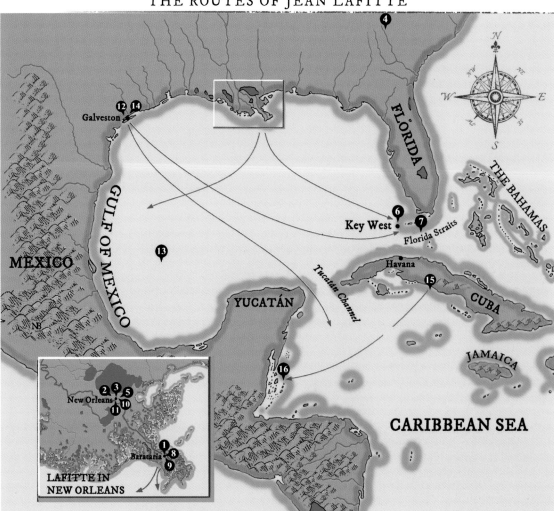

pirates on the Cuban coast. Although Gibbs and his men escaped ashore, Kearney succeeded in capturing or destroying all of his pirate squadron. However important this success was, it was still an isolated one. What was needed was a more organized response to the pirate threat in American waters.

Then in November 1822 the captain of the US naval schooner *Alligator* was killed in a brush with the Cuban pirate Domingo. This outraged public opinion in the United States. Consequently, four weeks later President Monroe ordered the formation of an anti-pirate squadron, charged with clearing the pirates from the waters around Cuba and the Gulf of Mexico.

1. 1809: Jean Lafitte establishes a smuggling operation based on the island of Grand Terre south of New Orleans.
2. 1810: Lafitte is named as a smuggler in official records, but the government fail to stop his goods from entering New Orleans.
3. 1812: Jean and his brother Pierre are now linked to an illegal slave-trading operation.
4. June 1812: The United States goes to war with Great Britain.
5. October: Lafitte's application for a letter-of-marque is rejected.
6. Spring 1813: Lafitte is identified as the perpetrator in a pirate attack – the capture of a Spanish slave ship off Key West.
7. Summer: More pirate attacks follow in the Florida Straits and the Gulf of Mexico.
8. September 1814: The Louisiana militia destroy Lafitte's base on Grand Terre, and Pierre Lafitte is captured.
9. September: Jean Lafitte rejects an offer from the British to assist them in an assault on New Orleans.
10. January 1815: The British attack New Orleans, and Laffite and his men side with the Americans to repulse the attack.
11. February: The Lafitte brothers are granted a pardon but are ordered to leave Louisiana.
12. 1817: Lafitte establishes a new base at Galveston (then known as Campeche) in what is now Texas.
13. 1818: Lafitte's ships continue their piratical attacks in the Gulf of Mexico, using forged letters-of-marque.
14. May 1821: The USS *Enterprise* bombards Galveston, and the pirate base is destroyed. The Lafitte brothers escape capture.
15. 1822: Rumours circulate that Jean Laffite is operating from a base on the southern coast of Cuba.
16. February 1823: It is claimed that Lafitte was killed during an attack on Spanish shipping in the Gulf of Honduras. This, though, has never been verified.

This was the largest peacetime assembly of American naval power. It was commanded by Commodore David Porter, a veteran of the War of 1812 and America's earlier campaign against the Barbary pirates. The fleet that congregated in Key West in Florida was perfect for the job.

Dubbed the 'Mosquito Fleet', it consisted mainly of small, shallow and fast schooners and brigs, supported by a paddle steamer and even a decoy merchant ship with hidden guns. Porter began operations in April 1823, and his first success came within days when two of his schooners captured a pirate ship off Matanzas in Cuba. Within a month Porter was able to write to the Secretary of the Navy, reporting that 'I can now say with safety that there is not a pirate afloat in this part of Cuba in anything larger than an open boat'. What he failed to add was that it was actually the British who had captured the flagship of Diabolito ('Little Devil'), the most notorious of all these Cuban pirates.

Cuba was a particularly difficult place to operate, as the Spanish resented the American presence, and some regional administrators condoned piracy. American consuls reported that the Spanish mayors in the ports of Matanzas and Caibarién were in league with the pirates, as was the governor of the western province of Pinar del Rio. Both areas lay close to the busy shipping lane of the Florida Straits. Certainly pirates such as Charles Gibbs appear to have bought

The pirate-hunting brig USS *Enterprise*, pictured off the coast of Cuba in 1821, attacking and destroying the flotilla of the troublesome pirate Charles Gibbs. Actions of this kind helped cleanse the Caribbean of piracy.

political protection in return for sharing their plunder with the local authorities. Another problem was that it was often difficult to tell the difference between pirates and local fishermen. However, as Porter's fleet began to gain the upper hand, Cuban merchants began lobbying the Spanish authorities to support his actions using their own military forces. By December 1823, when President Monroe announced his Monroe Doctrine, he noted 'the co-operation of the invigorated administration of Cuba'.

The Spanish soon began complaining that Porter was too successful. Many former pirates simply turned their backs to the sea and began new careers as Cuban bandit, operating on land. One of these was Charles Gibbs, one of the last of the Cuban pirates. After being driven ashore by Porter, he became a successful bandit. In 1830 he returned to sea, but was captured after leading a failed attempt to take over a ship. He was taken to New York to stand trial, where he confessed to the murder of over 400 people. He was hanged in Ellis Island early the following year. By then piracy had become a thing of the past. In fact, by early 1825 piratical attacks were virtually unknown in Cuban waters, and international shipping could once again pass through the Florida Straits without fear of attack.

THE *BLACK JOKE*

Although the pirate crisis had passed, a few isolated incidents of piracy still took place in the Caribbean or the Atlantic. These were made all the more shocking because of their rarity, and consequently the small-time pirates who still remained at large were given more notoriety than they probably deserved. One of the worst of these was Benito de Soto, a Spanish-born seaman who convinced his shipmates to turn piracy. In late 1827 he was serving on board an Argentinian slave ship, the *Defense de Pedro*, which had sailed from Brazil to the west coast of Africa, and was anchored off Luanda in Angola. Supported by the first mate, de Soto staged a mutiny and took over the brig. The captain and his loyal crew members were stabbed and thrown overboard. De Soto showed a sense of irony when he renamed the ship the *Burla Negra* (*Black Joke*).

In 1827 the Spanish-born Benito de Soto turned to piracy after leading a mutiny, and so began a violent piratical career that ended three years later on the gallows at Gibraltar.

The pirates sailed to the Caribbean, where the brig's cargo of slaves was sold in the slave markets of Santo Domingo. The pirates then headed south, working their way down the chain of the Lesser Antilles, chasing and capturing every ship they encountered. In every case the crew of the prize were murdered, and the ship burned or scuttled. This meant that there was nobody left to report the crime or describe who had attacked them. The only trail left by the *Burla Negra* was a string of missing ships.

After reaching Trinidad they continued on southwards, working their way down the South American coast towards Brazil and Argentina – the crew's home waters. By this time the authorities had worked out what was happening, and word was sent to the Latin American ports, warning merchantmen not to sail alone. In fact, the Brazilian government began organizing convoys as a means of protection, all because of one small pirate ship.

As de Soto found the seas empty of shipping, he decided to follow the transatlantic shipping route that led from Brazil towards the Cape of Good Hope. In the age of sail, ships travelling from Africa to the Indian Ocean would sail far out into the South Atlantic to take advantage of trade winds, which would then sweep them close to the Brazilian coast. From there westerlies would lead them south-east towards the southern tip of Africa. Similarly, ships heading toward Europe would follow another route closer to the African shore, but still keeping well out into the Atlantic. By operating where these two trade routes crossed, the *Burla Negra* would be in a perfect position to intercept shipping while keeping well away from land. As more ships started to disappear in the mid-Atlantic, the maritime governments began to become concerned

De Soto's *modus operandi* was to kill all his victims, leaving nobody behind who could link him to the pirate attack. Here he and his men execute the captain of the English merchantman *Morning Star* before locking everyone else in the hold and setting fire to the ship.

that a pirate was operating in the area. Consequently, homeward-bound British East India Company ships were ordered to wait at St Helena for a naval escort, which would then convoy them into safer waters.

On 21 February 1832, de Soto came across the *Morning Star*, a British barque returning home from Ceylon. The *Burla Negra* fired into the merchantman at point-blank range, killing several of her crew and forcing the *Morning Star* to heave to. De Soto ordered her captain to row over in his launch, and when he did the man was cut down by de Soto's cutlass, apparently because the pirate thought he took too long to comply. According to newspaper accounts, he cried, 'Thus does Benito de Soto reward those who disobey him', as he struck the British captain. The pirates then used the launch to board the *Morning Star*, where they embarked upon an orgy of destruction, killing several of the men, raping the women passengers and locking the survivors in the hold. This included a number of wounded British soldiers on their way home to be discharged. After looting the ship the pirates scuttled her, then rowed away to safety. De Soto sailed off, leaving the *Morning Star* sinking steadily. It was the same trick he had pulled several times in the past.

This time, though, it went wrong. The crew managed to free themselves, and were able to keep their ship afloat. The following day another ship appeared – a British merchantman – and the passengers and all but a skeleton crew were taken to safety. That meant that for once there were witnesses. News of the attack eventually reached Britain, where accounts of de Soto's rape of the female

Benito de Soto's ship *Burla Negra* ('Black Joke') overhauling the small British merchant ship *Morning Star*. This encounter proved to be de Soto's undoing, as after the pirates left their prize sinking the crew escaped from the hold, stopped the flooding, and so lived to testify to de Soto's identity and his crime.

Before locking the passengers and crew of the *Morning Star* in the hold, de Soto's men raped the women passengers. The women survived to tell of the atrocity, and the outrage that followed encouraged the maritime powers to crack down on this new wave of piracy.

passengers and the murder of wounded soldiers on board inflamed public passion. Overnight de Soto and his men became wanted criminals. Of course the pirates were oblivious to all this. They presumed that the crew and passengers had drowned, and that there was nobody left who could identify them.

Then came one of those strange coincidences. The surviving wounded soldiers had been dropped off in Gibraltar, where there was a large military hospital. By now it was early April, and the *Burla Negra* was cruising off the Spanish port of Cadiz, where the pirates hoped to sell their plundered cargo of silks and spices. Then a storm arose, and the *Burla Negra* was flung onto the lee shore. De Soto and most of his crew survived the disaster, and decided to make their way to the nearby port of Gibraltar, where they hoped to find another ship that they could take over once it put out to sea. The paths of one of the soldiers and the pirates crossed, and de Soto was identified and arrested. The governor agreed to extradite the prisoners to Cadiz, where they were duly tried, sentenced and hanged. The Spanish form of execution was unusual, involving the condemned man riding to the gallows in a cart, seated on his own coffin. After the noose was tightened the cart was pulled away, and the rope did the rest.

Another early 19th-century pirate who made the headlines was 'Don' Pedro Gibert, although he was singularly less successful than de Soto. Strangely enough, both pirates made the same mistake. They both left survivors behind who could identify them. Although it has been claimed that Pedro Gibert was the son of a Spanish nobleman, the title of 'Don' was something the Latin-American pirate adopted himself, rather than a rank that was his by birth. For a time he had sailed as a privateer, working for the junta that governed Colombia and preying on Spanish shipping in the Caribbean. However, by the late 1820s that was all in the past, and he had reinvented himself as a smuggler and illegal slave trader. He certainly had the perfect vessel for the job – a fast 150-ton Baltimore clipper (schooner) called the *Panda*, crewed by a dozen men who didn't have too many scruples.

Then in the early 1830s Pedro Gibert decided to try his hand at piracy. He already had a base – a secluded inlet somewhere on Florida's east coast, probably on or near the Saint Lucie River, which allowed easy access to the Bahamas Channel. On 20 September 1832 the American brig *Mexican* was passing through the Florida Straits, on its way from Salem, Massachusetts to Buenos Aires in Argentina. When Captain Isaac Butman spotted a schooner heading out from the Florida Keys to intercept him, he decided to alter course and keep his distance. The mystery vessel gave chase, and eventually the American brig was overhauled. Captain Butman tried to fire his guns, but the roundshot turned out to be the wrong calibre for the barrels. Realizing he was helpless, he went below and hid the ship's money chest – $20,000 in coin, with which he planned to buy his next cargo.

The mystery ship turned out to be the *Panda*. When Gibert and his men boarded the *Mexican* they locked up the crew in the forecastle, and then ransacked the ship. When they could not find any money the American captain was dragged out of the forecastle, then beaten and tortured until he told them where he had hidden it. Gibert now had what he wanted and prepared to return to the *Panda*. According to the American captain, when one of his crew asked what he wanted done with the prisoners, he replied, 'Dead cats don't mew. You know what to do.' However, rather than kill them outright, the pirates kept their prisoners locked up, then set fire to the ship. They then sailed away, leaving the American sailors to die.

However, one of the sailors managed to escape by squeezing out through a skylight. He freed his companions, and together they fought to bring the blaze under control. Somehow they managed it, but Butman made sure to keep a small fire going, so that the pall of smoke would still suggest that the *Mexican* was burning to the waterline. Once the pirate ship had sailed over the horizon the American sailors put the fire out completely, put their ship to rights, then sailed northwards again, away from the *Panda*. The *Mexican* eventually limped home, where news of the attack outraged the American public. Soon a worldwide hunt was under way for Don Gibert and his pirate crew.

Unable to return to Florida, Gibert decided to try his luck on the far side of the Atlantic. Eight months later, in early June 1833, Gibert was off Cape Lopez on the West African coast, where he planned to collect a cargo of Gabonese

slaves – a trade that was now officially banned, although illegal trading still continued. This meant that amongst other nations, Britain maintained an anti-slavery patrol in the area, in which warships looked out for illegal traders just like Gibert. Of course they were also well aware of Gibert and his activities, as the British Admiralty had already notified its captains to watch out for the pirates. The 10-gun brig HMS *Curlew*, commanded by Captain Henry Trotter, had been on slave patrol for three years, and so when its sailors sighted the *Panda* anchored off the Nazareth River (now the Olibatta, the northern mouth of the Ogowe River in Gabon) they realized she was a slaver. Although most of the pirates escaped ashore, Gibert and a dozen others were captured.

In 1832 the American brig *Mexican* was overhauled and captured by the pirate schooner *Panda*, commanded by Pedro Gibert, one of the last pirates of the era. Although it was set on fire, the crew survived, and once the pirates left they doused the flames and so were able to testify against Gibert and his men.

Trotter soon realized who his prisoners were. The *Panda* was destroyed by an accidental explosion, but the pirates were duly brought to Britain, where their capture was reported to the American ambassador. The brig HMS *Savage* then transported the prisoners to Massachusetts, where they stood trial in November 1834. In a Boston courtroom the pirates were faced by the crew of the *Mexican* they had left to die. The outcome was inevitable. While two of the pirates were acquitted and six more were given long prison sentences, Gibert and three others were sentenced to death. On 11 June 1835 Gibert and his companions were hanged – the last pirates to be executed on American soil. The pirate attack perpetrated by these men was really an isolated case, as by that time piracy on the high seas had become a thing of the past – at least in American waters. However, the great expansion of maritime trade in the 19th century meant that merchant ships began regularly to sail through other waters that were far from safe.

BROOKE AND THE MALAY PIRATES

While piracy was a worldwide phenomenon, it rarely had a global impact. Instead, incidents of piracy tended to flare up in different regions and then die away when maritime powers in the area found a way to deal with the problem. However, the growth of maritime trade in the 18th century meant that European and American merchants began to establish trade routes across the globe, and this in turn brought them into contact with regional pirates whose influence had rarely been felt beyond their own shores. Similarly, these foreign ships were seen as lucrative prizes for many who would otherwise have been content to eke out a peaceable living from the sea.

James Brook arrived in Sarawak as a trader in 1838, and he soon became the ruler of the small state on the coast of Borneo. As the raja of Sarawak he prosecuted a relentless war against local Dyak pirates.

For example, the Angrian dynasty that operated off the west coast of India in the early 18th century would hardly have been noticed by non-Indian historians had they not begun to prey on European East Indiamen. As a result, the British undertook a major campaign against the Angrian pirates during the 1750s, and their fleets and bases were destroyed. Similarly, the pirates who operated in the Red Sea and the Persian Gulf had little impact on the world until European traders became the victims of piratical attacks. The result was a string of punitive expeditions, which culminated in the British launching a large-scale assault on the Arabian pirates in the years following the end of the Napoleonic Wars.

The growth of trade with China in the 19th century meant that a new series of trade routes were opened up beyond the Spice Islands of the East Indies. This brought European and American ships and their crews into contact with a new set of pirates – those who operated in the waters of the South China Sea, the Philippines and the Malay Archipelago (now Indonesia). For the most part these were coastal pirates, operating within tightly confined geographical areas. However, some of these regions, such as the Malacca Strait between the Malay Peninsula and Sumatra, or the Makassar Straits between Borneo and the Celebes, became maritime bottlenecks, where these European traders sailed close to the shore. This made them tempting prey for the Malay pirates.

During his travels through the Malay Archipelago in the late 1850s, the British naturalist Alfred Russell Wallace described his encounter with local pirates:

Opposite us and along the coast of Batchian, stretches a row of fine islands completely uninhabited. Whenever I asked the reason why no one goes there to live, the answer was always, 'for fear of the Maguindanao pirates.' The scourges of the archipelago wander every year in one direction or the other, making their rendezvous on some uninhabited island, and carrying desolation to all of the settlements around … their long well-manned praos escape from the pursuit of a sailing vessel by pulling away right into the wind's eye, and the warning smoke of a steamer generally enables them to hide in some shallow bay or narrow river or forest covered inlet until the danger is past.

In another passage he wrote:

A small prao arrived which had been attacked by pirates and had a man wounded … The natives were of course dreadfully alarmed as these marauders attack their villages, burn and murder and carry away their women and children as slaves … They had four large war boats and fired a volley of musketry as they came up and sent off their small boats to attack. Two other praos were also plundered and the crews murdered to a man.

James Brooke, aided by sailors and marines from HMS *Dido*, attacks a Dyak pirate stronghold on the Saribas River in south-western Borneo. The action, fought in May 1843, ended with the destruction of the pirate base.

The coast of Borneo, the Celebes (now Sulawesi), Sumatra, Java and the Philippines were all perfect pirate havens, where a lack of central authority and easy access to these maritime bottlenecks meant that piracy thrived. The exceptions were a few small enclaves controlled by Europeans, such as the trading posts established by the Dutch, or else areas where strong tribal leaders managed to keep the pirates at bay using their own forces. The head-hunting Dyaks (or Dayaks) of Borneo were generally acknowledged to be the worst pirates in the region, and these were the fierce raiders described by Wallace. They ranged throughout the region, and developed a name for attacking European shipping sailing between Borneo and the Malay Peninsula.

Then there were the Ilanun people from the Philippines, who harassed Spanish shipping operating in Philippine waters. They also launched slaving raids throughout the area, selling their captives in the slave markets of the East Indies. Another formidable group were the Balanini or Sulu pirates from the north of Borneo (now Sabah). Their main stronghold was on the island of Jolo,

Dyak pirates ambush ship's boats and local canoes manned by sailors and marines from the British gunboats *Iris* and *Phlegethon*, during a punitive expedition against a Dyak pirate stronghold in Borneo in 1846.

in the Sulu Archipelago off the north of Borneo, although they operated throughout the region. Other pirate communities included the Bugis of Sulawesi, who divided their time between trading and piracy and were described by Wallace as 'the most mercenary, bloodthirsty, inhuman race', while the Atjeh (Achin) and Riau pirates operated in the strategic Malacca and Sunda Straits – on either side of their home island of Sumatra. For the most part these pirates used *proas* (also known as *praos*, *praus* or *prahus*) – shallow drafted canoes – although some variants were also employed, such as the *corocoro*, a fast sailing vessel fitted with outriggers, which could be powered by sail or oar.

While the Dutch generally tolerated these pirates as long as their own ships were not attacked, the British proved more proactive. The most celebrated European pirate hunter of the time was Sir James Brooke (1803–68), the 'White Rajah of Sarawak'. As the effective ruler of a small state in the middle of the Malay Archipelago, Brooke waged a private war against the 'Sea Dyaks' during the 1840s and 1850s, supported on occasion by the Royal Navy and by the Dutch. However, it was not until 1861 that a joint Anglo-Dutch force was sent into the region to stamp out piracy in the archipelago, and this, combined with similar Spanish expeditions, finally managed to subdue the pirates. Although the threat of pirate attacks remained, these were no longer considered a serious threat to European shipping. That, after all, was the main reason why most outsiders cared about the Malay pirates in the first place.

A Dyak warrior of Borneo, as depicted in an early 19th-century European engraving. They comprised dozens of sub-groups, some of which were seagoing peoples, and who, during the 19th century, relied largely on piracy for their livelihood.

In July 1845, James Brooke guided a Royal Naval punitive expedition into Marudu Bay in northern Borneo to assault a Dyak stronghold there. This sketch of the defences during the attack was drawn by a surgeon accompanying the attacking force, as reported by the crews of the British gunboats *Nemesis* and *Pluto*.

Chapter Nine

THE CHINESE PIRATES

PIRACY IN THE SOUTH CHINA SEA

Over the centuries piracy ebbed and flowed around the world, appearing and disappearing according to the whims of circumstance and the effectiveness of good government and naval power. However, in Chinese waters the threat of piracy remained constant for seafarers for more than a thousand years, probably longer. The first recorded incidence of piracy in the South China Sea took place in AD 589, around the time the emperor Wen unified China under the banner of his Sui Dynasty. It is almost a certainty, though, that piracy flourished long before, as the fragmented petty states provided pirates with the perfect political climate. Minor warlords dominated long stretches of the Chinese coast, their ships trading, raiding or conducting piratical attacks with equal ease. It was only when the emperor Wen and his dynasty managed to

A giant statue of Koxinga dominates a rocky headland on the Chinese island of Gulangyu, opposite the city of Xiamen. As well as being a Ming loyalist, Koxinga ruled a vast piratical and mercantile empire. In Chinese waters, trading, politics and piracy were often closely entwined. (Photo by Zhang Peng/LightRocket via Getty Images)

impose some degree of central authority that the power of these local warlords was temporarily checked. This proved short-lived, and so it was during the Ming Dynasty in the 13th and 14th centuries that Imperial authority was fully extended into China's coastal provinces. While this meant that these rulers acknowledged the emperor as their feudal master, it still did not mean they didn't involve themselves in piracy when it suited them. This might have been a golden period for China, as her merchants ranged as far as the Indian Ocean, but it was also a boom time for the pirates. It was the 15th century before the Chinese emperors came up with a reasonably effective solution. They simply paid the local rulers to suppress piracy in their own waters. As many of them were the same people who were responsible for the attacks, the policy was bound to work, at least in part. The Chinese government continued to adopt this pragmatic approach for the next five centuries.

In fact, the whole business of piracy was different in China from anywhere else in the world. For a start, piracy was highly organized. Rather than operating in individual ships, pirates congregated into large fleets. Instead of occupying small pirate havens, Chinese pirates tended to control large sections of the coast. Some of these pirate leaders were provincial landowners or governors, and so were also being paid by the Chinese authorities to suppress piracy in their own waters. This, of course, didn't stop them franchising out their pirate activities, or simply ordering their fleets to range further afield. For the most part these Chinese pirate confederations kept well away from politics, and ruled their pirate fiefdoms as independent states.

Chinese pirates operated more like a maritime mafia than anything else, using intimidation to extort protection money from coastal communities and from mariners, often over a wide area. Here, a Chinese pirate attacks villagers who refused his protection, wearing the head of a decapitated foe around his neck in order to intimidate any villagers who survived his assault.

Their strength lay in numbers. Both regional rulers and the emperor lacked the naval strength to do more than patrol their own sea lanes. As a result, for five centuries the pirates were allowed to operate virtually unchecked. It was not until the Europeans arrived with their steam-powered warships that the problem was finally dealt with.

Of course, China was not the only country in the Far East to suffer from piracy. The waters around Japan were plagued by pirates well into the 16th century. Another pirate 'hot-spot' was the coast of what is now Vietnam. Before the 10th century the region was just another Chinese province, but from AD 939 onwards it ran its own affairs, at

In 1627 Pieter Nuijts of the Dutch East India Company became the governor on Formosa and imposed trading tariffs on the Chinese and Japanese merchants. Effectively, they saw this as a Chinese pirate-style protection racket, and in 1628, when they refused to pay, the Dutch seized their ships. An irate Japanese merchant and privateering leader responded by seizing Nuijts by force and holding him until all his ships were released by the Dutch.

least until the French arrived in the 19th century. This said, the Vietnamese still had to pay an annual tribute to the Chinese emperor, and the country remained divided into small semi-autonomous provinces, similar to those found along the Chinese coastline. Local rulers used piracy as a means of protecting their own fiefdom at the expense of their neighbours. Piratical activity reached a peak during the Tay Song Dynasty (1778–1802), a period of widespread rebellion and decentralization. Even the reunification of Vietnam by the Nguyen Dynasty did little to check the influence of these small pirate kingdoms. It was only through the intervention of the European powers (primarily the French) that the power of the Vietnamese pirates was finally broken.

The arrival of the first Europeans in the late 16th century brought traders into contact with these pirates, and, just like the Chinese and Vietnamese rulers themselves, the Europeans had to reach some form of accommodation with them in order to trade. Their arrival coincided with the rise of the first large-scale pirate 'empire' – that of the Chinese warlord Ching Chih-lung (or Zheng Zhilong, 1604–61), who operated in Fujian province. His power showed that, in China, piracy and politics were intertwined, since Ching combined his role as a pirate leader with those of a province administrator, a leading merchant trader, and even an admiral in the Imperial navy! His son, Zheng Chenggong (nicknamed Koxinga) would expand this pirate empire into what was effectively the most powerful maritime power in the South China Sea.

This continued until the European powers sent powerful modern warships into Chinese waters. The successful defence of European trading enclaves during the Opium Wars of the mid-19th century was due to the presence of these naval forces, and these European squadrons remained there afterwards, protecting the interests of European merchants against local warlords and pirates alike. Their technological advantage over the Chinese (and Vietnamese) pirates meant that relatively small naval forces were able to conduct punitive expeditions that succeeded in destroying the naval power of these pirate kingdoms. This allowed European commerce to prosper without the constant threat of attack. In effect a combination of colonial police work, maritime steam power and shell-firing naval ordnance brought an end to a thousand years of pirate domination in the South China Sea.

KOXINGA

Zheng Cheggong (1624–62), better known as Koxinga, was loyal to the old Ming Dynasty and fought doggedly against the new Qing emperors, as well as the Dutch, who increasingly threatened his far-flung trading empire. While his rivals branded him a pirate, in fact he was a privateer, albeit one fighting on his own terms for a dynasty that had been driven from power.

The first of the three great Chinese pirate empires was based in Fukien province, opposite the island of Taiwan. Ching Chih-lung was a surprising pirate chief. After all, he was more of a merchant than a sea robber. He served his business apprenticeship with a Chinese trading magnate, working both in Japan (where he found a wife, Tagawa Matsu), and with Dutch merchants, who had recently established an outpost on the Penghu (Pescadores) Islands in the Formosa (now Taiwan) Strait. He may well have dabbled in piracy during the early 1620s, using the Dutch port as a base and acting more as a Dutch privateer than as a pirate.

When his trading mentor died in 1623, his merchant fleet and escorting war junks were passed to Ching. He established himself in Taiwan, but a growing rivalry with the Dutch encouraged him to move his operation to Amoy (Xiamen), the main port in the Amoy Islands (then called the Zsu-ming prefecture), and other ports in Fukien. While the mercantile arm of his maritime empire suffered from Dutch competition, the Europeans were traders, not pirates, and as long as Cheng avoided attacking Dutch ships, his pirate fleet was able to operate without restriction. One of his most daring ventures was a large-scale raid on shipping in the mouth of the Yangtse River. This secured his reputation as the unrivalled master

In 1661 Koxinga attacked the Dutch base in Formosa in support of a local rebellion. The following year he captured Fort Zeelandia and drove the European settlers from the island. Here, he is shown at the height of the siege, ordering the Dutch missionary Anthonius Hambroek to offer his terms to the fort's garrison.

of the Chinese seas. Within a decade his pirate war junks cruised as far afield as the Vietnamese coast and the Yellow Sea, and merchant ship owners were forced to pay him protection money to remain in business.

They were not the only ones who paid Ching off. In 1641 the Ming emperor Zhu Youjian (Chongzhen) needed help in countering the revolt that would eventually cost him his throne. Consequently he appointed Ching as his 'Admiral of Coastal Waters', and put him in charge of the suppression of piracy. The pirate chief was even paid an Imperial salary for three years, until the Manchu rebels captured Beijing and Zhu Youjian was forced to commit suicide. Ching Chih-lung aligned himself with the Ming successor Prince Tang in 1645. He ruled Fukien in the name of the doomed Ming Dynasty, but in 1649 he was persuaded to change sides, so allowing the Manchus to capture the province. His actions helped secure the end of Ming resistance, and therefore the new Manchu (Qing) Dynasty rewarded Ching for his efforts.

He remained in charge of Fukien for another two decades, until in 1661 he was summoned to Bejing. There the great pirate chief was held accountable for his son's actions, and he was executed. His son, Koxinga, was born in 1624, most probably during his father's stay in the Japanese port of Nagasaki. He was raised in Fukien, and during the late 1640s he took part in his father's military campaign on behalf of the Ming Dynasty. From around 1650 onwards, he also ran the twin family businesses of trade and piracy, leaving his father free to concentrate on his political responsibilities.

THE JUNK

For centuries the junk was the mainstay of Chinese and South-East Asian maritime shipping, equally suitable as a merchant trader or as a pirate ship. It was the Portuguese who first coined the name *junco*, a derivative of the Indonesian *djong*. The junks used by the pirates of the South China Sea were little different from the junks encountered by Marco Polo centuries before, and their motor-powered descendants can still be seen today.

Most pirate junks were converted from trading junks, armed with several guns (including numerous small swivel pieces called *lantakas*), and crewed by as many as 200 men. Some of the largest pirate junks were over 100ft (30.5m) long, with a beam of 20ft (6m), and carried three masts. The largest seagoing pirate junks had a substantial cargo space in the hold, part of which was used to store powder and shot. Junks were also divided into numerous small compartments below decks, which offered some form of protection against flooding if they were hit by enemy shot. This made them a lot less fragile than they looked.

Although the Europeans sometimes described junks as being primitive craft, mariners recognized that they were ideally suited to the waters of the South China Sea, being fast, reliable and commodious.

Much has been written about Koxinga the pirate chief, the Taiwanese hero and Ming loyalist. Although many of the legends that surrounded him fail to stand up to historical scrutiny, the pirate chief certainly became a figurehead for anti-Manchu resistance, and the defender of the older Ming civilization. One of these legends describes how he captured the city of Chinchew (Quanzhou) from the Manchus, only to find that his mother had died during the siege. As the story goes, he went to the temple, then burned his old clothes as a symbol, and declared his intent: 'In the past I was a good Confucian subject and a good son. Now I'm an orphan without an Emperor – I have no country and no home. I have sworn to fight the Manchu army to the end, but my father has surrendered and my only choice is to be a disloyal son. Please forgive me.'

At first he operated in Fukien, enjoying the protection of his father. However, as the new commander of the family's pirate fleet, he concentrated his attacks on Manchu shipping. He also masterminded a series of amphibious attacks by Ming rebels against Manchu territory. Inevitably the overwhelming military might of the Manchus meant that eventually he had to abandon the mainland of Fukien. So he took refuge just off the coast in Amoy (Xiamen), a port in the Amoy Islands, where the Manchus were unable to reach him. A military

The Chinese port of Amoy (now Xiamen) in Fujian province was used as a base by Koxinga for his attacks on both the Qing Dynasty and the Dutch. This Dutch engraving of the port dates from 1665. By then, Koxinga had moved his base to Taiwan.

stalemate followed that lasted for a decade, although Koxinga still served as a focal point for anti-Manchu resistance.

The high point of this struggle came in 1659, when he led a pirate fleet up the Yangtse River as part of a combined rebel assault on the Manchu capital of Nanking (Nanjing). The enterprise was a disaster, as the Manchus were able to trap the pirate fleet in the river and then destroy it. Koxinga managed to escape, but the rebel cause was lost. While Koxinga's anti-Manchu resistance is verified by historical sources, the suspicion is that his exploits have been exaggerated by later historians. He is often portrayed as a sort of Chinese Robin Hood figure, whereas the truth was probably quite different.

The Dutch traders who operated in the region certainly painted a somewhat different picture. Although they describe Koxinga as a rebel, they suggest that politics were only a secondary concern for him. First and foremost, Koxinga was a pirate. The Amoy Islands just off the coast of Fukien provided him with an ideal base for operations. While the Manchus dominated the mainland, including his father's province of Fukien, Koxinga ruled the seas – and ran his pirate empire. He continued his father's policy of offering protection money to merchants from Korea to Vietnam, while his pirate junks attacked anyone who

THE RAIDS OF KOXINGA

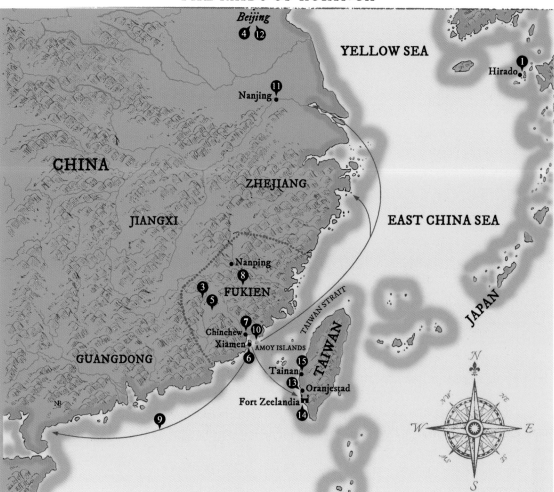

refused to pay. Unlike his father, Koxinga was prepared to take on the Dutch, who reported to Amsterdam that Koxinga's pirate junks regularly attacked Dutch shipping, off the new Dutch colony of Taiwan. For more than a decade Koxinga maintained complete control over the coastal waters from the Mekong Delta to the mouth of the Yangtse.

The disaster at Nanking in 1659 meant that for the first time, Koxinga was placed on the strategic defensive. His naval power had been weakened, and there was now no guarantee that the Manchus would not commit their overwhelming resources to an assault on the Amoy Islands, whose proximity to the Chinese mainland made them an obvious target. He also lost his one ally in

KEY

•••• Border of Fukien province   ◄──── Raids against the Manchu and the Dutch   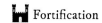 Fortification

1. 1624: Kuo Hsing Yeh (or Koxinga) is born in Hirado in Japan.
2. Around 1631: Koxinga's father Ching Chih-lung establishes his trading and smuggling business in Fukien province.
3. 1641: Koxinga's father is made an admiral by the Ming emperor.
4. 1644: Manchu invaders capture Beijing and depose the emperor. Ching Chih-lung remains loyal to the old Ming dynasty.
5. 1646: The Manchus conquer Fukien and force Ching Chih-lung to accept their authority.
6. Early 1647: Koxinga refuses to submit, and establishes a Ming rebel base at Chinmen (Xiamen) in the Amoy Islands. He begins attacking Manchu ships and garrisons.
7. Late 1647: Koxinga's mother commits suicide in Chinchew, rather than surrender to the Manchus.
8. 1650: Koxinga takes over his father's trading empire and concentrates on building up its piratical and smuggling operations.
9. 1651: Koxinga's pirate junks are now extorting protection money throughout the South China Sea. Only Manchu officials and the Dutch in Taiwan refuse to pay.
10. 1656: The Manchus attempt to invade the Amoy Islands, but are repulsed by Koxinga's forces.
11. 1659: Koxinga attacks Nanjing (or Nanking), but is repulsed by the Manchu garrison.
12. 1661: In response to the raid, Ching Chih-lung is executed in Beijing.
13. April 1661: Koxinga besieges the Dutch settlement of Oranjestad (now Tainan) in Taiwan.
14. February 1662: The Dutch stronghold of Fort Zeelandia outside Oranjestad surrenders to Koxinga, the Dutch colonists capitulate, and Taiwan now falls to the Chinese pirate and warlord.
15. July: Koxinga dies in Tainan, but his son takes over his empire. He would continue its piratical activities for another four decades.

Fukien when, in 1661, the Manchus executed his father in retaliation for his son's resistance. This meant that Koxinga needed a more secure base.

In 1661 he launched an amphibious attack on Formosa, landing on the southern tip of the island near the modern city of Kao-hsiung. The Dutch had built a powerful fortress – Fort Zeelandia – on a sandy spit which defended their main settlement of Oranjestad (Orange City, now Tainan). On 30 April Koxinga blockaded the settlement with a fleet of 400 pirate junks, while his army of 25,000 men laid siege to the fort. The siege that followed lasted for nine months, but with no prospect of relief and most of his 2,000-man garrison stricken by thirst, hunger and disease, Governor Coylett had no option but to surrender. On 1 February 1662 the Dutch surrendered Formosa to Koxinga, who accepted control of the island in the name of the Ming Dynasty.

The capture of Formosa was a triumph for the pirate chief, but he didn't live long enough to enjoy the spoils of war. Later that year he died of malaria, although there were rumours that his death was the result of a seizure following a disagreement with his son. Today, Zheng Chenggong (Koxinga) is seen as a

In 1806, pirates from Cheng Yih's Red Flag Fleet attacked a cutter belonging to the East India 'country ship' *Tay* and captured Chief Mate John Turner and six Lascar seamen. Turner was held captive for several months, and later wrote an account of his ordeal.

hero, both in Taiwan and in mainland China, where his reputation as a defender of Ming culture and civilization seems to have outweighed his crimes as a pirate warlord. Taiwan even boasts a shrine to Koxinga, which makes him the only pirate ever to be considered a religious deity. After his death Koxinga's pirate empire was taken over by his eldest son Zheng Jing (1642–81) who held Formosa against the Manchus for two more decades. However, he was unable to hold together the great pirate fleet, and it fragmented soon after Koxinga's death. This left Formosa open to invasion, and in 1681 the Manchus overran the Amoy and Penghu Islands and then attacked Formosa. Cheng Ching died fighting the invaders, and although his followers continued fighting for another two years after his death, the island eventually fell to the Manchus.

THE GREAT PIRATE CONFEDERATION

After the collapse of the great pirate empire of Koxinga, piracy in Chinese waters became a fragmented business, in which no one pirate chief or warlord was able to unite the various groups under a single banner. This lasted for a century, a period when individual provincial rulers acted as both pirates and traders, and when their influence extended no further than the boundaries of their own territorial waters. Then Cheng Yih appeared, and within a decade he had created a pirate empire that rivalled that of Koxinga.

As the son of a Chinese pirate operating in Vietnamese waters, Cheng Yih (or Zheng Shi, 1765–1807) was born into the business. His family had been pirates for generations. This was a time when Vietnam was in turmoil, as the Tay Son rebels were busy wresting control of the country from the Nguyen lords, who had ruled it for centuries. By the time the conflict ended the pirate had taken advantage of the chaos to become the leading maritime power in Vietnam. However, the re-establishment of order meant that his presence would soon be considered a threat to the country's new rulers. So in 1801 he moved his operation along the coast to the Chinese province of Guangdong (Kwangtung), a major centre of the opium trade.

In April 1804 he blockaded the Portuguese trading port of Macao and defeated a small Portuguese squadron sent to drive him off. This prompted the British to escort shipping in the waters off Hong Kong, Macao and other European enclaves on the Chinese coast. However, the threat posed by Cheng

Although these pirates wear Indian headgear, they purport to depict the Chinese pirates attacking a local East India company trader off Canton in 1809. The pirates often held European sailors for ransom.

THE ROUTES OF THE GREAT PIRATE CONFEDERATION

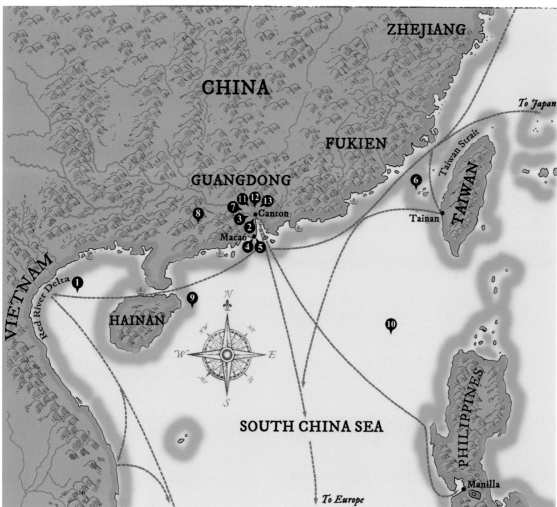

Yih was still growing. In 1805 he formed a pirate confederation, uniting the Chinese pirates who operated along the coast of the South China Sea into one mighty pirate empire. He divided this force into six fleets, each known by a colour – black, white, red, blue, yellow and green. Each fleet was also given a particular area to operate in, which helped ensure that the fleets would not fight each other or interfere in each other's operations.

Cheng Yih retained a merely nominal control over the other pirate fleets, but he kept his original fleet for himself. This force of some 200 pirate junks became the 'Red Flag Fleet', and was based in the provincial capital of Canton (now

KEY

⟵ Trade routes   🚢 Pirate fleet base

1. Spring 1801: In Vietnam's Red River, Cheng Yih inherits his father's pirate fleet.
2. Summer: Cheng Yih moves his pirate operation to Canton, in Guangdong province.
3. October: Cheng Yih marries Cheng Shi, a brothel 'madam' from Canton.
4. March 1804: His pirate fleet blockades the Portuguese port of Macao, as the Europeans refuse to pay protection money.
5. September: The pirates drive off a Portuguese squadron sent to drive them away from Macao. The protection money is paid.
6. October: Cheng Yih expands his protection money operation to include Fukien and Taiwan. His ships now control the whole coast from the Yellow River to the Red River.
7. 1805: Cheng Yih's confederation now consists of six pirate fleets, the largest of which is his own Red Flag Fleet, based in Canton.
8. 1806: The pirates attack villages in Guangdong in order to establish their control of the whole coastal region of the province.
9. 1807: Cheng Yih is lost at sea off Hainan, and his Red Flag Fleet is taken over by his wife. She is generally known as 'Madam Cheng'.
10. 1808–09: Madam Cheng takes control of her husband's pirate confederation.
11. September 1809: Madam Cheng's pirates attack British ships off Canton and hold their crews hostage. This provokes a major diplomatic incident.
12. Summer 1810: A European naval force destroys the Red Flag Fleet off Canton, and then hunts down and destroys the other fleets of the confederation.
13. October: The Chinese emperor offers the pirates an amnesty, and Madam Cheng accepts. She retires from piracy to concentrate on running other business interests, including opium smuggling.

Guangzhou). By the time of his death in 1807, Cheng Yih's Red Flag Fleet had trebled in size to some 600 pirate junks, crewed by around 30,000 men, making it the largest pirate fleet in the South China Sea. Of course this was only part of his power base – in time of need he could also count on the rest of his pirate confederation, whose commanders had agreed to help each other in time of difficulty. That meant that Cheng Yih could call upon as many as 1,200 junks and 150,000 men. This made it the largest pirate confederation in history. Protection money was demanded from Chinese merchants and coastal communities, and Cheng Yih's junks seemed able to roam at will, attacking ships or demanding payment with complete impunity.

The reason Cheng Yih could get away with this was that the Chinese government had failed miserably in all its attempts to deal with piracy. In fact, it seemed more intent on limiting the

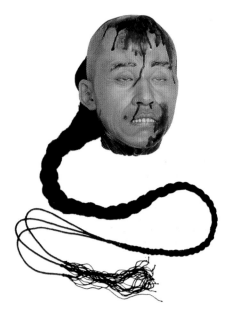

impact of European traders than on protecting its own national trade routes. Any Imperial response to the pirate threat required the support of provincial governors, many of whom were either in league with the pirates or were pirate leaders themselves. If an Imperial force was gathered for a punitive expedition, Cheng Yih simply matched it with a much larger pirate fleet, and the emperor's commanders were forced to back down. The arrangement was that if one pirate fleet was threatened, then the other coloured fleets would come to its aid. In effect this meant that the pirate confederation was invulnerable to attack. However, after his attack on the Portuguese, Cheng Yih was at pains to discourage attacks on European traders. After all, while he might be able to deal with the forces of the Chinese emperor, the combined naval might of these foreigners might be a different matter entirely.

Cheng Yih was at the height of his power when he died in late 1807, probably by being washed overboard during a storm. His wife Cheng Shi (or Zheng Yih Sao, which means 'wife of Cheng Yih') took over control of the Red Flag Fleet, and somehow managed to hold together the rest of the pirate confederation. She is also sometimes referred to as the 'Widow Cheng', or as 'Madam Cheng'. She was aided in this takeover by Cheung Po Tsai (or Chang Po), the young male lover (and adopted son) of her husband Cheng Yih, who duly transferred his allegiance and affections to the pirate leader's wife. According to tradition, Madam Cheng first came to the attention of the pirate leader when she worked as a prostitute in Canton. She went on to rule a vast pirate empire.

The East India Company's paddle-wheel warship *Nemesis*, pictured here in the pirate den of Anson's Bay near Canton, destroying a fleet of pirate junks. The pirates were unable to match the manoeuvrability and modern firepower of these British steam-powered gunboats.

Madam Cheng proved to be a natural pirate leader, and over the next few years she developed a reputation for ferocity and skill, building up the Red Flag Fleet and its confederate fleets into a force of 800 pirate junks. For the next three years she completely dominated the coastal waters from Hainan as far as Formosa. Also, unlike her husband, Madam Cheng refused to be

Arguably the most powerful pirate of all time was Cheng Shi, also known as Zheng Yih Sao, or more commonly as Madam Cheng. As the wife of a pirate leader, on his death in 1807 she inherited his Red Flag Fleet, which she expanded into a unified force of 300 ships and up to 20,000 men. However, from 1810, after a string of battles with both the Portuguese and the forces of the Qing emperor, she accepted an amnesty and retired from the sea.

intimidated by the Europeans. In September 1809 she kidnapped a group of seven British seamen from an East Indiaman anchored off Canton. They were eventually released after a ransom was paid, and one of them, Richard Glasspole, left an account of his experiences. He described the code of laws under which Madam Cheng governed, in which theft, disobedience or rape was punishable by death, and lesser crimes such as desertion involved the cutting off of an ear, a thumb or even a limb. The result of this severity, according to Glasspole, was to create a force that was disciplined, resolute and united.

However, the whole pirate empire started to break down. Unable to defeat the pirates on the high seas, the Chinese authorities adopted a 'carrot and stick' approach. First came the stick – supervised by Pai Ling, the new provincial governor of Guangdong. He declared war against the pirates operating around Canton, and crucially solicited European help to defeat them. First he resettled thousands of inhabitants of coastal settlements further inland, thereby denying the pirates a source of revenue and provisions. Supported by European warships, the Cantonese fleet cleared the local waters of pirates by the end of the year. Then came the carrot. The emperor offered a pardon to all Chinese pirates, and the terms were generous enough to be tempting. One of the first to accept the offer was Cheung Po Tsai, who defected to Pai Ling in early 1810, taking most of the Red Flag Fleet with him. This was a severe blow to Cheng Shi. Her world was rapidly falling apart.

The confederation was in disarray, as many pirate captains saw the benefits of accepting the pardon, which opened up lucrative Imperial markets that had hitherto been denied to them. Worse, the five remaining coloured banner fleets began fighting one another, as some accepted the pardon – and Imperial rewards – while others held out. Some, like Cheung Po Tsai, became pirate hunters, and actively campaigned against their former comrades. By the end of the year Cheng

Shi was forced to admit defeat, and she accepted the pardon herself. However, she was allowed to retain her own small force of ships and men, and she remained an influential figure in Guangdong; for the next three decades she ran the biggest opium smuggling operation on the Chinese coast. For his part, Cheung Po Tsai went on to become a highly respected Imperial admiral, although it was suggested that he never quite turned his back on his old piratical ways.

SHAP-'NG-TSAI

The threat of piracy receded slightly during the early 19th century, but it never completely went away. The Chinese policy of bribing regional officials continued to reap dividends. However, three decades after the collapse of Cheng Shi's great pirate confederation, the Europeans and the Chinese had come to blows, the friction being caused by the import of Indian opium into China on board British ships. When the Chinese seized ships carrying the drug, the British reacted with military force, initiating a conflict known as the First Opium War (1839–42). It ended with the Chinese being forced to sign a humiliating trade agreement that further opened up the country to European trade. Hong Kong Island was occupied by the British in 1841, and was formally ceded to Britain a year later. Canton also became an open port, and by 1843 it had become the centre of a thriving opium trade. From there the drug was smuggled along the coast to other ports, and by encouraging smugglers the trade also encouraged piracy, an occupation adopted by many smugglers in their spare time.

The pirate leader Chui A-poo pictured here was the deputy of the great 19th-century pirate chief Shap-'ng-Tsai, but he also commanded his own substantial pirate fleet. His lair was at Bias Bay (or Daya Bay) to the east of Hong Kong, a place that remained a pirate haven until the early 20th century. Chui A-poo was eventually defeated by a British naval expedition in 1849. He was subsequently arrested, and died in prison.

While the Chinese navy should have been powerful enough to deal with this problem, its recent encounter with the Royal Navy had left it demoralized and in no condition to fight a major anti-piracy campaign beyond the waters surrounding the major ports. Shap-'ng-Tsai was one such smuggler-turned-pirate, who was based in Tien-pai (sometimes called Tin Pak – now Dianbai) in the western corner of Guangdong province, 175 miles (282km) west of Hong Kong. He offered protection to smugglers in exchange for money, and during the 1840s this business expanded until he was able to extort payment from coastal shipping operating between Hainan Island and Canton.

By 1849 his fleet had grown to 70 pirate junks, and his protection racket had been extended as far as Vietnam. Then he made the mistake of attacking 'treaty' vessels – the European and American carriers who shipped opium into the 'treaty ports'. He captured one American and

This watercolour sketch ʰ Naval Surgeon Edward Cree shows 'a boatload of piratical rascals', captured survivors of the destruction of Shap-'ng-Tsai's pirate fleet in Vietnam's Red River (Hong Ha) Delta in October 1849.

three British opium-carrying clipper ships, which led to a panic in the treaty ports that disrupted trade. If Shap-'ng-Tsai had limited his piratical attacks and the extortion of protection money to Chinese victims, then the foreigners would probably have left him alone. However, an attack against Western ships was a different matter.

In September 1849 the Royal Navy commander of the Hong Kong Squadron was given orders to attack the pirate lair – a punitive expedition that had been demanded by the East India Company, whose shipping had been disrupted. Consequently, the Scottish-born Commander John Hay led a squadron of steam warships into Tien-pai, only to find that the pirates had already fled. Tipped off by his spies in Hong Kong, Shap-'ng-Tsai had led his

In October 1849 a Royal Naval squadron entered Bias Bay and destroyed Chui A-poo's fleet of pirate junks. The British also went ashore to destroy the pirate's lair, including its warehouses and shipyard.

Shap-'ng-Tsai's elaborate pirate flag was captured by the British in October 1849, after the destruction of the pirate fleet in the Red River. It depicts T'ien Hou, a mythical heavenly empress, the calmer of storms and the protector of mariners. It is now in the collection of the National Maritime Museum in Greenwich.

Following the destruction of Shap-'ng-Tsai's pirate fleet by the Royal Navy in October 1849, local Cochin villagers attacked many of the survivors in retribution for the pirates' own depredations against their fishing community. The scene was sketched by a British naval surgeon whose ship HMS *Fury* took part in the battle.

pirate fleet westwards towards the safety of Haiphong in Vietnam, leaving Commander Hay with little to show for his efforts except the recapture of a hundred trading junks.

According to Admiralty law these captured junks were now prizes of the Royal Navy, and once the expedition returned to Hong Kong they were sold in auction to the highest bidder. In this case the bidder turned out to be none other than an agent of Shap-'ng-Tsai, who simply bought his prizes back again. It was soon clear that a second naval expedition would be needed to deal with the pirate fleet, so once again Commander Hay was ordered into action.

In late October his squadron tracked the pirates down in the Red River (Hong Ha) Delta, just north of the Vietnamese port of Haiphong. First Commander Hay blockaded the river mouth to prevent any escape, and then he led part of his fleet into action against the pirates. For this operation his three steam warships (including the East India Company armed paddle-steamer *Phlegethon*) were supported by a squadron of Imperial Chinese junks. The pirates were taken by surprise and their junks were still at anchor when Hay arrived. The battle was one-sided, and by the end of the engagement 58 pirate junks had been captured or sunk, and 1,800 pirates killed.

As for Shap-'ng-Tsai, he escaped in a small junk, one of six to survive the battle. The British were unable to pursue him far up the Red River, so he got clean away. The Chinese then solved the problem of the pirate still being at large by offering him a pardon. Not only did Shap-'ng-Tsai accept it, but he went on to hold a commission in the Imperial navy, helping to scour Chinese waters for pirates. The incident also led to a permanent Royal Navy presence on the Chinese coast, and over the next few years it continued its anti-piracy operations, working in conjunction with the Chinese government and the East India Company. Consequently, by the mid-19th century the waters of the South China Sea were deemed to be largely clear of organized piracy, a victory achieved through a combination of Chinese pragmatism and Western firepower.

The aftermath of the execution of pirates on the beach at Kowloon in the Hong Kong colony, 1891. The sentence of beheading was carried out by British soldiers.

Chapter Ten

MODERN PIRACY

DANGEROUS WATERS

Piracy is not a thing of the past, a romanticized form of crime from the pages of history. It still happens every day, and the victims don't always live to tell the tale. In recent years it has hit the headlines, as even the largest super-tankers have fallen victim to pirate attack. As an example, in 2018 the International Chamber of Commerce (ICC) issued a warning that off Nigeria, 'all waters remain risky'. It added that off Port Harcourt and Bonny Island 'There has been a notable increase in attacks, hijackings and the kidnapping of crews ... vessels are advised to take additional measures in these high-risk areas.'

Over the past few decades organizations like the ICC have been monitoring pirate attacks, and have identified clear pirate 'hot-spots' where attacks are commonplace events. The waters of Indonesia, Somalia, Bangladesh, West Africa (especially Nigeria), the Philippines, and Venezuela have all been identified as high-risk areas. In 2017 there were 180 incidents worldwide, which is actually fewer than any year

An armed sailor from Benin's Force Navale keeps an eye on a pair of moored tankers during a naval patrol of the Bight of Benin. This region of the West African coast is becoming a major pirate 'hot-spot'. (Photo by jason florio/Corbis via Getty Images)

since 2010. However, while some areas such as the waters of Malaya have become safer, others, such as the Philippines, are now major pirate 'hot-spots'.

Piracy in these dangerous waters is not a new phenomenon. In the early 19th century the waters of the Persian Gulf were plagued by pirates, and it took a major initiative by the British East India Company to eradicate the threat they posed. The same was true in China during the early 20th century, when a collapse of central authority led to rule by local warlords – a situation reminiscent of the one described in the previous chapter. The maritime powers – mainly represented by the Royal Navy and the US Navy – took an active part in eradicating piracy on the Chinese rivers, as they did in other pirate 'hot-spots' of the pre-war world such as the Malay Archipelago, Central America and the Philippines. For the most part these pirate attacks were isolated incidents, or at worst they represented a temporary resurgence in maritime crime. Other piratical acts were also reported around the globe – the attack on a British merchant freighter in a small North African port, the plunder of an Australian fishing boat in the South Pacific, or the murder of a lone American yachtsman off the coast of Cuba. None of these incidents warranted the dispatch of a punitive expedition, but, when required, the maritime powers considered anti-piracy operations to be part of their job.

Previously, the most vulnerable type of mariner was the yachtsman. Nowadays even the crews of the largest vessels in the world are placing themselves at risk when they sail into these dangerous waters. Before World War II, 'modern' piracy was virtually unknown, and only sporadic incidents were reported around the world. Since then it has been on the increase, and within the past three decades the number of reported incidents has mounted dramatically. There are various reasons for this. First, the post-war trend is for navies to become smaller and more specialized. While in the past the maritime powers had the ships to patrol likely trouble spots, and could always 'send a gunboat', now merchant ships are largely left to their own devices on the high seas. Many smaller governments lack the resources or authority to patrol their own waters, let alone to hunt for pirates on the high seas. As in any other time, piracy thrives when there's a lack of a strong government, supported by an effective judicial system and navy.

A pirate in the Philippines uses an outboard-powered outrigger canoe to attack passing ships, and to hide in among the numerous islands, bays and shoals in the region.

These pirates based in the Niger Delta of Nigeria portray themselves as insurgents – members of MEND (Movement for the Emancipation of the Niger Delta). While numbers of attacks have declined since 2008, some MEND attacks now take place far out in the Gulf of Guinea.

Modern-day pirates now enjoy all the advantages of technology – radios, radar, satellite navigation, automatic weapons and high-performance boats. This gives them an advantage over their historical predecessors. Above all, there is a lack of regulation on the high seas due to a shortage of interest, of international goodwill and of resources. The erosion of national maritime fleets has been partly to blame. These days the majority of the world's merchant shipping sails under flags of convenience, especially those of Liberia, Panama or Honduras, rather than under the merchant marine flags of the major maritime

In many cases, the Somali pirates used captured fishing vessels as mother ships for smaller speedboats, allowing them to attack targets far out into the Indian Ocean. Here, members of an anti-piracy patrol stop a suspected pirate mother ship, some 120 miles (193km) from the Somali coast.

PIRATE OF MALAYSIA AND THE PHILIPPINES

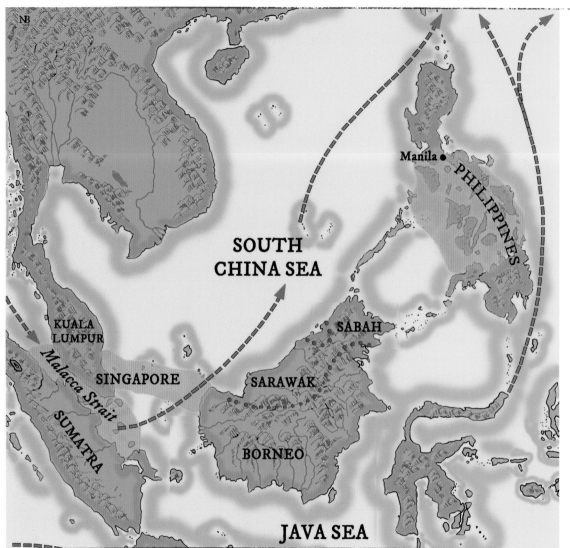

powers. In fact, it's only comparatively recently that piracy has been regarded as a serious form of international crime, worthy of combating on the international level. Meanwhile the pirates have prospered.

In 1985, the first year the ICC began recording pirate attacks, there were some 50 recorded incidents of piracy around the world. This total increased steadily every year – just over 200 in 1998, 300 in 1999 and on to a peak of 445 in 2003. The number of attacks then declined due to international involvement in anti-

KEY

●●●●● Country borders   ◄ ― ― Shipping routes   ▮ Pirate 'hot-spots'

This region has long been a pirate 'hot-spot'. Until 2005 the Malacca Strait was plagued by pirates, but a major international naval effort led to the eradication of much of this threat. These waters are still heavily patrolled. The Malaysian islands at the southern base of the South China Sea have seen a significant rise in piratical activity, and the International Maritime Bureau consider this a high-risk area. Since 2000 there has been a marked increase in piratical activity in the waters of the Philippines, and much of this has been linked to rebel groups, who see piracy and kidnapping as a useful means to raise funds. Recently, attacks have even taken place in Manila Bay, one of the busiest harbours in Southeast Asia.

piracy operations, so that by 2013 it was down to 264 attacks. These are only incidents involving registered ships – they ignore the hundreds, if not thousands, of attacks against yachts, small fishing boats or other vessels not big enough to make the grade. Ten years ago, a third of these attacks took place in the Malacca Strait. Today these waters see just a couple of incidents, while Indonesia has become the new world hot-spot, with 38 attacks registered in 2017.

However, the news is not wholly bad. In the last few years the number of incidents has been on the decrease. According to the Piracy Reporting Centre of the International Maritime Bureau (IMB), a wing of the ICC, there were 329 attacks in 2004, but for ten years after that numbers steadied at around 250 attacks a year. From 2016 this total has been decreasing. The agency credited the improving situation to better levels of international co-operation, particularly the presence of international anti-piracy patrols off Somalia, and in other pirate 'hot-spots' around the world.

Disregarding the risks inherent in sailing through the waters of a modern war zone, until recently the most dangerous stretch of water in the world was generally regarded to be the Malacca Strait, the 550-mile- (885km-) long waterway separating the Malay Peninsula and the island of

Sumatra. More than 50,000 ships a year pass through these waters, making it one of the busiest maritime bottlenecks in the world, as well as the most dangerous. Many of these ships are the largest vessels afloat, the super-tankers and bulk carriers that dwarf even the largest ocean liner. A quarter of the world's annual oil supply passes through these waters, the equivalent of 11 million barrels of oil each day. Ships have to slow down while they thread their way through such a busy waterway, which makes them vulnerable to attack by well-armed pirates operating in fast speedboats or inflatables.

The good news is that by 2007 there were only 11 pirate incidents in this strategic narrow waterway. By 2014 this had dropped further, and today attacks are virtually non-existent. While much of the credit for this lies with the large-scale naval and intelligence-gathering campaign waged by the international maritime community, the authorities were unable to stamp out piracy altogether. It almost looks as if the local pirates are biding their time, waiting for the warships to go away. In this respect they are little different from the pirates of the 'Golden Age', avoiding areas where the navy is known to patrol, and either moving elsewhere to continue their trade, or else adopting more legitimate pursuits until the situation improves.

The obvious effect of this is that piratical incidents have been on the increase in the neighbouring waters of Indonesia, with 108 attacks recorded in 2015 alone. It still tops the list of the world's pirate 'hot-spots'. However, a campaign by the Indonesian navy meant that attacks decreased by half the following year. Another pirate 'hot-spot' is Chittagong in Bangladesh, where 46 attacks were recorded in 2006. The port was viewed as the most dangerous anchorage in the world, but today fewer than a dozen incidents are logged, thanks to improved port surveillance. Although almost all of these attacks were conducted by opportunistic small-time pirates armed with knives and metal pipes, the trend is certainly a worrying one. Other 'hot-spots' highlighted in the IMB's latest report are the waters of Nigeria (33 attacks), India (14), Malaysia (7), Venezuela (12) and Somalia (5).

Another danger spot that rapidly climbed the piratical league table was the coast of east Somalia. The threat of piracy in this region was first highlighted in 1989 when the German-built cruise ship *Seabourn Spirit* was attacked on the high seas, some 70 miles (113km) off the Somalian coast. Just before 6am on 5 November two speedboats approached the liner, having been launched from a mother ship. The boats raked the liner with machine-gun fire and rocket-propelled grenades (RPGs), and one crewman was injured. Fortunately, the well-trained crew of the liner were able to prevent the attackers from boarding. Somalia is now

In 2004 internationally organized anti-piracy patrols were established in the Malacca Strait, and since then the presence of small patrol craft like these rigid raiders have played their part in making these busy waters much safer.

regarded as a particularly dangerous region, in which 19 major attacks were reported in 2005 alone. The country exists in a political vacuum, and the lack of a functioning government makes it easier for pirates to use it as a base.

One of these attacks took place on 27 June 2005, launched against the Kenyan-owned MV *Semlow*, which was transporting a cargo of rice to Somalia as part of a UN food programme designed to relieve tsunami victims. Somalian pirates attacked and captured the ship under cover of darkness as she approached the port of Harardhere, and her ten-man crew were held hostage for over three months. As one of the captured crewmen reported: 'These pirates are worse than the pirates we read about in history books … These Somali pirates are better armed, and they want ransom, not just our goods.' The lack of authority in the country means that it is difficult for the international maritime community to offer any firm response, apart from patrolling the international waters off the coast, warning passing shipping, and hoping that the Somalians will one day be able to police their own waters. Unfortunately, many so-called government organizations are either pirates themselves, or represent a local warlord. In November 2006 the crew of the cargo vessel MV *Veesham* were bemused when the ship was boarded and captured by a group of ten Somalian pirates, who sailed their prize into the Somalian port of Obbia. There a group of militia loyal to the Union of Islamic Courts recaptured the ship after a protracted gun battle, and returned it to their former owners. In places like Somalia, it is often very difficult to work out who the 'good guys' really are.

PIRATES OF SOMALIA AND BANGLADESH

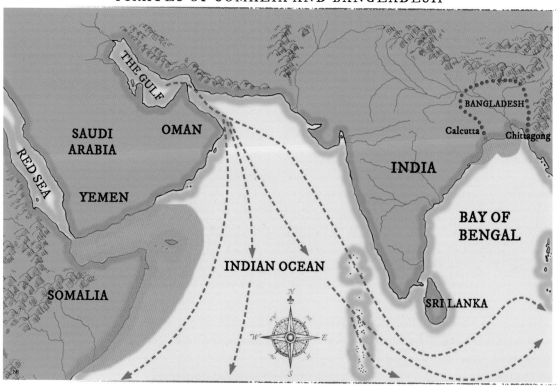

In April 2009 the cargo ship MV *Maersk Alabama* was captured by pirates 240 miles (386km) off the coast of Somalia. The crew were held for ransom, but were rescued by the US Navy, and the pirates were arrested. This incident was dramatised in the film *Captain Phillips* (2013). (ROBERTO SCHMIDT/AFP/ Getty Images)

KEY
●●●●● Country borders   ◄ – – Shipping routes   ▮ Pirate 'hot-spots'

Since 2002, the waters of the Gulf of Aden and off the coast of Somalia have been described as some of the most dangerous in the world. For more than a decade Somalia was the world's leading pirate 'hot-spot', with attacks occurring far out into the Indian Ocean. However, since 2009 a major stepping up of international naval patrols, combined with satellite surveillance and the introduction of armed detachments on merchant ships have dramatically reduced the size of the problem. While Somali pirates continue to pose a threat to shipping, the number of attacks has fallen dramatically. Another budding 'hot-spot' is the coast of Bangladesh. There, attacks have been carried out on shipping anchored off the coast, particularly in the bustling port of Chittagong. Again, an international response has been coordinated, and the International Maritime Bureau is monitoring its progress.

The capture of the MV *Maersk Alabama* by Somali pirates in 2009 not only captured world attention and spawned the film *Captain Phillips* (2013) starring Tom Hanks, it also led to an increased international awareness of the problem. Even more resources were allocated to deal with the pirate threat. Since then, extensive patrolling by warships, the presence of armed mercenaries on merchant ships, and a concerted international effort to curtail the power of local warlords have all had a major impact. The result was that by 2012 the number of attacks had been reduced to less than a dozen a year. Even then, most of these were thwarted by prompt action by anti-piracy patrols. The result is that what was once a headline-grabbing threat to maritime trade is now a thing of the past. Of course, attacks still continue elsewhere.

TACTICS AND TERRORISM

In his book *Dangerous Waters*, author John S. Burnett highlighted the problem:

There has been traditionally an ill-defined distinction between piracy and terrorism. Following the attacks on the World Trade Center and the Pentagon, governments worldwide finally began to take notice that there had been a war at sea long before September 11. The inevitable conclusion was reached – there is very little difference between the two crimes. The International Maritime Bureau and others in the maritime industry have called the bombing of the USS *Cole* in Aden harbour an act of piracy. The attack hammered home that we can no longer afford to ignore piracy, or deny its close relationship with terrorism. The stakes are too high.

On Christmas Day 2010, the Taiwanese deep sea fishing trawler *Shiuh Fu No. 1* was captured by pirates off Somalia. They beached the vessel and held her and her crew for ransom, which was duly paid, and the ship and crew were released in 2012. Here, a Somali pirate stands guard over the beached vessel a year after her capture.

In other words, many pirate attacks were probably the work of 'terrorists' – men who attacked for political or religious reasons instead of just for plunder. It was only after the event that the Western world woke up to the fact that piracy had become as much a tool of the terrorist as hijacking or bombing.

In the charged political atmosphere following 11 September 2001 and the Anglo-American invasion of Iraq, it is sometimes difficult to tell where piracy stops and terrorism begins. In the Western press the term 'terrorist' has been increasingly applied to pirates, regardless of their political or religious motives. In many cases, once these highly publicized attacks were investigated by the IMB, it was clear that profit rather than political gain was the only motive. One of the big problems is the official definition of piracy as an attack that takes place on the high seas. Many incidents that occur within a harbour, or even within a country's 12-mile (19-km) limits, are deemed local crimes rather than piratical acts, or can even be labelled as terrorist attacks in an effort to whip up world opinion. In other places the waters in which attacks take place are disputed by neighbouring countries, so it is often unclear exactly who should control them. This can sometimes lead to situations in which the supposed 'good guys' are just as likely to attack passing shipping for political or monetary gain as any local pirate crew. For instance, in Somalia the lack of a functioning government means that even semi-legitimate organizations such as the local coastguard took part in attacks. Groups such as the National Volunteer Guard, the Somali Marines and the Somali Coastal Defence Force were all identified as pirates, operating under the smokescreen of legitimacy. For example, in 2000 the MV *Bonella* was attacked off the Somalian coast by 26 pirates in two speedboats. The merchant captain later said, 'I told them that we didn't have any money, but the general of the Somali Coastguard cocked his pistol and pointed it by my head saying: "Captain, no ship travels without money. Do you really want to lose your life just as I am about to set your ship free?"' The pirates kept the captain and crew prisoner for five days while they tried to use her to capture other passing ships. When they found she was too slow, the pirates plundered her and left.

Clearly this 'Trojan Horse' approach – using an innocuous-looking vessel as a lure – is a tactic that has proved popular. In January 2006 the USS *Winston S. Churchill* intercepted an Indian freighter that had been captured off the Somalian coast several days earlier. The pirates were reportedly using her as a base for other attacks. Numerous similar examples were recorded, both off Somalia and in Indonesian waters. Typically, a fishing boat would serve as a base ship, allowing small inflatables crewed by pirates to carry out attacks far from shore.

In recent years the Chinese Coastguard has been involved in a number of incidents, which are either the result of official Chinese policy (which is unlikely), or the actions of Chinese officials who adopt a cavalier approach to their work. It is also possible that these represent the actions of real pirates, who use the Chinese as a cover for their illegal activities. For example, in June 1995

Somali pirates being arrested by US Special Forces during an anti-piracy patrol in the Gulf of Aden. The stepping up of international anti-piracy patrols in the region from 2009 has had a dramatic impact in curtailing the threat posed by pirates in Somali waters.

a Chinese customs cutter stopped the Panamanian-registered freighter MV *Hye Mieko* in international waters. The freighter had sailed from Singapore two days before, bound for Cambodia with a cargo of cigarettes and cameras.

A dozen men in Chinese uniforms seized the vessel, and sailed it over 900 miles (1,448km) through international waters until it reached the Chinese port of Shanwei. There the vessel was impounded on 'suspicion of smuggling'. The Chinese subsequently denied any knowledge of the customs cutter, and charged the vessel's owner with trying to smuggle cigarettes into China. Clearly the Chinese government does not engage in piracy, but evidently some official sanctioned the operation and covered it up. Since 2010, though, the Chinese authorities and the Chinese navy have conducted a widespread anti-piracy operation in their home waters, and so after 2014 no more incidents have been reported.

One equally worrying trend is the changing nature of modern piracy. Whereas in the past most attacks involved the temporary seizure of a ship while it was plundered, more recently the trend has been to augment this with kidnapping or hostage-taking – which only serves to blur the boundaries between piracy and terrorism even more. In 2006, 188 pirate attacks involved the taking of crew members or passengers as hostages, while 77 involved outright kidnapping. Of these, almost half of the hostages were taken in Somalian waters, although Indonesia came a close second. Over the past ten years, the majority of pirate attacks have involved kidnapping or ransom. Insurance companies have worked closely with the leading maritime powers and international organizations to counter this, but the trend continues in areas where the pirates can retreat to a secure base, where their hostages can be held until a ransom is paid.

In this respect the pirates are simply acting in a manner reminiscent of the Cilician pirates who plagued the Ancient Mediterranean – the people who took Julius Caesar hostage and held him to ransom. Hostage-taking is generally seen as a criminal act, not a terrorist one.

Kidnapping is a different matter. Of the 199 reported incidents worldwide in 2017, ten maritime kidnappings took place in the Philippines, while 65 people – mainly oil workers – were kidnapped off the coast of Nigeria. By contrast there were 91 hostage-takings during the same year, most of which took place in Malaysia or Somalia. The big difference between hostage-taking and kidnapping is that while the former is usually resolved after the payment of money, kidnapping is often accompanied by political as well as monetary demands.

An example was the capture of the Sri-Lankan-registered tanker *Aris 13*, which was boarded by Somali pirates in the Gulf of Aden on the evening of 14 March 2017. All eight of her crew were taken hostage, but they and their ship were released two days later after the vessel's owners paid a ransom. Two weeks and 3,000 miles away, the Malta-registered bulk carrier *Eleni M* was also taken by pirates. Four of them boarded her from a small speedboat, 32 miles (51km) off the port of Bonny, on the Nigerian coast. This time the pirates left the ship alone, but took her seven-man crew. They were still being held prisoner by a Biafran separatist organization a year later.

The situation in Nigeria is a little different from that encountered elsewhere in the world. There, several organizations see piracy and kidnapping as a useful means to obtain both funds and political concessions. Organizations such as the Movement for the Emancipation of the Niger Delta, the Indigenous Peoples of Biafra and the well-armed Niger Delta People's Volunteer force have all been linked to piratical attacks and the kidnapping of foreign oil workers. Usually, though, the local political situation is muddled and attacks are made without declarations of loyalty, so that the real identity of the culprits is often unclear.

In some cases, the victims have even included members of the Nigerian armed forces, charged with protecting foreign oil workers from attack. It seems that the disruption of oil production was the primary objective behind the attacks and kidnappings, which suggests that either the pirates have a political agenda, or they are simply being destructive – just like the pirates of the 'Golden Age' who destroyed ships' cargoes for the sheer hell of it. In this case, though, the point is that they often see themselves as striking back at the oil companies they perceive as exploiting the region.

The danger is that the use of piracy as a political weapon will become more popular with anyone from terrorist groups, local guerrillas or even states with an extremist religious or political agenda. In international law 'maritime terrorism' is defined as a piratical act intended to influence a government or group of individuals. This means that legally the rebels in the Niger Delta are effectively terrorists as well as pirates, regardless of the more complex economic or diplomatic issues involved. The problem for sailors and oil workers alike is that while regular piratical attacks are dangerous enough, in this new form of piracy the stakes are much higher.

Pirates operating in the Niger Delta see themselves as freedom fighters, and specifically target both Nigerian military targets and the facilities and ships of the oil companies they blame for robbing them of the area's natural resources. For these men, piracy is seen as a political tool.

Chapter Eleven

PIRATES IN FICTION

Long John Silver has a lot to answer for. In *Treasure Island*, published in 1883, the Scottish author Robert Louis Stevenson (1850–94) created the ultimate pirate, the figure everyone thought of when a mental image of a pirate was conjured up. Of course, fictional pirates existed long before *Treasure Island*. At the same time as Captain Johnson's pirate biography was proving a runaway success in early 18th-century London, a play called *The Successful Pirate* was drawing crowds to the Drury Lane Theatre – a production based on the exploits of the 'Red Sea Roundsman' Henry Every. This meant that even while the last of the pirates of the 'Golden Age' were still at large, the business of romanticizing them had already begun. In the early 19th century, romantic fiction writers and poets rediscovered piracy as a source for dramatic plots and exotic locations. For example, Lord Byron's poem *The Corsair* (1814), Sir Walter Scott's novel *The Pirate* (1821) and Giuseppe Verdi's opera *Il Corsaro* (1848) all provided the same

The Walt Disney version of *Treasure Island*, released in 1950, made a star of Robert Newton (centre), who played Long John Silver. Newton played the part using a thick Dorset accent, and this established how most people imagine pirates speak. (Photo by Walt Disney/Getty Images)

ABOVE The modern
perception of the way pirates
look was for the most part
shaped by the American artist
Howard Pyle (1853–1911),
and to a lesser extent by
Frank Schoonover (1877–
1972). For want of a better
look, Pyle based his pirates on
contemporary Spanish bandits.

ABOVE RIGHT Another
major 19th-century influence
on the 'pirate look' was the
theatre. Costumes for Gilbert
& Sullivan's comic opera
Pirates of Penzance introduced
skull and crossbones symbols
on pirate hats, and this
remained in vogue. This
version purports to depict the
American privateer John Paul
Jones, who of course never
wore such an outlandish
costume.

thing – a sanitized, rose-tinted view of the pirate world, in which pirates were romantic heroes and rebels against authority rather than simply a bunch of unwashed cutthroats.

Treasure Island was probably the most influential children's book ever published, and it first appeared as a serial called *The Sea Cook, or Treasure Island* in a children's magazine called *Young Folks* (1881–82). This original title showed that, at least in Stevenson's mind, Long John Silver, rather than Jim Hawkins, the boy hero, was the central character. For Stevenson, his hero was not a romantic figure, but a frightening symbol of pirate reality – a man who would make you walk the plank rather than wax lyrically about the freedom of the open sea. In *Treasure Island*, Stevenson introduced all those other elements of piracy that have now become the bedrocks of pirate mythology. He was responsible for putting parrots on pirate shoulders, for wooden legs, black eye patches, the Black Spot, and of course 'fifteen men on a dead man's chest'. Above all, it was Stevenson who came up with the idea of buried treasure, and maps where 'X' marks the spot.

Actually, the real inventor was probably Lloyd Osbourne, Stevenson's American stepson. Stevenson and his family were spending a late summer holiday in Braemar, in the Scottish Highlands, and the Scottish weather was proving as fickle as ever. One day Stevenson came across the 13-year-old Lloyd colouring in a map he'd drawn – the map of an island. As Osbourne later recalled:

Stevenson came in as I was finishing it, and with his affectionate interest in everything I was doing, leaned over my shoulder, and was soon elaborating the map and naming it. I shall never forget the thrill of Skeleton Island, Spyglass Hill, nor the heart-stirring climax of the three red crosses! And the greater climax still when he wrote down the words 'Treasure Island' at the top right-hand corner! And he seemed to know so much about it too – the pirates, the buried treasure, the man who had been marooned on the island. 'Oh, for a story about it,' I exclaimed, in a heaven of enchantment, and somehow conscious of his own enthusiasm in the idea.

Within three days Stevenson had penned the first three chapters, and the rest of the family helped him steer the plot to its climax. Within weeks the first chapters were offered to the editor of *Young Folks*, and within two years *Treasure Island* appeared in print. The rest is history.

Treasure Island has never been out of print, and remains one of the best-loved books of all time. There have been over 50 film and television versions of the story, from the first silent *Treasure Island* (1920) to the latest French adaptation – *L'Île aux Trésors* (2007), or the Italian TV animated version *L'isola del tesoro* (2015). Of these, probably the most notable is the Walt Disney version, filmed in 1950 – the first live action film ever attempted by the studio. Child actor Bobby Driscoll played Jim Hawkins, while the British-born Robert Newton came up with the definitive portrayal of Long John Silver, complete with his strong West Country accent and all those guttural utterances of 'Arrrr, Jim lad'. These were immediately added to Stevenson's caucus of pirate

To many, Robert Louis Stevenson's *Treasure Island* is the ultimate pirate adventure story. It also introduced many of the most persistent pirate myths, including buried treasure and pirate maps. Both were the invention of the author.

The great Scottish-born adventure novelist Robert Louis Stevenson (1850–94) did much to develop our modern fascination with piracy when he wrote *Treasure Island*. It first appeared as a serial in the children's magazine *Young Folks* between 1881 and 1882. It was first published as a book in 1883, and has remained in print ever since.

In Walt Disney's film version of *Treasure Island*, released in 1950, the part of the pirate Long John Silver was played by Robert Newton. He came from Dorchester in Dorset, and so for the part he reverted to his local accent. It has remained the standard form of 'pirate speak' ever since.

myth, and every self-respecting pirate impersonator for the past six decades has aped Newton's manner of speech. Newton made his name playing these rough, wizened characters, and six years later he revisited the role (and the accent) when he played the lead in *Blackbeard the Pirate*. Incidentally, both the actor Oliver Reed and the self-destructive The Who drummer Keith Moon described the hard-drinking Newton as a role model.

The next great work of pirate fiction was *Peter Pan*, written by another Scotsman, J. M. Barrie (1860–1937), and first performed in London in 1904. Barrie first wrote the play as a novel, *The Little White Bird*, and then adapted the work for the stage. The story of the boy who refused to grow up proved an instant success, and Captain Hook became an instantly recognizable pirate villain, although he and his crew were portrayed more as figures of fun than as real pirates – a far cry from the dangerous villains who populated *Treasure Island*. As well as pirates with hooks instead of hands, the stage version of *Peter Pan* also gave us pirate hats emblazoned with the skull and crossbones, and walking the plank. While no self-respecting pirate of the 'Golden Age' would have bothered with such nonsense, they have become just as much part of the whole pirate image as Stevenson's piratical affectations.

Within a decade the popular perception of the pirate would change yet again. Instead of villainous cutthroats or comic buffoons, the new breed of fictional pirates would be true heroes – youthful, quick-witted, honourable, clean-cut Englishmen who fought for a higher cause, who righted wrongs, and who saved

Another Scotsman who heavily influenced our view of pirates was J. M. Barrie (1860–1937), who wrote *Peter Pan*, first produced as a play in 1904. It was Barrie who invented the whole myth about pirates making their victims 'walk the plank'.

aristocratic ladies in distress. The man responsible for this was Rafael Sabatini (1875–1950), an Anglo-Italian author who single-handedly invented the genre known as the 'swashbuckler'. While his books have been derided as being a '*Boy's Own*' style of adventure fiction, Sabatini anchored his piratical world in the writings of Exquemelin and Johnson, although his heroes were entirely of his own invention. His first successful novel was *Scaramouche* (1921), set in the French Revolution, but the following year he produced *Captain Blood*, which set the standard for the swashbucklers that followed. His other pirate novels included *The Sea Hawk*, *The Black Swan* and two more Captain Blood books.

His success came just at the right time. *Captain Blood* was published two years after the release of the first film version of *Treasure Island*, and Hollywood immediately realized the potential of Sabatini's novel. *Captain Blood* first appeared on the silver screen in 1924, with Warren Kerrigan playing the title role. While the film itself was uninspiring, it led to two more – *The Sea Hawk* (1924) and more memorably *The Black Pirate* (1926), in which Douglas Fairbanks played the swashbuckling hero. He was the first screen hero to stick a knife in a sail and slide down to the deck, and he also walked the plank, killed a pirate captain in a sword duel, and rescued the princess. The floodgates had been opened, and the pirates of the silver screen would remain a staple of Hollywood for another three generations.

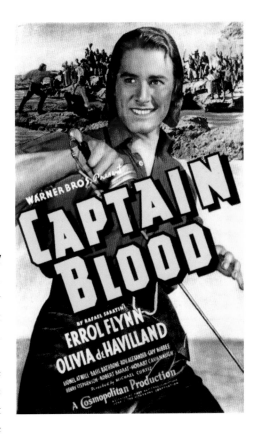

The 1930s and 1940s saw a profusion of talking-picture 'swashbucklers', many of which were based on Sabatini's novels. The best of these was probably the talking-picture remake of *Captain Blood* (1935), which launched the career of the unknown Errol Flynn as the swashbuckling hero. He returned to piracy in *The Sea Hawk* (1940), a wartime patriotic romp that owed little to Sabatini's original book. Another piratical classic of the time was *The Black Swan* (1942), in which Tyrone Power played a fictional pirate serving alongside a bombastic Sir Henry Morgan, while other mainstays of the genre – Maureen O'Hara and Anthony Quinn – both made their first appearance under the black flag.

In 1922 the Italian-born novelist Rafael Sabatini published *Captain Blood*, a rip-roaring adventure novel that featured a gentleman-turned-pirate. More than anyone else, Sabatini introduced the word 'swashbuckling' to the world, a term which was later adopted by Hollywood when it transferred Sabatini's books to the silver screen. *Captain Blood* was released in 1935.

Although the pirate genre continued into the early 1950s, tastes were changing, and the tendency was for these later pirate films to parody what had come before. For example, in the *Crimson Pirate* (1952) Burt Lancaster reprised Fairbanks' earlier role in *The Black Pirate*, but as a former circus acrobat he

RIGHT The 'swashbuckling' novels of Rafael Sabatini were brought to an audience through cinema. They served as the perfect vehicle for Errol Flynn, whose career was launched following his appearance in the title role of *Captain Blood*.

FAR RIGHT The influences of artists like Pyle and Schoonover, combined with the romanticism of Barrie, Sabatini and Stevenson, and the allure of pirate swashbucklers, all helped create a rose-tinted view of piracy that appealed to adults and children alike, but relied more on myth than fact to support it.

placed an even greater emphasis on swinging on ropes and sliding down sails. However, there was one last piratical hurrah, with Robert Newton appearing in both *Blackbeard the Pirate* (1952) and *Long John Silver* (1954), and the ageing Errol Flynn and Maureen O'Hara enjoying one final pirate romp in *Under All Flags* (1952). These were the last of their kind – for two decades at least one or two swashbucklers had come out every year, but from the late 1950s they became a rarity.

While most swashbuckling heroes were fictional, sometimes they crossed paths with real pirates – Blackbeard, Morgan, Kidd and others. In most cases these historical pirates were simply there to be outsmarted by our piratical heroes, two-dimensional villains who come across as even more bumblingly incompetent than Captain Hook or more fundamentally evil than Long John Silver. A prime example is the film *Captain Kidd* (1945), in which Charles Laughton portrayed the unfortunate privateer as an evil schemer. By contrast, one of the few swashbucklers in which the actual hero was based on a real pirate is *The Buccaneer*, in which the part of Jean Lafitte was played by Frederic March in the 1938 version, and by Yul Brynner in the 1958 remake. Even then the screen pirate was shown as a suave gentleman – two terms that were probably never applied to the real pirate.

For almost half a century piracy was never really considered a box office draw. Of course there were pirate films – *Swashbuckler* (1976) with Robert Shaw, *Yellowbeard* (1983) with Peter Cooke, *Pirates* (1986) with Walter Matthau, *Hook* (1991) with Dustin Hoffman and *Cutthroat Island* (1995) with Gina Davis were probably the most notable of these. There were a few others, including at least three versions of the Robert Louis Stevenson classic, one of which was *Muppet Treasure Island* (1996), in which even Tim Curry was unable to break completely from the Robert Newton version of Long John Silver. While some of these were competent enough films in their own right, none of them took the box office by storm.

Then along came Johnny Depp. The idea of basing a film on a rather dated Disney attraction may have been strange enough, but Depp's portrayal of a pirate captain – foppish swagger, slurred speech and rather camp demeanour – sent alarm bells ringing in the Walt Disney Studios. They need not have worried. *Pirates of the Caribbean: The Curse of the Black Pearl* (2003) proved a smash hit and earned Disney a small fortune. The sequels *Pirates of the Caribbean: Dead Man's Chest* (2006) and *At World's End* (2007) were equally successful. *On Stranger Tides* (2011) and *Dead Men Tell No Tales* (2017) were less so, possibly because they had moved even further away from their pirate roots, and concentrated on the undead, transforming ships and fantasy legends, rather than the swashbuckling theme that underpinned the original Disney ride.

While the myth that pirates made their victims walk the plank was first proposed by J. M. Barrie in *Peter Pan* (1904), this dramatic notion was repeated by illustrators such as Howard Pyle, so that today it is an integral part of our image of piracy.

However, the adventure series *Black Sails* (2014–17) showed that piracy was still attractive to audiences, and that they didn't need zombies or magic to augment the story. In effect, as a historical drama set firmly in the 'Golden Age', *Black Sails* represents a return to real pirates. The series was actually a prequel to Robert Louis Stevenson's *Treasure Island*, and skilfully integrates fictional characters from the novel such as Long John Silver and Billy Bones into the world of the pirates of New Providence. Woodes Rodgers, Edward Teach, Charles Vane, 'Calico Jack' Rackam, Anne Bonny, Mary Read and Benjamin Hornigold were all there, and, better still, they bore more than a passing resemblance to their historic counterparts. While by necessity the plot deviated from history, it remains the most accurate attempt yet to recreate the pirates of the 'Golden Age' for the camera.

Howard Pyle's painting 'So the Treasure was Divided' was produced to illustrate a story called 'The Fate of a Treasure Town', about a buccaneering raid, first published in *Harpers Monthly* magazine in 1905. It remains one of Pyle's classic pirate scenes.

For his part, Johnny Depp was hailed as having reinvented the screen pirate – a new combination of Errol Flynn, Robert Newton and everybody else. When reporters asked him whom he used for inspiration, Depp named Keith Richards as his role model, mixed with a touch of Iggy Pop and Errol Flynn. He added that pirates were 'like the rock stars of their time', which goes a long way towards explaining why he chose that particular persona. In fact just about the only person he didn't cite was Captain Charles Johnson. Despite this, both Robert Newton's Long John Silver and Johnny Depp's Captain Jack Sparrow owe more than a passing nod to Johnson's descriptions of pirates such as Blackbeard and Bartholomew Roberts. In fact, it could be argued that compared to Blackbeard, with his wild beard, burning pieces of slowmatch stuck in his tricorne hat and ferocious eyes, Jack Sparrow looks positively mundane. That remains one of the charms of these characters – pirate reality will always be every bit as colourful as pirate fiction.

CONCLUSION

The Real Pirates of the Caribbean

For a pirate historian, one frequently asked question is whether you feel any affinity for the pirates of the 'Golden Age', for men like Blackbeard, or 'Calico Jack' Rackam, or 'Black Bart' Roberts. If you think about it, it's a strange question. It assumes that just because you try to learn what you can about a person, you somehow approve of what they did. Robert Graysmith, who wrote about the 'Zodiac Killers' in San Francisco, was frequently presented with the same question. Even Truman Capote was asked the same thing when *In Cold Blood* was published in 1966. The difference is, unlike these other criminals, our pirates did not commit their crimes within living memory. This somehow makes the question less personal, less of an accusatory suggestion of complicity. The simple answer is no, I don't feel any affinity for them, and if I were given the chance I probably wouldn't like to meet them either, especially on the high seas. However, I do admit to being fascinated by them, by their crimes and by their lives. I want to know what drove them to follow the life they chose, and how they expected things to turn out.

What is interesting is that when Alexandre Exquemelin first published *Buccaneers of America* in 1678, and Captain Charles Johnson *A General History of the Robberies and Murders of the Most Notorious Pyrates* in 1724, both men were almost certainly asked the same question. Both books were written at the very end of the two great pirate eras – the age of the buccaneers and the 'Golden Age of Piracy'. Seamen who had been the victims of pirate attacks were still walking the streets, and might well have been the first to accuse Johnson of romanticizing the criminals he wrote about. In fact, buccaneer attacks and pirate incidents were still taking place. This immediacy might well have been part of the reason why both books were such an instant success. However, this does not explain why the books were quite so popular, and why they have remained in print ever since. The likelihood is that people in late 17th-century

Amsterdam or early 18th-century London were just as fascinated with pirates as we are today. Many of the reasons for their appeal have already been mentioned – men who rejected the constraints of a law-abiding society, who lived life to the full, who sailed away to exotic destinations, who took whatever they wanted … everything that the average book reader might have dreamed about, but was never going to do. By reading about pirates they were living pirate lives by proxy, and mentally escaping to a bold new world of adventure. It is much the same today. It's fairly easy to see why children have always had a strong fascination with piracy, or why the subject has long been a staple of junior fiction. Pirates were anti-authoritarian figures, who were allowed to stay up late and weren't made to have a bath. The attraction for adults runs along similar lines – the autonomy of the individual, the freedom from social obligations and the ability to escape the banality of modern life are all important. Adult and child alike see pirates as exotic, romantic and free-spirited.

Unfortunately, most of this image is the work of pirate fiction rather than fact. Most people don't want to consider that pirates were simply sailors who rebelled against a brutal and oppressive system of labour. The romanticism of piracy ignores the fact that conditions were still harsh, that fever and disease were commonplace, or that life expectancy was measured more in months than in years. Pirate historians such as David Cordingly, Peter Earle, Benerson Little, Robert Ritchie, Jan Rogozinski, Richard Zacks and I have all done our best to strip the fact from the fiction, but we are all swimming against the tide. Although we keep telling people that pirates didn't walk the plank, bury treasure, draw maps showing where the plunder was buried or routinely capture galleons filled with pieces-of-eight, most people simply don't want to know. The pirates of popular myth are too entrenched to challenge, and the best we can hope for is to make a few people aware that there was another, less romantic, side of the pirate coin.

When most people think about historical rather than fictional pirates, they think of the people described by Captain Johnson. These all date from one brief historical period, the so-called 'Golden Age of Piracy', which at most lasted for 40 years, between 1690 and 1730. In fact, this period was probably a lot shorter – and the real pirate heyday only lasted for one brief decade, from 1714 to 1724. This was the period of Blackbeard, 'Black Bart' Roberts, Charles Vane, 'Calico Jack' Rackam, Anne Bonny, Mary Read, 'Gentleman' Stede Bonnet, Howell Davis and several others. Piracy had existed since man first launched a dugout canoe, so why are we so obsessed with a few characters who lived in the early 18th century? I suppose the real answer is publicity. These people were written about by Captain Johnson, and their activities have been the inspiration for most of the pirate fiction out there, including *Black Sails* and even the *Pirates of the Caribbean* film series.

While this book certainly concentrates on this important period, it also covers other crucial pirate eras, such as the age of the Elizabethan 'sea dogs', the buccaneers and the 19th-century pirates of the South China Sea. In a way these are easier periods to deal with, as the reader is less encumbered by the baggage of pirate mythology. Although this book will never seriously erode the popular image of the pirates of the 'Golden Age', it may allow readers to question some of these myths, and give them a glimpse of the real pirates of the Caribbean. If this has allowed you to understand these people a little more clearly, to understand how they operated and even what drove them, then this book has achieved its purpose.

NOTES

Full publication details are provided the first time a work appears in a chapter's endnotes; thereafter only the author's name is given, unless more than one work by the same author is quoted in the chapter.

Chapter One: Pirates of the Ancient World

Page 9: 'It is now believed that these pirates became assimilated...' George Bass, *A History of Seafaring* (London, 1972), p.20.

Page 11: 'Although effectively the sea raiders operated like hostile migratory tribes...' Bass, pp.20–21.

Page 14: 'Herodotus provides us with vivid accounts of pirate attacks...' H.A. Ormerod, *Piracy in the Ancient World: An Essay on Mediterranean History* (Chicago, 1967), pp.22–25, 90–98.

Page 17: 'As a result, Roman attitudes hardened...' Ormerod, pp.190–204.

Chapter Two: Medieval Pirates

Page 24: 'A chronicler described the raid...' Angus Konstam, *The Historical Atlas of the Viking World* (New York, 2002), pp.60–63.

Page 24: 'In 820 a cleric wrote in the *Annals of Ulster*...' Quoted in Konstam, p.64.

Page 24: 'During the late 830s the Viking leader Turgeis...' Ibid, p.65.

Page 30: 'Today Klaus Störtebeker is something of a German hero...' Störtebeker has even been immortalized in a poem, *Die Hölle von Helgoland* (1924) by Walter Göttke. Göttke also adapted the poem as a song.

Page 33: 'Eustace was captured ...' This account of Eustace's activities is extracted from the writings of Matthew Paris, available online (www./standish.stanford.edu/). Also see Glyn Burgess, *Medieval Outlaws: Eustace the Monk and Fouke Fitz Waryn* (London, 1997), pp.32–78.

Page 35: 'Probably the most notorious Irish pirate...' For a full account of the life of Gráinne Ní Mháille, see Anne Chambers, *Granuaile: Ireland's Pirate Queen c.1530–1603* (Dublin, 2003).

Chapter Three: The Sea Dogs of the Renaissance

Page 39: 'While the English regarded Sir Francis Drake...' J. H. Parry, *The Spanish Seaborne Empire* (London, 1966), pp.137–51; Timothy R. Walton, *The Spanish Treasure Fleets* (Sarasota, FL, 1994), pp.30–35.

Page 42: 'So the safe arrival of a treasure fleet...' Walton, pp. 44–64; Angus Konstam, *Spanish Galleon, 1530–1690* (Oxford, 2004), pp.17–19.

Page 45: 'For the first time, the rest of Europe understood...' David Cordingly (ed.), *Pirates: Terror on the High Seas* (Atlanta, GA, 1996), p.18; Hugh Thomas, *The Conquest of Mexico* (London, 1993), pp.568–69.

Page 46: 'After plundering what he could...' Juliet Barclay, *Havana, Portrait of a City* (London, 1993), pp.33–52.

Page 54: 'Hawkins then embarked on a third attempt...' For a fascinating account of Hawkins' third voyage, see R. Unwin, *The Defeat of Sir John Hawkins* (London, 1960).

Page 56: 'The *Jesus of Lubeck* was trapped...' Unwin, pp.152–60.

Page 62: 'In December 1577 Drake sailed from Plymouth...' Lloyd Hanes Williams, *Pirates of Colonial Virginia* (Richmond, VA, 1937), pp.80–117; Angus Konstam, *Elizabethan Sea Dogs, 1560–1605* (Oxford, 2000), pp.29–30.

Page 64: 'Despite this, Drake planned to attack Santo Domingo...' Williams, p.141; David Cordingly, *Under the Black Flag: The Romance and the Reality of Life Among the Pirates* (London, 1995), pp.31–32; Konstam, *Elizabethan Sea Dogs*, pp.43–44.

Page 67: 'Few would have guessed it at the time...' Konstam, *Elizabethan Sea Dogs,* pp.44, 62–63.

Page 68: 'As the sun rose, the Spanish captain Don Pedro de Valdés...' Angus Konstam, *The Armada Campaign, 1588* (Oxford, 2001), pp.37, 41.

Page 69: 'The Spanish ship was taken after an epic fight...' Ibid., p.41.

Page 69: 'Not all of these privateers were successful...' Kenneth R. Andrews, *Elizabethan Privateering during the Spanish War, 1585–1603* (Cambridge, 1964), pp.134–36, 199–204.

Page 69: 'In 1595, Elizabeth's advisor William Cecil devised a plan...' For a detailed account of the Cadiz Expedition, see Williams, pp.158–60; Arthur Nelson, *The Tudor Navy: The Ships, Men and Organisation, 1485–1603* (London, 2001), pp.124–30.

Page 70: 'Drake found San Juan too well defended to attack...' Nelson, pp.193–202.

Page 71: 'The ships arrived back in Plymouth in April 1596...' Ibid., pp.202–03.

Chapter Four: Mediterranean Corsairs

Page 77: 'The Spanish followed their Reconquista...' John F. Guilmartin, *Gunpowder and Galleys* (London, 1974), pp.61–41; John F. Guilmartin, *Galleons and Galleys* (London, 2002), pp.126–36.

Page 80: 'In a Mediterranean world filled with black hair...' Jan Rogozinski, *Pirates! An A–Z Encyclopedia* (New York, 1995), pp.16, 178–79; David Cordingly (ed.), *Pirates: Terror on the High Seas* (Atlanta, GA, 1996); Angus Konstam, *The History of Shipwrecks* (New York, 1999), pp.46–47.

Page 82: 'As the new beylerbey, Hızır 'Barbarossa' became the head...' Rogozinski, p.179; Konstam, p.47.

Page 84: 'The Barbarossa brothers were only the first of many Barbary corsairs...' Rogozinski, pp.349–50.

Page 86: 'He took part in the disastrous battle of Lepanto in 1571...' Guilmartin, *Galleons and Galleys,* pp.137–51. For a full account of the battle, see Angus Konstam, *Lepanto 1571: The greatest naval battle of the Renaissance* (Oxford, 2003).

Page 92: 'For example, in 1643, seven women petitioned the English Parliament...' Quoted in Christopher Lloyd, *English Corsairs of the Barbary Coast* (London, 1981), pp.72–82.

Page 92: 'For instance, in April 1655 the English admiral Robert Blake...' Lloyd, p.97; J. R. Powell, *Robert Blake, General-at-Sea* (London, 1972), pp.252–72.

Page 94: 'A second conflict (known as the Algerine War)...' For an account of the American attacks against the Barbary States see Joshua London, *Victory in Tripoli* (Hoboken, NJ, 2005).

Chapter Five: The Buccaneers

Page 97: 'The Dunkirkers, however, were unable to halt the steady expansion...' David Cordingly, *Under the Black Flag: The Romance and the Reality of Life Among the Pirates* (London, 1995), pp.12–13. For an appraisal of the Dunkirk privateers see C. R. Boxer, *Dutch Seaborne Empire, 1600–1800* (London, 1965).

Page 100: 'Then someone dreamed up the idea of depopulation.' Pablo E. Pérez-Mallaína, *Spain's Men of the Sea: Daily Life on the Indies Fleet in the Sixteenth Century* (Baltimore, MD, 1998), pp.50–52, 95–98; J. H. Parry, *The Spanish Seaborne Empire* (London, 1966), pp.262–64. For an examination of Spanish policies see Timothy R. Walton, *The Spanish Treasure Fleets* (Sarasota, FL, 1994).

Page 106: 'If Exquemelin is to be believed...' Alexandre O. Exquemelin, *Buccaneers of America* (Amsterdam, 1678, reprinted New York, 1969), pp.67–69.

Page 109: 'In other words, Dutch, English and French buccaneers...' For a detailed overview of the military campaigns of this period, see John A. Lynn, *The Wars of Louis XIV, 1667–1714* (London, 1999).

Page 110: 'The reason for it was largely economic...' Cruz Apestegui, *Pirates of the Caribbean: Buccaneers, Privateers, Freelooters and Filibusters, 1493–1720* (Barcelona, 2002), pp.151–56. In addition see Paul Sutton, *Cromwell's Jamaica Campaign* (Leigh-on-Sea, 1990).

Page 111: 'Captain Johnson was probably a pseudonym...' For a detailed discussion of the identity of Captain Johnson, see Angus Konstam, *Blackbeard: America's Most Notorious Pirate* (Hoboken, NJ, 2006), pp.1–4.

Page 112: 'Myngs returned to Jamaica in August 1662...' Dudley Pope, *Harry Morgan's Way* (London, 1977), pp.96–98.

Page 114: 'As for Port Royal, the town prospered.' David Cordingly and John Falconer, *Pirates: Fact & Fiction* (London, 1992), pp.38–39; Cordingly, pp.49–50.

Page 116: 'Merchants turned to more legitimate pursuits...' Pope, pp.349–56; Apestegui, pp.174–80.

Page 117: 'After a bout of heavy drinking...' Cordingly, pp.50–51. Another account of Braziliano's debauchery is found in Exquemelin, pp.81–82. Also see Angus Konstam, *The History of Shipwrecks* (New York, 1999), pp.86–87.

Page 120: 'However, as Exquemelin put it...' Exquemelin, pp.79–80. Also see Konstam, *The History of Shipwrecks*, pp.86–87.

Page 122: 'On other occasions he would resort to...' Exquemelin, pp.106–07, p.193; Konstam, *The History of Shipwrecks*, pp. 82–83; Apestegui, pp.160–61.

Page 126: 'Morgan's subsequent actions pushed the boundaries…' Pope, pp.149–50. Also see David F. Marley, Pirates: *Adventurers on the High Seas* (London, 1995), pp.48–50.

Page 128: 'Meanwhile Morgan wrote to the governor of Panama...' Marley, p.50. Also see Exquemelin, pp.138–39; Pope, pp.168–69.

Page 129: 'Admiral Campo's first move...' Exquemelin, p.154.

Page 132: 'Then, on 24 June he was forced to issue a proclamation...' Quoted in Marley, p.54.

Page 133: 'On 9 July 1670, Modyford proclaimed...' For a full account of the political situation see Pope, pp.217–19.

Page 134: 'On 6 January 1671 Bradley landed...' Exquemelin, p.193.

Page 140: 'They headed south past the East Indies...' A detailed account of Dampier's voyage is provided in Diana and Michael Preston, *A Pirate of Exquisite Mind: The Life of William Dampier* (London, 2004).

Page 142: 'The story would inspire Daniel Defoe...' Ibid., pp.329–30.

Page 143: 'Part of this impetus came from colonization...' Although Exquemelin deliberately omits mentioning much about French buccaneering activities in the Caribbean, Louis le Golip, *The Memoirs of a Buccaneer* (London, 1954) provides a useful account. The subject is also discussed in depth by both Marley and Apestegui.

Page 144: 'Once the tempest passed...' Exquemelin, p.223.

Chapter Six: The Golden Age of Piracy

Page 152: 'This meant that when the War of the Spanish Succession (1701–14) began...' For a broader account of these conflicts, see John A. Lynn, *The Wars of Louis XIV, 1667–1714* (London, 1999).

Page 154: 'Often this action came about when the benefits of illicit trade...' Angus Konstam, *Blackbeard: America's Most Notorious Pirate* (Hoboken, NJ, 2006), pp.41–43.

Page 155: 'It sped back to Havana with the news...' Ibid., pp.36–40.

Page 157: 'Consequently, on 5 September 1717...' Captain Charles Johnson, *A General History of the Robberies & Murders of the Most Notorious Pyrates* (London, 1724, reprinted by Lyons Press, New York, 1998), pp.13–14. Also see Konstam, p.107.

Page 161: 'Charles Vane was quickly gaining a reputation...' Johnson, pp.103–10. Also see Konstam, pp.158–59.

Page 161: 'As the pursuit continued...' Johnson, p.107.

Page 165: 'As Captain Vernon, a naval officer based in Jamaica...' Quoted in Konstam, p.117.

Page 166: 'Woodes Rogers responded by naming them all as pirates...' See Konstam, p.120.

Page 167: 'As Captain Johnson put it, they...' Johnson, p.121.

Page 168: 'As for Anne Bonny...' Ibid., p.131.

Page 169: 'The public was shocked that two women...' Ibid., p.131.

Page 170: 'Johnson makes little mention of the pregnancy...' Ibid., p.131.

Page 171: 'A victim of Rackam said of the women...' Quoted in David Cordingly, *Under the Black Flag: The Romance and the Reality of Life Among the Pirates* (London, 1995), p.64. This and all other information concerning the trial is drawn from the transcript of the proceedings, published in 1721.

Page 172: 'So our hero, Captain Teach, assumed the cognomen of Blackbeard...' Johnson, p.60.

Page 172: 'Johnson claims that Teach 'sailed some time out of Jamaica in privateers'...' Ibid., p.46.

Page 174: 'In a letter to officials in the Carolinas Munthe reported that...' Quoted in Konstam, p.64.

Page 174: 'At the time Teach was still cruising in concert with Hornigold...' Johnson, p.46.

Page 175: 'After mentioning the *Revenge*, it said that…' Quoted in Konstam, pp.69–70.

Page 177: 'Teach detained all the ships and prisoners...' Johnson, p.49.

Page 178: 'The [Carolina] government were not long in deliberating...' Ibid., p.49.

Page 181: 'Consequently, the North Carolina Maritime Museum...' The excavation of the wreck and the conservation of finds was undertaken through the co-operation of the state of North Carolina, academic archaeological teams and the salvors who originally located the wreck. The conserved collection is now displayed in the state-run museum.

Page 183: 'Maynard recorded the conversation...' Quoted in Konstam, p.251.

Page 183: 'As the two sloops crashed into each other...' Johnson, pp.56–57.

Page 187: 'At his trial the judge described him...' Ibid., pp.63, 77.

Page 188: 'On board the Pirate Sloop is Major Bennet...' Quoted in Konstam, p.70. Also see Johnson, p.64.

Page 189: 'That was when he learned that Blackbeard had absconded...' Johnson, p.65.

Page 192: 'So, on 13 November, Stede Bonnet...' Ibid., p.79.

Page 194: 'They vilify us, the scoundrels do...' This speech was included in the original 1724 version of Johnson (Chapter 28). Quoted in David Cordingly (ed.), *Pirates: Terror on the High Seas* (Atlanta, GA, 1996), p.111.

Page 197: 'Johnson claimed that: 'Worley and his crew...' Johnson, p.273.

Page 204: 'Effectively, this took all winter.' Ibid., pp.286.

Page 207: 'Pyrates and Buccaneers, are Princes...' Ibid., pp.180–81.

Page 228: 'There the Dutch authorities pardoned the mutineers...' Ibid., p.268.

Chapter Seven: The Pirate Round

Page 234: 'However, Tew had no intention of limiting his attacks...' The account of his decision to turn pirate was described in detail in the original 1724 version of Captain Charles Johnson, *A General History of the Robberies & Murders of the Most Notorious Pyrates* (London, 1724, reprinted by Lyons Press, New York, 1998) (Chapter 22). The account is also quoted in David Cordingly (ed.), *Pirates: Terror on the High Seas* (Atlanta, GA, 1996), p. 122; Jan Rogozinski, *Pirates! An A–Z Encyclopedia* (New York, 1995), pp.337–38.

Page 235: 'As Johnson put it, 'This differing of opinion'...' Johnson, p.34.

Page 237: 'This 'struck such a terror in his men'...' Ibid., p.35. For a further interpretation of the relationship between Tew and Every, see Cordingly, pp.147–51.

Page 243: 'The governor described them as 'men of desperate fortunes'...' Quoted in Richard Zacks, *The Pirate Hunter: The True Story of Captain Kidd* (New York, 2002), p.20.

Page 246: 'There was a brief exchange of curses...' Johnson, p.352.

Page 249: 'The whole trial had lasted just three days.' Ibid., p.358.

Page 251: 'It is little wonder it came to be associated with a pirate utopia.' Ibid., pp.35–40. The theme of Madagascar as a pirate utopia is explored in Cordingly, pp.124–39; Jan Rogozinski, *Honour Among Thieves* (London, 2000), pp.165–84.

Page 254: 'As the Scottish captain wrote in his report...' Johnson, pp.85–87.

Page 255: 'There he 'subsists at present'...' Ibid., p. 89.

Chapter Eight: The Last of the Pirates

Page 260: 'What all these wars meant for sailors...' An account of the privateering elements of these wars is provided by David Cordingly (ed.), *Pirates: Terror on the High Seas* (Atlanta, GA, 1996), pp.164–87; David J. Starkey, E. S. van Eyck and J. A. de Moor (eds), *Pirates and Privateers* (Exeter, 1997), pp.10–28.

Page 263: 'For instance, in February 1819 the *Boston Daily Advertiser*...' Quoted from the *Boston Daily Advertiser*, February 1819. Also see Colin Jameson, 'Porter and the Pirates', in *Florida Keys Sea Heritage Journal*, 4:4 (1994), pp.4–11.

Page 265: 'Laffite set fire to Campeche.' Jameson, p.14. Also see Cordingly, pp.82–84.

Page 269: 'De Soto showed a sense of irony...' Angus Konstam, *The History of Shipwrecks* (New York, 1999), pp.160–61.

Page 274: 'Alfred Russell Wallace described his encounter...' Alfred Russell Wallace, *The Malay Archipelago* (London, 1869), Vol. I, pp.264–65.

Page 275: 'A small prao arrived...' Ibid, pp.264–65.

Page 275: 'The coast of Borneo...' Cordingly, pp.189–92.

Page 276: 'Other pirate communities included…' Ibid, p.147.

Chapter Nine: The Chinese Pirates

Page 282: 'Ching Chih-lung was a surprising pirate chief.' Tonio Andrade, 'The Company's Chinese Pirates' in the *Journal of World History* (December 2004), Vol. 15, No. 4, pp.415–44.

Page 284: 'As the story goes, he went to the temple...' Ibid., p.421. Also see Jonathan Clements, *Pirate King: Coxinga and the fall of the Ming Dynasty* (Stroud, 2004), pp.126–127.

Page 289: 'Then Cheng Yih appeared, and within a decade...' David Cordingly (ed.), *Pirates: Terror on the High Seas* (Atlanta, GA, 1996), pp.220–25.

Page 292: 'She was aided in this takeover by Cheung Po Tsai...' Ibid., pp.229–31.

Page 294: 'From there the drug was smuggled along the coast...' Ibid., pp.233–35.

Chapter Ten: Modern Piracy

Page 299: 'In recent years it has hit the headlines...' A fascinating account of modern piracy is provided by John S. Burnett in *Dangerous Waters* (New York, 2002). Also see Jay Bahadur, *The Pirates of Somalia* (New York, NY, 2011), and the reports published by the International Marine Bureau, a department of the International Chamber of Commerce. These are available on-line at www.iccwbo.org and www.icc-ccs.org/imb/overview.php.

Page 303: 'According to the Piracy Reporting Centre...' IMB Annual Piracy Reports, 2004–17.

Page 304: 'Other 'hot-spots' highlighted...' IMB Piracy Report, 2017.

Page 305: 'As one of the captured crewmen reported...' IMB Piracy Report, 2006.

Page 307: 'There has been traditionally an ill-defined distinction...' Burnett, p.284.

Page 309: 'The merchant captain later said...' IMB Piracy Report, 2001.

Page 309: 'The pirates were reportedly using her as a base...' US Navy Report, published on their official website (www.navy.mil), Story Number NNS060121-01.

Chapter Eleven: Pirates in Fiction

Page 313: 'For example, Lord Byron's poem *The Corsair* (1814)...' For a more detailed look at the role of literature in our perception of piracy see David Cordingly and John Falconer, *Pirates: Fact & Fiction* (London, 1992), pp.10–12, 37, 49, 54.

Page 317: 'The floodgates had been opened...' A brief account of 'Pirates of the Silver Screen' is provided by Cordingly and Falconer, pp.68–69, and David Cordingly, *Under the Black Flag: The Romance and the Reality of Life Among the Pirates* (London, 1995), pp.174–76. Jan Rogozinski, *Pirates! An A–Z Encyclopedia* (New York, 1995) provides a catalogue of pirate films.

SELECT BIBLIOGRAPHY

Albury, Paul, *A History of the Bahamas* (London, 1975)

Andrews, Kenneth R., *Elizabethan Privateering during the Spanish War, 1585–1603* (Cambridge, 1964)

Apestegui, Cruz, *Pirates of the Caribbean: Buccaneers, Privateers, Freebooters and Filibusters, 1493–1720* (Barcelona, 2002)

Baer, Joel, *Pirates of the British Isles* (Stroud, 2005)

Bass, George, *A History of Seafaring* (London, 1972)

Boxer, C. R., *Dutch Seaborne Empire, 1600–1800* (London, 1965)

Bradford, Ernle, *The Great Siege, Malta, 1565* (London, 1961)

Burg, B. R., *Sodomy and the Pirate Tradition* (New York, 1983)

Burgess, Glyn, *Medieval Outlaws: Eustace the Monk and Fouke Fitz Waryn* (London, 1997)

Burgess, Robert F. & Clausen, Carl J., *Florida's Golden Galleons: The Search for the 1715 Spanish Treasure Fleet* (Port Salerno, FL, 1982)

Burnett, John S., *Dangerous Waters* (New York, 2002)

Chambers, Anne, *Granuaile: Ireland's Pirate Queen c.1530–1603* (Dublin, 2003)

Clements, Jonathan, *Pirate King: Coxinga and the Fall of the Ming Dynasty* (Stroud, 2004)

Clifford, Barry, *The Pirate Prince: Discovering the Priceless Treasures of the Sunken Ship Whydah* (New York, 1993)

Clifford, Barry, *The Black Ship: The Quest to Recover an English Pirate Ship and its Lost Treasure* (London, 1999)

Cordingly, David, *Under the Black Flag: The Romance and the Reality of Life Among the Pirates* (London, 1995)

Cordingly, David (ed.), *Pirates: Terror on the High Seas* (Atlanta, GA, 1996)

Cordingly, David & Falconer, John, *Pirates: Fact & Fiction* (London, 1992)

Dodson, Leonidas, *Alexander Spotswood: Governor of Colonial Virginia* (Philadelphia, PA, 1932)

Earle, Peter, *The Sack of Panama* (London, 1981)

Earle, Peter, *Sailors: English Merchant Seamen 1650–1775* (London, 1988)

Earle, Peter, *The Pirate Wars* (London, 2003)

Exquemelin, Alexandre O., *Buccaneers of America* (Amsterdam, 1678, reprinted New York, 1969)

Forbes, Rosita, *Sir Henry Morgan: Pirate and Pioneer* (Norwich, 1948)

Gerhard, Peter, *Pirates of New Spain, 1575–1742* (New York, 2003)

le Golip, Louis, *The Memoirs of a Buccaneer* (London, 1954)

Gosse, Philip (ed.), *The History of Piracy* (New York, 1925, reprinted by Rio Grande Press, Glorieta, NM, 1988)

Gosse, Philip, *The Pirate's Who's Who: Giving Particulars of the Lives & Deaths of the Pirates & Buccaneers* (New York, 1925, reprinted by Rio Grande Press, Glorieta, NM, 1988)

Guilmartin, John F., *Gunpowder and Galleys* (London, 1974)

Guilmartin, John F., *Galleons and Galleys* (London, 2002)

Hayward, Arthur L. (ed.), *Lives of the Most Remarkable Criminals* (London, 1735, reprinted by Dodd, Mead & Co., New York, 1927)

Hympendahl, Klaus, *Pirates Aboard!* (New York, 2003)

Johnson, Captain Charles, *A General History of the Robberies & Murders of the Most Notorious Pyrates* (London, 1724, reprinted by Lyons Press, New York, 1998)

Konstam, Angus, *The History of Pirates* (New York, 1999)

Konstam, Angus, *The History of Shipwrecks* (New York, 1999)

Konstam, Angus, *Elizabethan Sea Dogs, 1560–1605* (Oxford, 2000)

Konstam, Angus, *The Armada Campaign, 1588* (Oxford, 2001)

Konstam, Angus, *The Historical Atlas of the Viking World* (New York, 2002)

Konstam, Angus, *Lepanto 1571: The greatest naval battle of the Renaissance* (Oxford, 2003)

Konstam, Angus, *The Pirate Ship, 1660–1730* (Oxford, 2003)

Konstam, Angus, *Spanish Galleon, 1530–1690* (Oxford, 2004)

Konstam, Angus, *Blackbeard: America's Most Notorious Pirate* (Hoboken, NJ, 2006)

Lee, Robert E., *Blackbeard the Pirate: A Re-appraisal of his Life and Times* (Winston-Salem, NC, 1974, reprinted John F. Blair, Winston-Salem, NC, 2002)

Little, Benerson, *The Sea Rover's Practice: Pirate Tactics and Techniques, 1630–1730* (Dulles, VA, 2005)

Little, Benerson, *Pirate Hunting* (Dulles, VA, 2010)

Lloyd, Christopher, *English Corsairs of the Barbary Coast* (London, 1981)

London, Joshua, *Victory in Tripoli* (Hoboken, NJ, 2005)

Lynn, John A., *The Wars of Louis XIV, 1667–1714* (London, 1999)

Marley, David F., *Pirates: Adventurers on the High Seas* (London, 1995)

Mather, Cotton, *The Tryals of Sixteen Persons for Piracy* (Boston, MA, 1726)

Mather, Cotton, *The Vial Poured upon the Sea: A Remarkable Relation of Certain Pirates* (Boston, MA, 1726)

May, W. E., *A History of Marine Navigation* (Henley-on-Thames, 1973)

Moore, John R., *Daniel Defoe, Citizen of the Modern World* (Chicago, 1958)

Nelson, Arthur, *The Tudor Navy: The Ships, Men and Organisation, 1485–1603* (London, 2001)

Ormerod, H. A., *Piracy in the Ancient World: An Essay on Mediterranean History* (Chicago, 1967)

Parry, J. H., *The Spanish Seaborne Empire* (London, 1966)

Pawson, Michael & Buisseret, David, *Port Royal, Jamaica* (Oxford, 1975)

Plutarch, *Lives of Alexander the Great and Julius Caesar* (reprinted London, 1886)

Pope, Dudley, *Harry Morgan's Way* (London, 1977)

Powell, J. R., *Robert Blake, General-at-Sea* (London, 1972)

Preston, Diana & Michael, *A Pirate of Exquisite Mind: The Life of William Dampier* (London, 2004)

Rediker, Marcus, *Between the Devil and the Deep Blue Sea: Merchant Seamen, Pirates and the Anglo-American Maritime World, 1700–1750* (Cambridge, 1987)

Rediker, Marcus, *Villains of all Nations: Atlantic Pirates in the Golden Age* (Boston, MA, 2004)

Reinhardt, David, *Pirates and Piracy* (New York, 1997)

Ritchie, Robert C., *Captain Kidd and the War against the Pirates* (Cambridge, MA, 1986)

Rogozinski, Jan, *Pirates! An A–Z Encyclopedia* (New York, 1995)

Rogozinski, Jan, *Honour Among Thieves* (London, 2000)

Sanders, Richard, *If a Pirate I Must Be* (London, 2007)

Stanley, Jo, *Bold in her Breeches: Woman Pirates across the Ages* (London, 1995)

Starkey, David J., van Eyck, E. S. & de Moor, J.A. (eds), *Pirates and Privateers* (Exeter, 1997)

Stevenson, Robert Louis, *Treasure Island* (London, 1883)

Sutton, Paul, *Cromwell's Jamaica Campaign* (Leigh-on-Sea, 1990)

Talty, Stephan, *Empire of Blue Water* (New York, 2007)

Unwin, R., *The Defeat of Sir John Hawkins* (London, 1960)

Wallace, Alfred Russell, *The Malay Archipelago* (London, 1869)

Walton, Timothy R., *The Spanish Treasure Fleets* (Sarasota, FL, 1994)

Woodbury, George, *The Great Days of Piracy in the West Indies* (New York, 1951)

Zacks, Richard, *The Pirate Hunter: The True Story of Captain Kidd* (New York, 2002)

INDEX